Critical Inventions

General Editor: John Schad
Lancaster University

PUBLISHED

D1615046

GIVEN: 1° Art 2° Crime
Modernity, Murder and Mass Culture
Jean-Michel Rabaté

Heidegger's Bicycle
Interfering with Victorian Texts
Roger Ebbatson

FORTHCOMING

The English Question; or, Academic Freedoms
Thomas Docherty

The Prodigal Sign
Kevin Mills

Rapture: Literature, Secrecy, Addiction
David Punter

Someone Called Derrida
An Oxford Mystery
John Schad

John Schad is Professor of Modern Literature at the University of Lancaster. He is the author of *The Reader in the Dickensian Mirrors* and *Victorians in Theory*, the editor of *Dickens Refigured*, Thomas Hardy's *A Laodicean*, and *Writing the Bodies of Christ*; and co-editor of *life.after.theory*. His latest work, *Queer Fish: Christian Unreason from Darwin to Derrida*, was published by Sussex Academic in 2004.

Voor Yvonne van der Loo

HEIDEGGER'S BICYCLE
Interfering with Victorian Texts
Roger Ebbatson

sussex
ACADEMIC
PRESS

Brighton • Portland

2 4 6 8 10 9 7 5 3

First published 2006 in Great Britain by
SUSSEX ACADEMIC PRESS
PO Box 139
Eastbourne BN24 9BP

and in the United States of America by
SUSSEX ACADEMIC PRESS
920 NE 58th Ave   Suite 300
Portland, Oregon 97213-3786

British Library Cataloguing in Publication Data
A CIP catalogue record for this book is available from the British Library.

Library of Congress Cataloging-in-Publication Data
Ebbatson, Roger.
    Heidegger's bicycle : interfering with Victorian texts /
    Roger Ebbatson.
    p. cm. — (Critical inventions)
    Readings and interpretations of Victorian literary texts
    based in German critical thinking.
    Includes bibliographical references and index.
    ISBN 1-84519-104-8 (acid-free paper) —
    ISBN 1-84519-105-6 (pbk. : acid-free paper)
    1. English literature—19th century—Criticism, Textual.
2. English literature—Explication. 3. Hermeneutics.
4. Phenomenology and literature. 5. Philosophy in
literature. I. Title.
PR468.T48E33 2006
820.9′008—dc22

                                                    2006017722

Typeset and designed by SAP, Brighton & Eastbourne
Printed by The Cromwell Press, Trowbridge, Wilts.
This book is printed on acid-free paper.

Contents

Series Editor's Foreword

In the book that follows, Roger Ebbatson reminds us of Walter Benjamin's remark that 'your name is your destiny'. If Benjamin is right, then it was Ebbatson's destiny to write about Robert Louis Stevenson's novella *The Ebb-Tide,* as he does here in a book that is marked throughout by a certain ebbing, or declining – a sense of an ending, if you will. This is, in part, an effect or trick of the period of which he writes, since Ebbatson is with Kierkegaard in seeing the nineteenth century as characterised, above all, by 'sympathetic melancholy'. This is nowhere more evident than in the 'melancholy, long, withdrawing roar' of the ebbing 'Sea of Faith' in Matthew Arnold's 'Dover Beach'; however, Ebbatson's account of the ebbing tide that was the nineteenth century takes us to a beach or coastline that is hard to place, that never quite feels like the little England of conventional Victorian studies. For, time and again, Victorian England here turns, quite bizarrely, into twentieth-century Germany – here Victorians such as Tennyson, Hardy and Conan Doyle are easily confused with Germans such as Benjamin, Adorno and (above all) Heidegger. It is no accident that Ebbatson is so concerned with Hopkins's poem *The Wreck of the Deutschland.* Working as he does at the coastal edge or limit of Victorian literature Ebbatson hears, or overhears, uncanny rumours of the wrecking of twentieth-century Deutschland – the wrecking that was to be presided over by National Socialism.

And what makes Heidegger the climactic figure for Ebbatson is that Heidegger takes ebbing to be the supreme philosophical fact of life, or Being. As Ebbatson points out, for Heidegger, '*Dasein* [being-there] is dying as long as it lives' – for Heidegger, living is dying. Indeed, he sees 'Being as falling'. It is inevitable that *Heidegger's Bicycle* should, like the Roman Empire, be characterised by both decline and . . . fall. Or perhaps that should be (to quote Dickens's Silas Wegg) 'Decline and Fall . . . off', since *Heidegger's Bicycle* never makes for an easy ride; indeed, at times, even Ebbatson falls . . . off. But so he must, for Germanic thought in general and Heidegger's thought in particular does, in the end, throw us completely off balance. Some bicycles are, as Heidegger writes (and Ebbatson cites), 'too rickety to ride'. Some, indeed, are too dangerous to ride. Ebbatson never forgets that Heidegger's thought helped lay down the tracks that led straight to the gates of Auschwitz.

These gates might seem a long way from Victorian England, but for Ebbatson the literature of Victorian England is a long way from itself; he believes it is a literature scarred by a terrible internal difference, or even indif ference – a Benjaminian 'space of resonance' that finds its echo within the appalling noises off of twentieth-century Germany. That is why Ebbatson feels compelled to adopt the unusual strategy of recycling Victorian writing through the bone-crunching machine of Germanic thought. The results are dramatic, perhaps even alarming, as it quickly becomes clear that Nietzsche is not the only German to 'philosophise with a hammer'; it turns out that to reread Victorian literature via Germanic thought is to take a hammer to that literature, to do a kind of a violence to it. In Ebbatson's hands, Heidegger's bicycle is at times a kind of weapon, something that he almost hurls at Victorian writing. Make no mistake, Ebbatson's school of criticism is the school of hard knocks. His aim, he confesses, is to effect 'cultural sabotage', to smash up a monumentalised account of Victorian England. He seeks, that is, to 'expose its jagged edges', a dangerous coast-line of perilous rocks and sand-bars, a coast-line on which is strewn the wreck of the thought of twentieth-century Deutschland.

In the end, though, it would seem to be a strangely spirit-ed coast since, as Ebbatson knows well, the wreck of German thought is, above all, the wreck of spirit or metaphysics. Ebbatson thus finally alerts us (almost unwittingly, I think) to the holy violence secreted within Victorian spirit or faith. He makes me think of Christina Rossetti's astonishing insistence that, 'Today, whilst it is still called today / Kneel, wrestle, knock, do violence, pray.' This very particular Victorian violence is something that hitherto we have overlooked, or censored. After *Heidegger's Bicycle* we can do so no longer. The school of hard knocks may yet surprise us.

JOHN SCHAD
Loughborough, January 2006

Prefatory Note

During the preparation of this book I have been extremely grateful for help and critical advice from a number of colleagues: Matthew Campbell, Anne Colley, Mariaconcetta Costantini, Robert Douglas-Fairhurst, Alan How, Catherine Neale, Derek Paget, Richard Pearson, Julia Reid, Angelique Richardson, Marion Shaw, Jane Thomas, and Saverio Tomaiuolo. Members of the Tennyson Society, the Richard Jefferies Society, the Thomas Hardy Society and the British Association for Victorian Studies have provided invaluable forums for the development of my ideas, and I have benefited from discussions of Jefferies with my student, Chen Ying (Grace). My greatest indebtedness, however, is to my editor, John Schad, whose unfailing support and critical acumen have been notably allied with a willingness to listen to my observations on the state of English cricket.

Earlier versions of two chapters have appeared elsewhere: the chapter on *The Ebb-Tide* was first published in *Figures of Heresy*, edited by Andrew Dix and Jonathan Taylor (Sussex Academic Press, 2006), and the chapter on *A Laodicean* in *Thomas Hardy and Contemporary Literary Studies*, edited by Tim Dolin and Peter Widdowson (Palgrave Macmillan, 2004). I am indebted to editors and publishers for permission to reprint this material.

The jacket/cover illustration "Nisqually Spit" is courtesy of Randall David Tipton, Portland, Oregon <randalldavidt@comcast.net>.

Bicycle Wheel, 1963 (mixed media) by Marcel Duchamp (1887–1968). Private Collection / Cameraphoto Arte Venezia / The Bridgeman Art Library.

Marcel Duchamp, *Bicycle Wheel*, 1963

Introduction

In *Heidegger's Bicycle* I will seek to chip away at the marmoreally institutionalised surface of a group of Victorian literary texts in a strategy of critical
'interference' based mainly in German critical thinking. My title relates to
two widely estranged textual 'moments' which I somewhat arbitrarily yoke
together. First, it glances at Heidegger's notion of existence ('*Dasein*') as a
kind of practical investment in the world which allows things to 'show up'
in significant ways, for example, 'as hammers that "nicely fulfil" their function, or as bicycles that are "too rickety to ride"'.[2] My chosen exempla are
thus seized upon for their usefulness-to-hand for my project. Secondly, I
allude to the murder of a cycling German teacher, one Herr Heidegger, in
the Sherlock Holmes canon, a death which I read as symptomatic of the
problematisation of the literary text by Germanic theory. Throughout my
study I take as a guiding principle Adorno's contention that 'once artworks
are entombed in the pantheon of cultural commodities, they themselves –
their truth content – are also damaged'.[3] This 'damage' occurs, Adorno
postulates, because 'the endless pains to eradicate the traces of making,
injure works of art and condemn them to be fragmentary'.[4]

The principle underlying my project here may thus be aligned with the
notion of translation as delineated by Walter Benjamin; in my view, the
critic is allied with the translator in looking for 'the echo of the original'.
In the readings that follow I locate myself 'not in the interior of the mountain forest of language itself but on the outside facing the wooded ridge',
seeking the Benjaminian 'resonance' emanating from my chosen texts.[5] My
breaking open of, for instance, Hardy's *A Laodicean* or Hopkins's 'The
Wreck of the Deutschland' is envisaged as a re-calling of the original by a
process of diversion or avoidance which will elicit a textual reverberation.
In looking for a deferral or multiplication of meanings I am seeking the
'alien' within the 'same' – the text echoing back with a ruptured or interrupted implication of meaning, a set of 'deliberately opened up antitheses'

in Benjamin's terms, which portend a type of textual demise. In laying stress on difference and disjunction I am wishing to tease out that difference from itself which inhabits the Victorian text, in an operation which verges upon paronomasia – a blossoming of meanings wrought through slight phonetical alteration. My wide-ranging deployment and (mis-)application of German critical theory would, I hope, serve my purpose in tearing open the density and imperviousness of signification in the nineteenth-century literary text. In other words, I wish to read, say, 'Crossing the Bar' or *The Ebb-Tide* as expressing, staging and yet repressing a crisis of signification which is also a crisis of similarity – the deathly sand-bar of the Laureate imperially refashioned in the South Seas as a type of rhetorical echo which multiplies into the wreckage-strewn pages of Hopkins's poetry.

I seek to convince the reader that my chosen texts are not merely randomly selected exempla, but that they are peculiarly pervaded by those gaps and interstices which expose the arbitrariness of naming: in each of these writings, I argue, the echo, mask or voice is broken or cut adrift so that, for example, Sherlock Holmes's forensic skills on an English moorside ineluctably calls up and foreshadows the evil of the Final Solution, or the passage-ways, turrets and crypts of Hardy's Somerset castle implicate seminal issues of middle-European modernism. Victorian literature places great emphasis upon the density and 'reality' of its self-referential function, and yet these exemplary texts tend to deny or cancel out what they should confirm through a kind of disruptive and reverberative echo. In place of an imposed meaning, Benjamin implies, there is the 'hindrance' or rupture which traverses all language:

> The chasm between the signifying written figure and the euphoric language sound compels the gaze to look into the depth at the moment when the fixed massif of the meaning of the word is torn up.[6]

Criticism, like translation, represents an entry (perhaps a Holmesian forced entry) into the text which ensures that the self-assurance of identicality of that text is shattered or torn apart so that the poem or novel appears alien to itself. We cannot enter 'the interior of the mountain forest of language' except by a roundabout path founded in errancy and miscomprehension. Paronomasia posits an adherence to the literalness of words which the critic must sweep away in a discrepant gesture. In *Heidegger's Bicycle*, I depart from the context in seeking to produce a shattered series of readings in which I turn away, utilising my German theoretical sources, from the scenario of referential language. The complex doubling of speaker positions in, for instance, 'The Loss of the Eurydice' or *The Ebb-Tide*, inaugurates a division which is at the heart of writing and critique – an acute sense of one's own voice as alien. For me it as if these texts, standing in the 'mountain forest of language', await their echoic call, and I often locate that call within the equally dense forest of German critical writing. The writing of the Victorian moment is the first, as I conceive it, undertaken at the precise juncture when the commodity, value and exchange dominate not only economic but also social relations and cultural superstructure. I understand my reading strategy as both enabling and disabling, my readings facilitating and withdrawing what is allowed to 'appear' in the text, creating and stifling meaning through a deliberate policy of dis-articulation. The echo or resounding of meanings becomes lost amidst the literary monuments which lie in ruins. This process implies the ruination of the text in the sense that Benjamin defines allegory as ruin. Criticism, Benjamin holds, is the mortification of the work, operating not by closure but through resonance and reverberation. The monuments of the Victorian literary 'heritage' from Tennyson to Conan Doyle thus take the form of shattered ruins or cultural remains, and I can only conceive of *Heidegger's Bicycle* as a kind of postscript which allows these echoes to be heard. The work of reading thus takes the form of a making present through deferral or distortion: the voice of the critic (here, my voice) does not give life to the dead but rather is a calling up of memories of what is to be discerned posthumously in the Benjaminian 'space of resonance' – that 'empty mussel shell' of the nineteenth century which Benjamin holds to his ear in *Berlin Childhood*.

In our confrontation with a massively present and institutionalised Victorian literary field, we must attend to Benjamin's contention that 'The way in which [the past] is celebrated as our "heritage" is more ominous than any oblivion'. What the celebratory misses are 'the jagged edges which offer a foothold to someone who wants to get beyond that work'.[7] If we do not wish, in Benjamin's phrase, to 'construct a continuity', we need to hold the text in a 'firm, apparently brutal grasp' which takes us 'beyond' the past. According to Benjamin, it cannot be a question 'of presenting written works in the context of their time, but of articulating the time which grasps them – namely ours'.[8] My aim in *Heidegger's Bicycle* thus accords with Irving Wohlfarth's Benjaminian call for a 'cultural sabotage' which 'aims to expose the jagged edges by which we may clamber beyond the slippery blocks of a monumentalised past'.[9]

It is a characteristic of the Victorian literary artefact, that it generates signifying systems which promptly disappear as soon as they are defined. In texts such as 'In the Garden at Swainston', *The Guilty River* or 'The Priory School' we may discover that which is exemplary, even if, as Benjamin contends, 'this exemplary character be admitted only in respect of the merest fragment': 'The value of fragments of thought is all the greater the

less direct their relationship to the underlying idea'.[10] My study, culminating in a reading of the Sherlock Holmes phenomenon, may appropriately
proceed by what Benjamin designates 'the art of interruption in contrast to
the chain of deduction',[11] but the critic needs, in a sense, to possess the
Nietzschean ability 'to read a text as text without the interference of an
interpretation'.[12]

Thus, rather than attempt to unify this set of readings into a coherent
whole in some kind of bogus 'reconciliation', I have preferred to view the
following chapters as offering a kind of 'constellation' which, whilst being
as it were random, at the same time avoids being entirely miscellaneous.
Adorno justly placed great emphasis upon the incommensurablility of
artworks; in his searching diagnosis, 'Every work is the mortal enemy of the
other', becoming comparable 'only by annihilating themselves, by realising
their life through their mortality'.[13] *Heidegger's Bicycle* offers, I hope, varia-
tions on a theme, being shaped and conceived as a series of responses to the
consequences of the Victorian force-field, atmosphere or *Stimmung* largely
perceived through the lens of German cultural theory. Adorno once spoke
presciently of that 'dissolution' of the 'layers' of the artwork 'which was
unforeseeable in the moment of the work's appearance'. We need to be alert,
to 'the petrification of works that have become transparent, their decrepi-
tude, and their falling silent'.[14] I am, then, addressing the issues of
modernity not as a term denoting a historical or cultural period but as an
ethos or problematic, a conjuncture in which, in Foucauldian terms,
mankind is compelled to 'produce him/herself'. Here I would concur with
Richard Bernstein's contention that

> There is no hidden essence to be discovered, there is no hidden depth
> revealing what we truly are, there is only the task of producing or inventing
> ourselves.[15]

The Victorians faced this task as they began to realise, under the impress
of philology, anthropology and Darwinism, that they inhabited an 'open
universe', a world of risk and chance which was uncannily unstable. Such
openness offered both threat and opportunity in the interplay between the
laws of nature and random contingencies. My intention in what follows is
to prise open my selected texts by showing up the internal fissures and
contradictions as well as the potential thematic similarities which their
reading demands. By placing my focus upon examples of Victorian writing,
rather than offering a historical survey, I attempt to apply a Benjaminian
methodology of allegorical (mis)reading. Rather than offer a comprehensive
account, *Heidegger's Bicycle* thus exposes the often contradictory valences of
these case studies. The internal relations and ambivalences of these texts are

set in relief by configuring them together in this way in a kind of critical montage.

Literary texts, as Paul de Man gnomically remarks, 'have to be read', but the 'possibility of reading can never be taken for granted'.[16] The readings undertaken below, from Tennyson to Conan Doyle, attempt to take into account Kierkegaard's sense of the '*sympathetic melancholy*' of the age. It is melancholy, Kierkegaard proposes, which is 'the defect of our time', and 'reverberates even in its frivolous laughter':

> Everything is cut away except the present; little wonder then that in one's constant anxiety about losing it one does lose it.[17]

It is, as Kierkegaard insists, the problem of choice which defines the period. As he perceives it, 'Choice itself is decisive for a personality's content', because 'in choice personality immerses itself in what is chosen'. Kierkegaard's analogy, I suggest, possesses a deep resonance for some of the texts encountered here – most obviously, Tennyson's 'fair ship', Hopkins's wrecks, or Stevenson's 'Farallone'. In Kierkegaard's terms,

> If you imagine a helmsman in his ship when it is just about to tack, then he may be able to say, 'I can either do this or that', but unless he is a pretty poor helmsman he will also be aware that the ship is still maintaining its normal headway, and so there is only an instant when it is immaterial whether he does this or that.

It is thus of the utmost importance 'to choose and to choose in time'.[18] Choice involves ethics, and it is this crucial insight which is involved and invoked in the Victorian literary text, poised as it is between the twin poles. To turn to Kierkegaard again, 'Either, then, one is to live aesthetically or one is to live ethically'. History is seen, according to this argument, 'under the category of necessity'.[19] The necessity invoked depends upon an under-standing of the complex relation between discourse and society, in ways which are helpfully defined by Timothy Reiss's sense of the term 'episteme' as marking 'an abstraction whose concrete side is named by the word *society*':

> Discourse and society are a total praxis, 'society' designating a kind of concrete anchorage of discourse, 'discourse' designating the way in which society makes itself meaningful to itself. [20]

My approach here is confessedly eclectic, drawing upon a variety of theoretical positions in my attempt to illuminate the objects of scrutiny, but my speculative bias is predominantly towards the Hegelian perspective of German cultural theory. I do not seek, or pretend to achieve, any degree of rigorous philosophical investigation, but I do aim at a dialectical confrontation between cultural/theoretical and literary texts, and I proceed entirely through an immersion in textual detail. The dialectical sentence operates figuratively in gesturing towards what Fredric Jameson designates the 'decipherment of experience which may be thought of as a hermeneutical exegesis of a text'.[21] The German tradition, as Jameson concedes, may be seen in Anglo-Saxon culture as 'obscure and cumbersome, indigestible, abstract' – in other words *'Germanic'* – but I follow his example in attempting, in this investigation of a group of nineteenth-century literary texts, 'to press beyond the individual, empirical phenomenon to its meaning'.[22] The connections which the Victorian writer sought to make between public and private are no longer available, and it is the role of Benjamin, Adorno or Heidegger to trace that movement of impossibility to its sources in metaphysical enlightenment. *Heidegger's Bicycle* modestly seeks to be, in Jameson's terms, *'diagnostic* as well as descriptive'.[23]

Thus I uncover, in an elegiac Tennysonian lyric, formal, psychological and historical elements which lay bare its origins in the secretive male brotherhoods of the mid-century and reveal the rivalrous and homosocial thematics invoked by the very form of the elegy. The marginalisation of woman inherent in the form is related here to the subtextual presence of a colonial project which both invokes and denies its homosexual motivation (chapter 1). These interrelated issues are carried further in the poetic figuration of the Victorian ship, in a strategy through which the material processes of the age are transmuted into the type of the spiritual in Tennyson. The ever-present risk of shipwreck, both literal and spiritual, stages a poetry of human crisis set against the divine in Hopkins, whilst at the end of the century divinity is transformed into human transcendence in the metaphysics of the endless voyage (chapter 2). In Hardy's *A Laodicean*, by contrast, it is the spiritualisation of money which is at issue in a novel which may be read through the lens of Simmel's sociology of exchange. The coalescence in this novel of erotic desire, money and property serves to hollow out the past whilst eliciting an empty or homogenous present. The labyrinthine structure of the castle, taken together with the plot reliance on telegraphy and gambling, points enigmatically towards the existential 'moment' of modernism. In Hardy's *Return of the Native*, in contradistinction, man seeks to retrieve his relations with the natural world in a physical gesture of communality which is framed and complicated, I suggest, by Marx's account of the capitalist transformation of nature, whilst in the same conjuncture Richard Jefferies stages a return to the earth whose poetic qualities may be read through Heideggerian aesthetics (chapter 4). It is German cultural theory and the myth of origins which also reveals the complex structure of Wilkie Collins's *The Guilty River*, in which the Gothic figure of the double is complicated by a racial and sexual ambivalence presented within the ruptured flow of history (chapter 5). Race and degeneration similarly come to the fore in Robert Louis Stevenson's *The Ebb-Tide*, a text embedded in notions of heresy, parody and Darwinian discourse; here, Stevenson presents a dramatic instance of 'imperial Gothic' and exposes the murderous underside of the missionary and trading enterprise in the South Seas (chapter 6). Finally, I read the Sherlock Holmes phenomenon as a foreshadowing of 'rationalised' race theory, and explore some of Conan Doyle's writings in connection with the vexed issue of Heidegger's 'silence' (chapter 7).

Heidegger's Bicycle does not present German cultural theory as the key to all mythologies, nor do I seek to promote any kind of totalising reading. Rather, the discrete but linked chapters might be envisaged as constellations, ruptures or moments of 'dialectics at a standstill' along the lines of a Poundian vortex – instants of illumination in which the text is wrenched out of context so as to afford a new perspective. My study seeks nothing more than to bear witness to such revelatory moments – Clym on the heath, George Somerset in the tower, the drowning sailors on board the 'Eurydice', and so on – and to reflect or transform some of the intensity of affect discernible, for instance, in the estranging observations of a neglected writer of crucial significance (as I have argued over many years)[24] for this period, Richard Jefferies. The lines from Jefferies that follow might be productively read through the estranging lens of Heidegger's concept of being as falling as a structural element of *Dasein*, or of Benjamin's *verfall*, the fall into a multiplicity of languages; nevertheless, something remains as a surplus. Timothy Clark remarks of these lines that, whilst tending 'towards a seemingly insignificant or even an ideally meaningless testimony', they are 'still uniquely odd': 'Is it about more, or about less, than what it is about?':[25]

> A swallow never hesitates, never looks before he leaps, threads all day the eye of needles, and goes on from half-past two in the morning till ten at night, without so much as disturbing a feather. He is the perfection of a machine for falling. His round nest is under the eaves, he throws himself out of window and begins to fall, fall, for twenty hours together.[26]

CHAPTER I

Tennysonian Shadows
'In the Garden at Swainston'

A shadow flits before me,
Not thou, but like to thee.
(Maud, II. 151–2)

Tennyson's elegy, 'In the Garden at Swainston', was composed in 1870, prompted by the death and, more specifically, the funeral on 31 May, of Tennyson's friend and neighbour in the Isle of Wight, Sir John Simeon (1815–70). The two men had first met in 1838, being introduced to each other by Thomas Carlyle. Simeon represented the Isle of Wight as a Liberal MP from 1847 to 1851, but on his conversion to Catholicism in that year he had taken the Chiltern Hundreds and retired to private life; he was re-elected in 1865. The Simeons called for the first time at Farringford in June 1854, and the two families became close; indeed Sir John, whom Emily Tennyson described as 'a friend who was to be so much to us both',[1] may have done something to mitigate the Laureate's antipathy to Catholicism. There was regular intercourse between the two neighbouring households, with the children becoming good friends, and Emily growing especially fond of the Simeons' eldest child, Louisa, who came to assume the role of surrogate daughter to her. Simeon was to remarry in 1862, only a year after his first wife's death, and the Tennysons struggled for a while to accommodate themselves to the second Lady Simeon. In relation to Sir John, Tennyson had become, Robert Martin observes, 'more confidential than with any person since Arthur Hallam',[2] and it was partly at Simeon's instigation that *Maud* was composed. The poet was thus deeply saddened by the news of Sir John's sudden death abroad, in Switzerland on 21 May 1870, at the age of fifty-five; as Emily commented of her husband later in that year, 'He has never got over our loss in May'.[3] Although burial was to be in the Barrington-Simeon family vault of the Anglican parish church at Calbourne, when the body was brought back to England it was first placed in the newly created Catholic chapel at Swainston Hall. Martin describes the corpse lying in state 'with lights burning' and 'a Roman Catholic priest in the room'. It was said that the 'shrieks and sobs were terrible', and Lady Simeon is reported to have thrown herself on the coffin in order to embrace it.[4] Such Romish excess was too much for the poet, and on the day of the funeral, borrowing a pipe, hat and cloak of Sir John's, he escaped into the garden and composed a first draft of the poem. Martin's account continues with a revealing anecdote:

> When young Simeon came to fetch him, he found Tennyson lying full length in Sir John's clothes beneath one of the cedars he had written about in *Maud*, smoking the pipe, tears flowing from his eyes. [5]

The Simeon family were avid bird lovers, and the Swainston nightingales were a particularly famous feature of their estate. Of this particular occasion Emily reported to Hallam Tennyson how 'nightingales were singing, beautiful roses were all about the house and garden and lilacs were in full bloom and the contrast only added to the sadness'. At the end of November she told him, 'Papa has done a little song about the day of our dear Sir John's burial'[6]:

> Nightingales warbled without,
>   Within was weeping for thee:
> Shadows of three dead men
>   Walked in the walks with me,
>   Shadows of three dead men and thou wast one of the three.
>
> Nightingales sang in his woods:
>   The Master was far away:
> Nightingales warbled and sang
>   Of a passion that lasts but a day;
>   Still in the house in his coffin the Prince of courtesy lay.
>
> Two dead men have I known
>   In courtesy like to thee:
> Two dead men have I loved
>   With a love that ever will be:
>   Three dead men have I loved and thou art last of the three.[7]

This 'little song' may be read formally, psychologically and historically. The poem possesses the formal properties of an elegy in which Tennyson ponders the relation of life to death, haunted by the 'shadows' of Arthur Hallam, Henry Lushington and Sir John Simeon, and hails the latter, who acted not only as master of the Isle of Wight foxhounds between 1854 and 1856 but also as master of the Newport freemasons' lodge prior to his conversion, as 'Master'. The politician is also designated 'Prince of

Courtesy', a title which, given King Arthur's sobriquet as 'the king of courtesy' in 'Balin and Balan' (l. 252), perhaps serves to emphasise Arthur
Hallam's continuing primacy in Tennyson's affections. Indeed, this poem
may possess deeper connections with the *Idylls*, especially in the context of
Margaret Cameron's photographic illustrated edition of 1875. The dead
were a popular photographic subject at this time, and it has been suggested
that 'The language of loss, for both photography and for Tennyson is encompassed by the word "shadow"'. The daguerreotype in particular 'gave new
meaning to the concept of shadow and loss as the person is reduced to a
shadow floating on glass'[8] – Elizabeth Barrett Browning for instance expos-
tulated on 'the fact of the very shadow of the person lying there fixed for
ever!'[9] Indeed, photography's origins were conceived, in Fox Talbot's terminology, as the 'Art of fixing a Shadow', a process in which, he argued, that
'most transitory of things, a shadow, . . . may be fixed forever'.[10] Cameron's
curiously 'unfocused' photographs, like Tennyson's poem, served to create
a texture in which, in Alison Chapman's words, 'the subject is fading, transitory and elusive'.[11] However, it may also be the case, as Roland Barthes
suggests, that 'photography has something to do with resurrection'.[12] John
Rosenberg intriguingly suggests in connection with the *Idylls* that 'the *idea*
of Arthur as Tennyson envisioned him carries with it a strong supposition
of nonbeing, of a ghostly presence made all the more vivid by virtue of its
absence'.[13]

Whilst the nightingales sing of mating and a sexual love which 'lasts
but a day', the poet here commemorates 'a love that ever will be' in celebrating the gift of male friendship founded upon a cult of secrecy within
the clandestine brotherhoods of the freemasons and the Cambridge
Apostles.[14] 'In the Garden at Swainston' seeks to be read as a funerary elegy,
but one prompted by the retreat to the garden when faced with the figure
of the mourning woman, a retreat in which the poet adopts the mantle, hat
and pipe of the deceased, in a sense impersonating the dead man. The trope
of the garden functions potently in Tennyson's poetry throughout his career
as an often feminised image of refuge or retreat – we think, for instance, of
'Mariana', 'The Gardener's Daughter', *The Princess* or *Maud*: it offers an
image of a private enclave within the public world to which both the
laureate and politician perhaps reluctantly belonged, and embodies a sense
of tension between social responsibility and private feeling, engagement
and withdrawal, masculinity and femininity, which is always productive in
Tennyson's work. But the garden also suggests self-cultivation, and as
Darrel Mansell has observed of *In Memoriam*, the 'pull' of the elegy is towards
certain literary conventions, one of which is 'the contention of poetic rivalry
between the elegist and his now dead friend', a contention which ends with

the poet 'obliterating' his rival, 'honouring him by surpassing him'.[15] This obliteration is achieved, in a linguistic act of erasure, by reducing Sir John Simeon, and Tennyson's other subjects, Henry Lushington and Arthur Hallam, to non-existence, veritable 'Shadows of three dead men' – the framing of a statement which affirms that the men are both present and absent. Language cannot rid itself of what it declares non-existent, and this is one of the conundrums posed by the literary form of the elegy, a form always itself haunted by the ghosts of other pre-texts. Mansell suggests that saying anything at all about Hallam, in *In Memoriam*, 'does not make him disappear but does substitute him for a semiotic, a lost other',[16] and this applies equally to this much slighter poem in which the dead man becomes, as it were, 'merely words', a master who is both 'far away' and 'Still . . . in his coffin', where 'still' scrupulously enforces a double meaning.

Tennyson fled from Sir John's coffin at the spectacle of the candles, priest and mourning second wife, just as for many years he had avoided any sighting of Hallam's grave at Clevedon – an evasion which led him into a catalogue of faulty detail in *In Memoriam*. As in the case of Arthur Hallam, Sir John's body was brought back from abroad after sudden death, and once again, as in that more ambitious work, the formal structure of the elegy enables Tennyson to conceive the friend as text, a text, in Mansell's phrase, 'to be erased and overwritten'. George Steiner has argued that the 'lament for the poet gone is always autobiographical', because 'the mourner tenses his own resources against the ubiquitous blackmail of death'.[17] It is conventional in the elegy that nature join in the lament, a function both performed and refused by the nightingales here. The structure of the elegy, Mansell argues, is that of a tomb: the elegy, that is to say, constructs 'a house built for the dead friend', but also hints at 'the permanence of the elegist's own surpassing literary achievement',[18] as curiously signalled in this instance by Tennyson's wilful act of impersonation. The poem imagines loss of personal identity and dissolution of the self paradoxically accompanied by a shadowy reincarnation: by absenting himself from the scene of mourning, Tennyson is satisfyingly able to lose the object of the poem, just as he had fantasised, in *In Memoriam*, about Hallam's body being lost at sea. Here, Sir John is simultaneously in his coffin and walking through the shrubbery of his garden. Thus the elegist constructs his own memorial in a way which obeys the literary laws of elegy: Hallam's tomb at Clevedon, Mansell remarks, possessed a powerfully patriarchal authority, being chosen by Henry Hallam, who also composed the epitaph, and this leads Tennyson to do 'everything imaginable to rob this place of its authority':

He buries the body outdoors in grasses and clover sod; he appropriates,

cancels and overwrites the text of the memorial tablet, which he mis-locates;
he appropriates, cancels, and overwrites the very words of Arthur Henry
Hallam his subject – the remains of the paternally edited Remains.[19]

Whilst it was the continued publication of the *Remains* which, as Angela
Leighton observes, 'not only kept Hallam's death present, audibly in the
title, but also paradoxically kept Tennyson, the aesthetic poet, alive',[20] it is
also significant that these literary remains were subjected to severe paternal
censorship. In *Either/Or*, Kierkegaard appositely suggested that
'Posthumous papers are like a ruin', and went on, 'what haunt could be more
natural for the interred?'[21]

'In the Garden at Swainston' fulfils the major functions of the elegy
through the patterning device of repetitive iteration: thus we have the
variant lines about the nightingales, the three dead men/two dead men
contrast, and the re-emphasised 'shadows', all bound together by the
trimeter/hexameter rhythmic structure. As Peter Sacks remarks in his study
of elegy, repetition 'creates a sense of continuity, of an unbroken pattern
such as one may oppose to the extreme discontinuities of death'. The elegy,
Sacks reminds us, from its beginnings in ancient Greece, is 'legally
connected with the right to inherit', and comprises part of 'combative struggles for inheritance'.[22] As a poetic form, the elegy must have exerted a
peculiar attraction for Tennyson, deeply conscious as he was of being a
member of the 'disinherited' Somersby branch of the family, whose main
heritage was the famous 'black blood'. Sacks's argument that elegy enacts
the displacement of an actual father by an idealised totemic figure offers
resonant implications for the reading of Tennyson, but 'In the Garden' is a
text which also endorses Gerhard Joseph's contention that elegy, as the
literary expression of mourning, offers 'evidence of elaborate staying power,
the generation of far-off rather than merely short-term interest'. The elegy
stresses long-term attachment, as opposed to the endless substitutions of
erotic love, here embodied by the nightingales' warbling. What Joseph
designates the 'loss-into-gain economics' of elegy 'depends upon the expen-
diture of a good deal of time and psychic energy before a "*far-off*" interest
may be available to the writer'.[23] But if the elegy is literature that seeks to
forget, it might paradoxically re-enliven the dead, to the extent that the
'Shadows of three dead men/ Walked in the walks with me' in a risky, almost
Gothic, resurrection. As David Shaw has observed of Morris's Arthurian
poems, 'To banish a phantom by first evoking it is already to endow that
phantom with spectral life'.[24] In his student days, we may recall, Tennyson
had proved a thoroughly unsatisfactory Apostle: the Society's record book
notes that the youthful poet 'wrote and began to read a paper on "Ghosts",

but was overcome by nervousness, and tore up what he had written, throwing it in the fire'.[25] Thus the material entity, the paper itself, is reduced to ashes in a premonitory moment of dematerialisation which renders the argument ghostly: Tennyson's paper, marking both the outset and termination of his Apostolic career, becomes, as it were, the ghost of its own occasion. Around the same time, in the spring of 1831, Tennyson had slept in his father's bed just a week after Dr Tennyson's unlamented death, 'earnestly desiring to see his ghost, but no ghost came'.[26] There is a latent threat, Paul de Man has written, that the strategy of the elegiac form will bring the dead back to life so that, 'by making the dead speak', the 'living are struck dumb, frozen in their own death'. The necessary repetitions of elegy which are so marked a feature of this poem signal and obscure what de Man memorably terms the 'wound of a fracture that lies hidden in all texts'.[27] Elegy thus works to recollect the past whilst perjuring that past: elegiac language seeks unsuccessfully to restore an absent wholeness.

A second reading of 'In the Garden' may be proposed based in psychoanalytic theory. We have seen that elegy turns upon a struggle for inheritance, and that this was a subject of intense concern for Alfred Tennyson, but the poem might specifically be read in the light of Freud's proposal that the super-ego is made up of what he terms the illustrious dead in a kind of cultural reservoir or cemetery in which renounced love-objects might be interred. Through this process, psychoanalysis suggests, the father is displaced by an idealised hero-figure, and this is of course highly pertinent not only to the strategies of *In Memoriam* and *Idylls of the King*, but also to this lesser piece, though complicated in this instance by the displacement of the problematic figure of Dr Tennyson not by one love-object but by 'three dead men', a trio in which Hallam stands pre-eminent. In addressing the 'work of mourning', Freudian psychology shows how the experience of loss becomes expressed in figuration, as the elegist or mourner draws attention to his own powers of survival. Melancholia is identified with an ambivalently loved object with the result, Freud remarks, that 'The *shadow* of the object falls across the ego'.[28] Mourning requires that we detach our affections from the first love-object and attach them to a 'substitute', but this process is, in a Freudian reading, a necessarily painful one since the first object is that of the mother, and it is through the act of separation, begun in the mirror-phase, that we ultimately come to assume our adult sexual identity. As Peter Sacks observes, 'one of the most profound issues to beset any mourner and elegist is his surviving yet painfully altered sexuality', and traces of this sexual contestation are discernible in the poem. Sacks notes that the classical elegy is characterised by its pastoral context, its occluded sexual references to vegetation ritual, and its images of resurrection. Both the piping of the flute in Greek elegy, and the frequently invoked trope of cut flowers, he suggests, invoke a phallic frame of reference for the elegiac form together with the threat of castration – aspects of elegy, Sacks adds, which 'should not be slighted'.[29] This is borne out, for instance, by the moment in *In Memoriam* where the poet imagines himself in the graveyard at Clevedon, where 'since the grasses round me wave,/ I take the grasses of the grave,/ And make them pipes whereon to blow' (XXI, ll. 2–4). 'In the Garden at Swainston', in the density of its verbal and rhythmic realisation, brings together these crucial and defining elements: the pastoral context of the garden, the singing of the birds, and the hint of resurrection as the three dead men 'Walked in the walks with me'.

In this connection, Tennyson's adoption of the curious ensemble of metonymic objects – the dead man's pipe, hat and cloak – takes on a partic-ular resonance further complicated by an earlier incident when, walking in the New Forest in 1855, the laureate had lost an umbrella and a tobacco case given to him by Sir John. These circumstances are rendered more significant when we recall Simeon's double-edged gift of an invalid chair, in 1858, to Emily, who was then forty-five, in a gesture of friendship which served to confirm female incapacity and dependence. In his readings of phallic dream symbolism Freud comments that the tobacco-pipe represents 'the approximate shape of the male organ', and he offers a similar interpre-tation of dreams involving the hat and the overcoat; elsewhere in his study he makes the intriguing claim that 'the number three has been confirmed from many sides as a symbol of the male genitals'.[30] From the perspective of the Freudian 'family romance' we might see the 'Master' who is 'far away' as representing the symbolic father (a formidable amalgam of Dr Tennyson and Henry Hallam) whose threat of castration leads the child to choose substitute love-objects in place of the mother; but we also hear, in this version of the Tennysonian mantra, 'far, far away', an echo of the poet's visit to the empty Wimpole Street residence of the Hallams in *In Memoriam*: 'He is not here; but far away' (VII, l.9). The 'Shadows of three dead men' might also offer a Jungian resonance, hinting as they do at a disturbance of the poetic ego. The Jungian shadow 'is a moral problem that challenges the whole ego-personality' and to 'become conscious of it involves recognising the dark aspects of the personality as present and real'[31] – an acknowledge-ment, perhaps, which Tennyson would always resist. The 'degree of inferiority' with which the shadow is associated by Jung would mark the poet's relation with Hallam both living and dead, and *In Memoriam,* for instance, might be read as a massive resistance to, and projection of, these Jungian traits. As Jung puts it, the subject 'throws a very long shadow before he [sic] is willing to withdraw his emotionally-toned projections from their object'. In order to gain protection, the subject spins 'a cocoon, which in the end will completely envelop him'.[32]

At first sight this elegy in which a male poet mourns the deaths of three male companions appears to exclude and marginalise woman, the patriarchal/fraternal voice reducing her to silence and invisibility, whilst the poet contemplates the joys of comradeship with the dead. Tennyson's fascination with the lifeless male body has often been critically noted, but whilst sexual difference is seemingly occluded in this ode to likeness and comradeship, it returns in the interstices of the text, in the song of the nightingales, glancing as this does at Ovid's *Metamorphoses*, where Philomel, having been raped by her brother-in-law, is transformed into a nightingale. T. S. Eliot would later make striking use of this tale in *The Waste Land*, but another poem, 'Sweeney Among the Nightingales', appears to offer a parodic reinflection of Tennyson's poem:

> The host with someone indistinct
> Converses at the door apart,
> The nightingales are singing near
> The Convent of the Sacred Heart,
>
> And sang within the bloody wood
> When Agamemnon cried aloud
> And let their liquid siftings fall
> To stain the stiff dishonoured shroud.[33]

It is often forgotten, in relation to Ovid's tale, that the avenging sisters, Procne and Philomel, prior to their transformation into birds, contrive to trick King Tereus into cannibalistically eating his own son. Hallam Tennyson, we may reflect, was similarly 'devoured', reduced to a lifetime of filial conformity from the moment he was named after that most potent 'shadow' from his father's past. Through Tennyson's conjuration of the nightingales, therefore, woman here functions as the unmentioned oppositional signifier within male discourse, a discourse which seeks to evade sexual difference but is pervaded by a sense of the instability of gender definitions.

This is a poem which celebrates a 'masculine' patriarch (Simeon), a 'feminised' male (Hallam) and a potential homosexual (Lushington), and thus, in its textual unconscious, illuminates the oscillations in masculine identity within the period. The poet, fearful of the figure of the weeping woman, flees into a garden of same-sex brotherhood, his resultant elegy composed as an expression of mastery and absolute knowledge in formulating what Hélène Cixous nominates 'the empire of the self-same', an empire in which, she observes of the male writer, 'death is his master'.[34] The poet claims a universality for his utterance through the strategy of excluding woman, but the cost of this exclusion is signalled by troubling eruptions as the unconscious pierces the neutral or judicious tone of the text. The fourth figure in the poem is ostensibly that of the poet, but John Schad, in his reading of Christina Rosssetti, postulates the presence of a fourth figure 'conventionally (mis)interpreted not as *like* Christ but rather *as* Christ', adding that 'we may just interpret "him" as *her*, as the maternal "fourth" that lies within all "trinities"'. Schad claims that, in Irigarayan theory, 'the fourth figure would be "like the Son of God" because she is, in a sense, his (m)other'.[35] Woman inhabits the poem through her illusory absence, rendering problematic the claim to a relation based not in 'passion' but in 'courtesy'. Tennyson's poem is, like *In Memoriam*, a beautifully inflected expression of narcissistic self-reference which attempts to domesticate the strangeness of its sexual trajectory, a project whose difficulties are paradoxically registered in syntactical and rhythmic effects, word-play, repetition and the whole armoury of Tennyson's poetic mastery. This conflictual element may be traced back to the classical models which Tennyson so consciously inherited, and the reinflection of these forms through the rhythmical experience of his own national language – the establishment of the unit of metre in variable syllabic accentual patterns. In this sense Tennyson's poetry is generated out of a sense of exile from the parent body of Greek and Latin literature – 'the Master was far away'. The male poet who appears supremely 'at home' in his culture only sustains that authority through a series of exclusions or acts of censorship which circle ambiguously around the figure of woman and the 'mother-tongue'.

In her feminist reading of *In Memoriam*, Marion Shaw argues that loss 'is located within sexual difference', but that writing 'is also a kind of loss', because 'what was once part of the writer is now separate, different, spent', and she argues that 'this is doubly true of elegy'. She pertinently notes how, in Melanie Klein's reinflection of Freud, the sense of loss is related to infantile development in a process through which 'all females, in this imaginative scheme, become associated with loss and desire'. Woman is thus 'the symptom of the male speaker's (poet's) lack, which is a doubling-up of her role as the image of loss': woman, in this Kleinian scenario, is 'both stand-in for and cause of the loss'.[36] In the interloper figure of the second, 'belated' Lady Simeon embracing the coffin in a theatrical gesture offensive to reason and propriety we are presented with a figure of Kristevan abjection estranged from language and living precariously on the margins of existence. Lady Simeon exists in an abject borderline state from which the poet flees into the comforting stability of male comradeship, a stability rendered precarious, however, by his own sense of exile in the garden which may be characterised as a landscape of estrangement. Julia Kristeva argues that abjection enables us to differentiate between proper and improper, inside (the coffin) and outside (the garden), and that what we expel as waste or defilement becomes abject, but can never finally be expelled, and she relates this scenario ultimately to the maternal body. Abjection suggests, potently in Tennyson's case, the risks of a loss of self and absorption by the Other, and this poem takes as its occluded theme the ambivalence of the human subject who seeks to retain an autonomous identity even after death, but is also prone to invasion of the ego-boundary, experiencing what Kelly Hurley designates 'the vertiginous pleasures of indifferentiation'.[37] The writer is, in this theoretical argument, one who transfers his/her fears of an over-whelmingly present mother (at Eton, Arthur was nicknamed 'Mother' Hallam) through the power of metaphor into a literary text. The unspoken subject of the poem, in the light of Kristevan theory, thus takes the form of the 'derelict' female body defined against its polar opposite.

In his study of German tragic drama, Walter Benjamin pertinently observes that spirits emerge through 'an opening in the passage of time, in which the same ghostly image constantly reappears'. However, his further claim that 'The spirit world is ahistorical'[38] may be countered by a critical reappropriation of Tennyson's lyric. A materialist reading of the poem might begin by recalling the moment in 'Balin and Balan' where Sir Balin confronts Sir Garlon with the challenge, '"So thou be shadow, here I make thee ghost"' (l. 388). 'In the Garden' is a poem inhabited by Virgilian and Arthurian shadows which demand identification: one of them, Sir John Simeon, was a politician and man of property, the second, Henry Lushington, an agent of empire and member of the landed gentry, whilst the third, Arthur Hallam, dying propertyless and bequeathing only his literary 'remains', was the scion of two great Whig landed families, the Hallams and the Eltons. The fourth protagonist, Alfred Tennyson, trans-formed himself from self-styled 'penniless beggar'[39] to man of properties (Farringford, Aldworth) through a species of aesthetic self-help. The poem thus centres upon a distinct and formidable fraction of the Victorian elite, political, cultural and colonial. A historicised reading might then take as its starting point the contention in the *Communist Manifesto* that 'the ruling ideas of each age have ever been the ideas of its ruling class'.[40] As Isobel Armstrong has observed, in the 1830s the Cambridge Apostles, who were to exert so profound an influence upon the politics and culture of Victorian England, 'wanted a transformation of the mind of the country, but not through direct political change'. Rather, they sought, and to some extent achieved, what she terms a 'non-revolutionary transformation'.[41] However,

in Tennyson's vision here that hegemonic class is reduced or dislimned to a
set of 'shadows' whose spectral identity mirrors Marx's thesis as to the
ghostly or bodiless quality of money in the exchange economy, a spectrality
producing, in Jacques Derrida's terminology, 'not the lifeless body or the
cadaver' represented by Sir John 'in his coffin', but 'a life without personal
life or individual property',[42] manifested by these ambulatory shadows. If
in the trenchant exordium of the *Communist Manifesto*, 'A spectre is haunting
Europe',[43] that premonitory vision of communism has been ineluctably
conjured into being by what Derrida nominates an entire 'hauntology', and
all this happens as the 'alliance of the worried conspirators assembles, more
or less secretly, a nobility and a clergy – in the old castle of Europe, for an
unbelievable expedition against what will have been haunting the night of
these masters'.[44] It is in this precise historical and class sense that Simeon,
member of the secret order of masons, comes to be hailed as 'master' and
'Prince', his foxhunting proclivities uncannily echoed in Marx's depiction
of the 'powers' of Europe joining in a 'holy hunt' against the spectre of
Communism. Hallam, who advertised himself to an editor as being 'as good
a Tory as your heart can wish',[45] had characterised a life without religious
feeling as one of 'dreadful shadows'.[46] Tennyson's 'Shadows', men possessed
of cultural or material property who are not quite ghosts and not quite
bodies, are conjoined in what Derrida terms 'a secret alliance against the
spectre' of social revolution,[47] but this is an alliance compromised by the
'disincarnated' basis of their own money power. Indeed, Marx tellingly
remarks at one point, 'The body of money is but a shadow',[48] and the
Manifesto speaks of the leeching away of identity in bourgeois society so that
'capital is independent and has individuality, while the living person is
dependent and has no individuality'.[49] This is the puzzle of capital which
the poem enacts: as Derrida phrases it, how do 'living men, temporal and
finite existences, become subjected, in their social relations, to these spec-
tres that are relations, *equally social* relations among commodities?' In the
Marxist analysis, that is to say, and also in the trajectory of the poem, 'ghosts
that are commodities transform human producers into ghosts',[50] and this
applies to the poet himself as cultural producer or generator of 'cultural
capital'. Under the spectral threat of communism, Marx argued, men and
events appear 'as shadows that have lost their bodies',[51] and Derrida's interpretation of this phenomenon may illuminate our reading of the poem:

> The whole movement of idealisation that Marx then describes, whether it is
> a question of money or of ideologems, is a production of ghosts, illusions,
> simulacra, appearances, or apparitions . . . Later he will compare this spec-
> tral virtue of money with that which, in the desire to hoard, speculates on
> the use of money after death, in the other world.[52]

The radical threat is perhaps reflected in the addition to *Idylls of the King* composed precisely at this juncture, namely 'The Last Tournament', in which a debilitated King Arthur sets out to quell a rebellion by the Red Knight, who founds a counter 'Round Table in the North' in a tower 'full of harlots' in which the knights 'are all adulterers' (ll. 78, 81, 84). This strange episode, ominous in its implications for the Arthurian brotherhood, might well embody a covert response to the perceived dangers to the ruling classes of the Reform Bill in 1867, nominated by Coventry Patmore the 'year of the great crime'.

The historical perspective of 'In the Garden' may be further opened up by focusing upon one of Tennyson's three 'shadows', that of Henry Lushington. 'What *passions* our friendships were', Thackeray reflected of his days at Cambridge,[53] and this was especially true of the Apostles, where the pairing of friends was common practice. It was said that the relation between Lushington and his fellow-Apostle George Venables was so intense that Venables, whose passion was largely unrequited, was even jealous of Tennyson's affection for Henry, the poet's favourite among the Lushington brothers. After leaving university Venables, an able critic and journalist who advised Tennyson in the preparation of the manuscripts of the 1842 *Poems* and of *In Memoriam,* lived together with Lushington in apartments in the Temple in London. Tennyson was a frequent visitor, as he was to Park House, the Kent home of the Lushingtons, including Edmund, who married Cecilia Tennyson in 1842. It was Park House which furnished the primary model for the setting of *The Princess*, the second edition of which was dedicated to Henry. Lushington was called to the Bar and joined the Home Circuit, but his tendency to consumption stifled a promising legal or political career. Having evinced a deep interest in imperial matters in his book on the Afghan war, *A Great Country's Little Wars* (1844),[54] he was offered the post of chief secretary to the government of Malta by the Colonial Secretary, Lord Grey, in January 1847 – a post not dissimilar to that filled with surprising efficiency by Coleridge in 1804–5. This was a role which would place Lushington second in seniority to the governor at a time when the British Government sought to liberalise the government of the island. As John Waller remarks in his invaluable study of the Lushingtons, Henry 'desired, yet deeply feared to go',[55] but after a good deal of vacillation he set off in the autumn, finally arriving in Malta in January 1848 in the company of several of his sisters. Malta was a hotbed of intrigue at this juncture as the result of a constitutional battle between the ruling British Protestants and the Roman Catholic populace, a situation exacerbated by the intervention of one of the original Cambridge Apostles, George Tomlinson, who had been appointed Bishop of Gibraltar, a see whose seat was in Malta. Lushington found himself caught between the ardently protestant bishop and the Catholic Governor, Richard O'Ferrall, and as Waller observes, 'In the new colonial edifice, he would occupy a cornerstone position'.[56] The difficulties were exacerbated by the nationalist uprisings in Italy during 1847–8, Lushington's liberal sympathies being wholeheartedly with the *risorgimento*, whilst O'Ferrall supported the duplicitous Pope Pius IX. In May 1849 Lushington's duties increased, despite his chronic ill health, when it was determined to incorporate elected members in Malta's Council of Government – a move Lushington opposed. Whilst a liberal espousal of freedom marked his European policies, as expressed in his 1851 *Edinburgh Review* articles on Italian nationalism, when Lushington turned his attention to British India his tone was markedly different, a sign of the way in which the Victorian ruling elite tended to read history as a clash between classical Hellenic freedom and barbaric Eastern despotism. In his book *The Double Government*, published in 1853, he supported the supposedly divine right of the British to rule India, arguing

> If there is one lie more fatal to the hopes of India, and more monstrous in itself, than those of their own religions, it surely is comprised in this, – "We are as good as the English." [57]

The thesis is a familiar one, based upon an interpretation of the Other as plural, feminised, threatening and potentially overwhelming. England's mission in India, Lushington paternalistically believed, was 'not to crush, but raise'. With somewhat uncanny prescience, in *In Memoriam* Tennyson had anticipated, 'ere yet the morn/ Breaks hither over Indian seas', what he defined as 'That Shadow waiting with the keys/ To shroud me from my proper scorn' (XXVI, ll. 13–16). Despite the death in 1854 of his beloved sister Louy, who had always accompanied his tours of duty, Lushington remained in his post, a 'half-dead patriot',[58] fired up by the *imbroglio* of the Crimea. He was virulently opposed to Russian claims, and composed some sanguinary poems celebrating the Crimean campaign during 1855, at the same time as Tennyson was completing *Maud*. In his poem on the battle of Inkerman, Lushington wrote of the troops,

> Little then could aid us
> Bugle or command;
> Most was native manhood,
> And your own right hand.
> Back to back, each fighting
> For himself and all,
> Broken, yet together

> Like a shattered wall,
> In our ranks no bayonet
> Lacked its stain of gore,
> As through ten times our number
> Our bloody path we tore.[59]

In the dedication to Louy and Venables, Henry Lushington significantly described these poems as the 'shadow of a wreath of lilies to the dead' and 'the shadow of a wreath of honour to the living'[60] – a phraseology which may be echoed in Tennyson's elegy. But he did not live to see publication, falling ill on his return journey through France and dying in Paris, with Venables at his bedside, in Paris on 11 August 1855.[61]

Lushington's publications may be read as a minor contribution to the massive framing of discourse on orientalism during the eighteenth and nineteenth centuries; in this period there occurred an intersection of texts and objects within an increasingly pervasive strategy of European cognition of 'the east'. Knowledge of these other lands and cultures, as Edward Said has shown, took the dual form of representation and exercise of colonial power. The workings of colonial governance, to which Lushington contributed, drew sustenance from a range of texts (such as his own) which worked, Said argues, to 'create not only knowledge but also the very reality they appear to describe'. The kind of studies of Afghanistan or India in which Lushington engaged offered 'a political vision of reality whose structure promoted the difference between the familiar (Europe, the West, 'us') and the strange (the Orient, the East, "them")'[62] – a sense of difference so great in his case that he suspended his progressive liberal principles when engaged in this body of work. This suspension or abnegation is a marker of his status, as both administrator and writer, as a member of the colonial elite. Lushington was a representative of that educated class fraction which promulgated Britain's imperial policy at this juncture, a cadre which subscribed wholeheartedly to the sense of imperial mission formulated by Lord Grey:

> The authority of the British Crown is at this moment the most powerful instrument, under providence, of maintaining peace and order in many extensive regions of the earth, and thereby assists in diffusing amongst millions of the human race, the blessings of Christianity and civilisation.[63]

This mission was performed by an imperial bureaucracy recruited from Britain's dominant classes, and Henry Lushington aptly fits Thomas Richards's definition of those who compiled the 'imperial archive':

> The work of the Foreign Office was done by any educated person, however

unqualified, working in whatever department, stationed wherever, who felt he had to do it simply because he happened to be British. These people were painfully aware of the gaps in their knowledge and did their best to fill them in. The filler they liked best was information. From all over the globe the British collected information about the countries they were adding to their map.[64]

Lushington's writings on Afghanistan, India and the Crimea focus concerns about the successful implementation of law and authority whilst unconsciously mobilising a conflictual oscillation between desire and mastery in the colonial sphere. The project of orientalist discourse, as Catherine Hall observes, 'was to secure the binaries between East and West', an aim only realised 'by constant discursive work, fixing and refixing the boundaries between western rationality and oriental irrationality, western industry and oriental laziness, western self-control and the oriental lack of it'.[65] Lord Grey's mission statement, like Fitzjames Stephen's prescription for Indian governance of a 'compulsory gospel which admits of no dissent and no disobedience', is haunted by what Christopher Lane has defined as 'a corresponding impulse to self-dispossession whenever [the coloniser] bid for a country's possesssion'.[66] If, as has often been proposed, sexuality is historically constructed, in the Victorian period the unspeakability of homosexual desire would fuel a range of modes of homosocial exchange which are elegaically inflected in Tennyson's poem. Lushington's colonial career conformed to the conservative lineage of homosexual desire: his work of empire, both literary and administrative, illustrating 'homosexuality's ability to demonstrate what is precarious and *lacking* in heterosexual meaning and national formation'.[67] Certainly his uncertain health and submission to an unsuitable climate enact what Lane defines as 'the relation between imperialism and the death drive'. Thus Lushington's career, like that of countless other men, took the form of

> the service that colonialism performed in the realm of sexual fantasy, and the influence that all of those factors brought to bear on the symbolisation of masculinity and homosexuality during Britain's volatile years of world power.[68]

In conclusion, it is possible to read 'In the Garden at Swainston' as a Victorian double-poem, one which, whilst espousing fellowship and comradeship, arises out of a sense of inwardness and solipsism, of a fracture in bourgeois hegemony. The double-poem, according to Isobel Armstrong's definition, draws the reader's attention to problems of knowing and to the cultural conditions in which the subject or self is formed. She nominates the dramatic monologue as the defining type, but this definition is perhaps too narrowly conceived. Certainly 'In the Garden at Swainston' may be read, in her phraseology, 'as a symptom of the political unconscious and thus irrevocably blind to its own meaning', or indeed as no less than three 'concurrent poems in the same words'.[69] In his old age Tennyson lamented that 'a poet never sees a ghost',[70] but as Rosenberg suggests, 'he saw nothing but ghosts', and his finest poetry 'is about absence rather than presence, about vanished persons and shadowy places, particularly the long and vivifying shadow cast over his life by the passing of Arthur Hallam'.[71] This is just, but 'In the Garden' might, in the final analysis, be read as a supplement or footnote to that sense, in *In Memoriam*, of the poet's expulsion from an Edenic friendship:

> But where the path we walked began
>   To slant the fifth autumnal slope,
>   As we descended following Hope
> There sat the Shadow feared of man;
>
> Who broke our fair companionship,
>   And spread his mantle dark and cold,
>   And wrapt thee formless in the fold,
> And dulled the murmur on thy lip,
>
> And bore thee where I could not see
>   Nor follow, though I walk in haste,
>   And think, that somewhere in the waste
> The Shadow sits and waits for me.

(XXII, ll. 9–20)

CHAPTER 2

Fair Ships

A Victorian Poetic Chronotope

The Ship of Death

In *Culture and Anarchy* Matthew Arnold diagnosed as a 'besetting danger' the current British obsession with the machine: 'What is freedom but machinery?' he asked, going on, 'what is coal but machinery? what are rail-roads but machinery? what is wealth but machinery?'[1] This Victorian cultivation of machinery is evidenced nowhere more spectacularly than in the mechanical revolution in shipping during the period. The first steam-powered paddle-wheel vessels were trialled in 1802, and by the 1820s were operating across the Channel and on North-American rivers. The crossing of the Atlantic utilising partial steam-power was inaugurated in 1838, a development epitomised in Brunel's ship the *Great Western*. By the middle of the century wooden ships had attained their maximum size of 7000 tonnes, the last wooden three-decker being constructed in 1859. From the 1830s onwards, attention turned to the iron-built hull; furthermore, the instability under some sea conditions of the paddle-wheel vessel led to the development of the screw-propeller, which was utilised on the *Great Britain*, the first iron-built ship to cross the Atlantic. The Royal Navy began to adopt steam power, and the new mail routes to Asia led to the formation of the P & O Company. Increases in engine power paved the way for the construction of the transatlantic liner and the success of companies such as the Cunard line. Mass emigration to the United States, with large numbers uncomfortably housed in 'steerage', fuelled the need for larger vessels, whilst at the opposite end of the social scale the steam-yacht became an object of desire for the leisured classes. Whilst sailing ships such as the Baltimore clippers and the *Cutty Sark* continued to flourish, the overall tendency was towards ever larger steam-powered iron-hull vessels – a tendency which culminated first in the construction in 1904 of the *Lusitania* and *Mauretania* and ultimately, in 1912, of the *Titanic*.

Victorian poetry of ships and the sea condenses and refracts a large histor-ical and contradictory conjuncture, the replacement of mercantile capital embodied in sail by industrial capital embodied in steam. Culture in England, Arnold suggested, had 'a weighty part to perform, because here that mechanical character . . . is shown in the most eminent degree'.[2] This cultural nostrum, he argued, would counterbalance the material dogma of progress as enunciated by John Bright, who hailed 'the cities you have built, the railroads you have made, the manufactures you have produced, the cargoes which freight the ships of the greatest mercantile navy the world has ever seen' – all evidence in his eyes of British eminence.[3] 'He who works for machinery', Arnold ripostes, 'works only for confusion', a confusion to be counterbalanced by the famous nostrum of 'sweetness and light'.[4] The dialectical connection between mechanism and metaphysics is at the heart of Tennyson's trope of the ship. In his poetry, the positivist materiality of his age, made manifest in the developments in marine engineering, is haunted by its other to such a degree that the ship becomes the archetype of the spiritual:

> Sunset and evening star,
>   And one clear call for me!
> And may there be no moaning of the bar,
>   When I put out to sea,
>
> But such a tide as moving seems asleep,
>   Too full for sound and foam,
> When that which drew from out the boundless deep
>   Turns again home.
>
> (ll. 1–8)[5]

The insistence upon technology, the materialisation of the motif of the sea-voyage, the enabling mechanisms of steam, paddle-wheel and propeller become estranged and abstracted in Tennyson's poetry into a form of mourning, an anticipation of death. The ship functions as a token, even a fetish, which is transmuted into a trace of its material embodiment, just as 'Crossing the Bar' is a text haunted by ghostly hints and memories of a prior sea-going poem by his brother Charles:

> The brazen plates upon the steerage-wheel
> Flash'd forth; the steersman's face came full in view;
> Found at his post, he met the bright appeal
> Of morning-tide, and answer'd 'I am true!'[6]

The action represented by the sea-crossing becomes in effect the emblem of the removal of the signified: the bar which is crossed functions, linguistically, as the Saussurean bar between signified and signifier. As the signified, the ferry between the Isle of Wight and the mainland, fades out of the text, so the ship becomes as it were a ghostly trace or signifier. In enacting the 'crossing' from material to spiritual, the text creates its own demise:

> For though from out our bourne of Time and Place
>> The flood may bear me far,
> I hope to see my Pilot face to face
>> When I have crost the bar.

(ll. 13–16)

'Crossing the Bar' is essentially a poem of the border-line, the crossing of the sand-bar conventionally representing the passage from life to death, in a reversal of Swinburne's image, composed twenty years earlier in the *Songs Before Sunrise*, of 'birth's hidden harbour-bar'.[7] The imaginary border delineated here represents a topographical and somatic limit-situation projected as an 'in-between' state seeking a stable location which is forever postponed – what is the Pilot but a 'supplement' to the ship's captain? Linda Shires, noting the metrically 'compelling undersong' of such verse, points out how often Tennyson 'singles out the watery deep as a figure for this primal rhythm or pulse of time and timelessness'.[8] The dynamism of the discourse of Victorian progress and evolution leads towards a deterritorialisation, the projection of a seascape in which boundaries fade and dissolve, certainties of self and place destabilised in a crisis of (self-)representation. In *The Dialectic of Enlightenment*, Adorno and Horkheimer postulate that 'in the image of voyaging, historical time is detached from space, the irrevocable pattern of all mythic time'.[9]

Whilst Tennyson piously explicated the figure of the pilot in terms of a figure 'Divine and Unseen Who is always guiding us',[10] the wish to see him 'face to face' inevitably calls up memories of the more human image of Arthur Hallam, whose mythicisation had been undertaken in *In Memoriam*, where it is noted of the Son of God that we 'have not seen thy face' (Prologue, l. 2). Hallam was envisaged, in the argument of the poem, as a superior being who, Tennyson felt, 'still outstript me in the race' (XLII, l. 2), and it is this hidden or occluded sense of rivalry which troubles the ostensible serenity of the imagined voyage bringing home the corpse from Italy:

> Fair ship, that from the Italian shore
>> Sailest the placid ocean-plains
> With my lost Arthur's loved remains,
>> Spread thy full wings, and waft him o'er.
>
> So draw him home to those that mourn
>> In vain; a favourable speed
>> Ruffle thy mirrored mast, and lead
>> Through prosperous floods his holy urn.

(IX, ll. 1–8)

At first the ship sails smoothly on with 'sliding keel' under 'gentle winds', until

> I hear the noise about thy keel;
> > I hear the bell struck in the night:
> > I see the cabin-window bright;
> I see the sailor at the wheel.
>
> (X, ll. 1–4)

This increased sense of movement leads into the curious fantasy of a drowning corpse:

> > . . . if with thee the roaring wells
> > > Should gulf him fathom-deep in brine;
> > > And hands so often clasped in mine,
> > Should toss with tangle and with shells.
>
> (X, ll. 17–20)

The entanglement of the corpse's hands in seaweed and shells is both feared and desired, since it removes the elegiac subject from the human arena – Hallam as it were dies a second death. The act of memorialisation, the hymning of 'that noble breast' which satisfyingly 'heaves but with the heaving deep' (XI, l. 20), masks and disguises the covert rivalry between poet and critic which *In Memoriam* circles around. The elegist works like the translators who, in Paul de Man's phrase, 'kill the original, by discovering that the original was already dead'; but this act of remembering or translation 'belongs to the afterlife of the original, thus assuming and confirming the death of the original'.[11] The poem's inaccurately plotted sea-voyage projects fantasies of sorrow, passivity and rivalry as the poet imagines 'ocean-mirrors rounded large', sees 'the sails at distance rise', and as the breezes 'play/ About the prow', returns in a macabre and almost Gothic motif 'To where the body sits' (XII, ll. 9, 11, 19). The hidden charge of these lines, suffused as they are by the anxiety of influence, is traceable to the source of the 'ocean-mirrors' in an earlier poem, 'The Voyage', in which 'that smooth Ocean rounded large' is ominously traversed by 'the long sea-serpent',[12] its serpentine coils suggesting both the intertwining, quasi-familial dependence of the two Cambridge Apostles and the strangling, suffocating nature of that dependence for the youthful poet.

The homosocial problematics of *In Memoriam*, and the associated imagery of ships and the sea, seem to invite a reading informed by psychoanalytic theory. In Freudian dream symbolism, 'hollow objects' such as 'ships, and vessels of all kinds'[13] represent the uterus, and are thus inextricably linked with thematics of birth and sexuality. There is furthermore, Freud would propose, a linkage between the series water/urine/semen/amniotic fluid which subtextually underlies Tennysonian imagery here.[14] The funerary ship carrying Hallam's body from Livorno to Dover bears as cargo the corpse of a man characterised by a 'largeness of aspiration and moneyed culture'[15] which eluded the Somersby Tennysons. *In Memoriam* enacts a drama of return, a voyage towards a final home, but one which is interrupted and baffled by the imaginary sea-wreck and loss of the treasured corpse in a staging, not of the return of the repressed but the repression of the return. The journey takes on the tone of the uncanny, as *heimlich*, in Freud's terms, is translated into its opposite, *unheimlich*. One of the anxieties of the uncanny in Freud's essay centres upon the question of whether a lifeless object 'might not be in fact animate'[16] – an issue which the gratuitous drowning of the corpse seeks to settle. Whilst the poet asks the ship, 'Come quick, thou bringest all I love' (XVII, l. 8), and hails Hallam as 'More than my brothers are to me' (LXXIX, l. 1), the function of Hallam's corpse as Tennyson's double persistently haunts the text, hollowing out its insistent declarations of affection. That which is, in Freudian theory, 'familiar and old-established', is now alienated in a process Freud links with 'the return of the dead'.[17] In this scenario, which the poem seeks to resist, 'the dead man becomes the enemy of his survivor and seeks to carry him off' to the land of the dead.[18]

The Shipwreck

The trope of shipwreck, as George Landow observes, is pervasive in nineteenth-century painting and literature, and he reads it as signifying punishment, trial or spiritual education. Landow contends that 'whereas the traditional shipwreck takes place in the *presence* of God', for the Victorians 'it occurs in his *absence*'.[19] In this period of waning faith, he suggests, 'the shipwreck and its corollary of being stranded, drifting, or cast away are often used as paradigms to communicate experience of personal crisis'.[20] In the eighteen-forties particularly, as Froude maintained in his biography of Carlyle, 'the intellectual lightships had broken from their moorings . . . the lights drifting, the compasses all awry'.[21] Victorian historiography, it may be said, is often compromised by the wish ascribed to the Young Hegelians in Karl Löwith's account: 'To want to be oriented by history whilst standing in its midst would be like wanting to hold on to the waves during a shipwreck'.[22] But this existential account of shipwreck needs to be contextualised by the material history of navigation. Alison Winter suggests in her fine study of this issue that throughout the Victorian period 'the language of disordered compasses and lost ships was used to describe spiritual and intellectual uncertainties', but as she demonstrates, this metaphor was based in the everyday problems encountered in the navigation of the new iron ships.[23] Winter outlines the intense debate between ships' captains, scientists, underwriters and other interested parties regarding irregularities in compass readings caused by the development of the iron-clad steamship. In particular, she focuses upon the controversy between George Airy, the Astronomer Royal, and William Scoresby, a clerical ship's captain. Airy's solution to compass variation was a system of continual compass corrections carried out by technicians on the spot, a solution which reduced the decision-making role of the captains whose 'stupidity' Airy loftily deplored. Certainly this was a crucial issue: as Winter notes, the mid-century saw heightened awareness of shipwreck and navigational questions. In the period 1852–60 alone, for example, over 10,000 ships were wrecked and more than seven thousand lives lost; in one of the most spectacular accidents, the troopship *Birkenhead* was lost off the coast of South Africa with the loss of almost 500 lives. Some years earlier, the *Great Britain* had been grounded in 1846 off the coast of Ireland.

This seemingly endless chapter of accidents led to public scepticism about Airy's method and to the quasi-religious intervention of William Scoresby, who drew parallels between magnetism and mesmerism. Scoresby was opposed to adjustment of the ship's compass and called upon his wide seafaring experience in a campaign conducted against the increasing professionalisation of the scientific community. This contest, pertinently analysed by Winter, is crucial to any historically alert reading of Victorian shipwreck, historical, artistic or literary, and is subtextually present in Gerard Manley Hopkins's ruminations, in a sermon of 1881, about the human will possessing 'in its affections a tendency or magnetism towards which every object and the *arbitrium*, the elective will, decides which', and Hopkins adds, 'this is the needle proper'.[24] Such reflections bear out John Irwin's notion of 'a direct link between the letters of God's unutterable name and the four points of the compass'.[25] A year or two prior to this sermon, Hopkins had referred to Christ exerting 'a magnetic spell' on humanity, and argued that God's anger towards the rebel angels operated in the same way 'as a magnetic current is heightened', causing 'needles and shreds of iron' to 'rear, stare and group themselves . . . at the poles'.[26] That this figure was theologically persuasive for Tractarians is evidenced in Christina Rossetti's notation of errors in conceptualising the Trinity: 'well will it be for us if trembling between them our magnet yet points aright'.[27] Daniel Brown, in his analysis of Hopkins's debts to Oxford Idealism, usefully glosses this concept, demonstrating how the 'affective "freedom of field", through which the elective will ranges and comes to settle, parallels the electromagnetic or gravitational fields of force, the media in which the iron compass exists and acts'.[28] Hopkins's imagination, Brown argues, generates metaphors which characterise the human subject in terms of 'the "burl", the

taut rope, and the compass needle' in order to 'illustrate the integral relation that he sees personal instress to have to the all-encompassing field of
stress'. Brown offers an insightful account of the ways in which Hopkins
'elaborates his ontological monism as an economy of energy' so that the
poet's 'ontology of "instress" is concerned with open systems of energy'[29] –
an ontology nowhere more in evidence than in the two shipwreck poems.
'In watching the sea', Hopkins observes in 1872, 'one should be alive to the
oneness which all its motion and tumult receives from its perpetual balance
and falling this way and that to its level'.[30] God's participation in history
manifests itself as power articulated through water most dramatically in
Hopkins's shipwreck poetry, where it is conceived in mechanistic terms, as
Brown suggests, of 'hydrodynamic "pressure", "stress", and "force"'.[31]

Issues of technical and human failure at every level combined to tragic
effect in the winter of 1875, when the British-built screw steamship, the
Deutschland, sailed out of Bremen. The steel-constructed vessel, though ten
years old, had just been refitted with new engines, propeller and no fewer
than five compasses – a feature which Hopkins may subtextually refer to in
his allusion to the nuns as 'Five! The finding and sake/ And cipher of
suffering Christ' (st. 22), itself an echo of an earlier poem on the crucifixion:

> For us the Vine was fenced with thorn,
> Five ways the precious branches torn;[32]

On Sunday 5 December, encountering severe storms and heavy snow,
Captain Edward Brickenstein set the engines at full throttle, inadvertently
steering the ship onto the sandbanks at the mouth of the Thames and shattering the propeller. What ensued was a catastrophic series of blunders both
on board ship and on the English coast which meant that the ship was not
reached by rescue vessels for thirty hours. Given his father's career as an
insurance underwriter, and author of a textbook of instruction for master-
mariners, *The Port of Refuge* (1873), it is little wonder that Gerard Manley
Hopkins was spurred by this disaster to a rivalrous yet filial outburst of
poetry delineating the 'unchilding unfathering deeps' (st. 14). The nation-
alistically nominated *Deutschland*, carrying into exile the five Catholic nuns,
thus embodies the potent yet catastrophic law instigated through the
'name-of-the-father' in both state and family. The details of the actual shipwreck have been fully delineated elsewhere,[33] but what is worth stressing
in the text is the curious admixture of technical detail and metaphysical
rhetoric: Hopkins, for instance, accurately notates the circumstance of the
damaged propeller, 'the whorl and the wheel/ Idle for ever to waft her or
wind her with' (st. 14), or the decapitation of the sailor in his attempt to

save the nuns (st. 11). At the same time he offers a hermeneutic reading of the wreck as sign of England's potential spiritual redemption: 'is the shipwrack then a harvest, does tempest carry the grain for thee?' (st. 31). The Catholic resonance of Hopkins's concluding stanza, with its visionary conjuration of a new dawn for 'rare-dear Britain' (st. 35), consorts uneasily with the narrative of failure, death, delay and error – David Shaw has appositely noted 'the plenitude of stacked nouns that all but choke off life in the crowded final line'.[34]

Hopkins brilliantly but problematically seeks to integrate mechanical and human failings, meteorological disturbance and the circumstances of the wreck to a missionary world-view – he transforms the linguistic evidence of the *Times* reports into a new literary totality with its own coherence and dissonance, so that the poem functions not as description but as intervention. 'The Wreck' is an account of a physical and spiritual event relating to a collective subject, conscious and unconscious, which might be termed sacramental: the poem frames a 'possible consciousness' in response to the wreck in order to create an entirely new realisation of a conventional trope. The problematic of Hopkins's work, and of this text in particular, is generated by the impossibility of its reading and reception – what is broken or wrecked is the work of art in all its potentialities. This broken-backed state of the text is made literal as a failure of language and vision:

> But how shall I . . . make me room there:
> Reach me a . . . Fancy, come faster –
> Strike you the sight of it? look at it loom there,
> Thing that she . . .
>
> (st. 28)

Here the industrial terminology – 'strike', 'loom' – may be no accident. As Cesare Casarino observes in his study of Melville and Conrad, 'the modernist sea narrative anticipates in the nineteenth century many of the later tendencies toward narrative fragmentation and dissolution of early twentieth-century modernism'.[35] Accepting Foucault's definition of the ship as a heterotopian space, Casarino holds that 'the fabular language of representation falters, flounders, encounters the unspeakable, faces the unrepresentable' in these texts of the sea.[36] 'The Wreck of the "Deutschland"' seeks to imagine an escape from modernity towards an archaically framed new life of religious observance and ritual, and here Casarino's general definition of the sea narrative is germane:

> The very structure of the text seems to buckle down and crack at its seams under the enormous atmospheric pressures of capital, and the final product

of such metamorphic processes might well be one of the first specimens of an as yet unrecognisable and unprecedented literary form.[37]

The contextual implications of the text relate to the formation of the Prussian nation-state, the framing of the Falck laws and the concomitant expulsion of those 'Loathed for a love men knew in them,/ Banned by the land of their birth' (st. 21). This concatenation of events culminating on the Kentish Knock is evidence of that acceleration of capital fuelled by technical progress which Casarino defines, in Benjaminian terminology, as 'an attempt to rush ahead of the inescapable, unfathomable, and ominous gravitational pulls of a history of modernity increasingly apprehended as "one single catastrophe"'.[38] It makes no difference that the poem possesses a 'documentary' context, as may be seen in comparison with a dream or fantasy text, Herman Melville's 'The Berg' (1888):

> I saw a ship of martial build
> (Her standards set, her brave apparel on)
> Directed as by madness mere
> Against a stolid iceberg steer,
> Not budge it, though the infatuate ship went down.
> The impact made huge ice-cubes fall
> Sullen, in tons that crashed the deck;
> But that one avalanche was all –
> No other movement save the foundering wreck.
>
> (ll. 1–9)[39]

The blank and fatal imperviosity of the ice, and the contrast with the 'impetuous ship' which 'in bafflement went down', is ominously proleptic in its resonance. The berg's whiteness inevitably conjures up memories of Moby-Dick, whose whiteness Ishmael categorises as 'a dumb blankness, full of meaning, in a wide landscape of snows', and its theological signification is elaborated in his remarks about 'a colorless, all color of atheism from which we shrink'.[40] The berg stands, as it were, for the final limit of capital, but it is capital in crisis which motivates both poems. Melville's dream text, unlike Hopkins's 'factual' poem, eschews any metaphysical conclusion, paradoxically wedded as it is to an imaginary materiality which 'The Wreck' seeks to transcend: the concatenation of objective conditions – weather, human and mechanical failure – is spiritualised by Hopkins in a staging of the wreck as a vessel of conversion running on to the sandbanks of the secular liberal state – the Kentish Knock on which the *Deutschland* foundered is, after all, only a short distance from Dover beach with its 'melancholy, long, withdrawing roar'. Seven years before the wreck, Hopkins notes his anxiety that, under the impact of a Comtean Positivism, 'the end of all metaphysics is at hand', and projects this process in terms of that 'tide we may foresee' which would 'always turn between idealism and materialism'.[41] Melville, by contrast, stresses the meaninglessness of historical accident, and in his poem what is registered is a linguistic shock effect, the 'free' life of nature containing and emptying out the power of technology in a staging of the dialectic of self and other:

> Along the spurs of ridges pale,
> Not any slenderest shaft and frail,
> A prism over glass-green gorges lone,
> Toppled; nor lace of traceries fine,
> Nor pendant drops in grot or mine
> Were jarred, when the stunned ship went down.
> Nor sole the gulls in cloud that wheeled
> Circling one snow-flanked peak afar,
> But nearer fowl the floes that skimmed
> And crystal beaches, felt no jar.
>
> (ll. 10–19)

There is here no reconciliation between subject (ship) and object (berg) such as is available to Hopkins's theological reading of the scenario of shipwreck. Freed from the constraints of theology, Melville stages the collision of a warlike positivism with a somnambulistic nature. The berg is a concrete abstraction which restricts and overcomes dialectical thought and the human insistence on difference in an unravelling of comprehensibility that will be characteristic of modernism. It is as if the linear pattern of nineteenth-century historiography, the myth of technical progress, is shattered and fragmented in a poem which functions as a footnote to the definition of modern culture:

> Hard Berg (methought), so cold, so vast,
> With mortal damps self-overcast;
> Exhaling still thy dankish breath –
> Adrift dissolving, bound for death;
> Though lumpish thou, a lumbering one –
> A lumbering lubbard loitering slow,
> Impingers rue thee and go down,
> Sounding thy precipice below,
> Nor stir the slimy slug that sprawls
> Along thy dead indifferent walls.
>
> (ll. 28–37)[42]

In this conjunction of opposites, the 'administered society' of the ship, expressed in the formal ingenuity of the verse, is undermined and countered by the blank concretion of nature; a sense of dialectic is unavailable, visible only in its moment of ruin. Melville's vision is of a 'primal scene' already projected in an early Hopkins poem, 'I must hunt down the prize' (1864), where the poet desires to 'see the green seas roll/ Where the seas set/ Towards wastes where the ice-blocks tilt and fret,/ Not so far from the pole'. Both poems refract the mid-century public interest in Arctic exploration, and the controversy generated by the 1857 discovery of the remains of Sir John Franklin's expedition twelve years earlier.[43] In its whiteness the berg represents the realm of pure thought, its contradictory relation to the human not to be resolved, as in 'The Wreck', by recourse to Tractarian ideology.

In 'Sleep at Sea' (1862), Christina Rossetti offers an interesting variant of the Tractarian reading of the scenario of the shipwreck. Whilst 'the watchmen sleep',

> White shapes flit to and fro
> From mast to mast;
> They feel the distant tempest
> That nears them fast:
> Great rocks are straight ahead,
> Great shoals not past;
> They shout to one another
> Upon the blast.
>
> (ll. 9–16)[44]

The sleepers dream as the ship 'is driving, driving/ It drives apace' (ll. 29–30): 'From such a sunset/ When shall day arise?' (ll. 39–40). The spirits call '"Wake"' to 'heedless ears' (ll. 41–2), and then 'rise and go':

> Driving and driving,
> The ship drives amain:
> While swift from mast to mast
> Shapes flit again,
> Flit silent as the silence
> Where men lie slain;
> Their shadow cast upon the sails
> Is like a stain.
>
> (ll. 73–80)

The stern morality of the preacher, finally, defines that 'Vanity of vanities' (l. 85) which 'is the end/ Of all their ways' (ll. 87–8). Rossetti apparently offers an orthodox Christian warning about spiritual deafness, but also frames a language, in Adorno's terminology, 'constituted by a collective undercurrent' which manifests itself particularly 'in the case of those works popularly stigmatised as lonely and walled up in the ivory tower'.[45] Whilst the religious typology lends itself to the note of 'vanitas vanitatum' that pervades Rossetti's oeuvre, this is a critique, as Jerome McGann puts it, 'launched from the vantage . . . of the poet's "secret place"'.[46] The aesthetic of renunciation enables Rossetti, in Adorno's phrase, to 'diverge from empirical reality' in a trajectory which lays bare 'the affinity of artworks to the dream'. The scene of spiritual wreckage surveyed by 'Sleep at Sea' illuminates Adorno's argument that 'Only those artworks are enlightened that, vigilantly distant from the empirical, evince true consciousness' because they are determined 'by spirit'.[47] 'Sleep at Sea' inhabits that region of 'thresholds and borderlands, dream-states and twilight regions'[48] characteristic of the poet, and it is thus that Rossetti is enabled, as Dolores Rosenblum suggests, to 'create a self by abdicating the self' in a strategy of 'extreme alienation' contained within 'self possession'.[49] In contradistinction to Hopkins's theophany of shipwreck, for Rossetti the sailors' predicament acts as marker of a spiritual blindness in which only she, as poet, is able to keep watch over the 'face of the deep': 'In artworks nothing is literal, least of all their words; spirit is their ether, what speaks through them, or, more precisely, what makes artworks become script'.[50]

On 24 March 1878 a wooden-hulled frigate, the *Eurydice*, returning from a training cruise in the West Indies, was struck by a sudden squall and capsized with the loss of all but two of her over three hundred crew, the majority of them youths from Portsmouth. The *Eurydice* was an old-fashioned wooden ship whose guns had largely been removed, leaving the gun-ports open for ventilation. Sailing close to the cliffs of the Isle of Wight in bright sunlight, the captain was unable to observe an immense storm approaching from the land. The squall of wind, rain and snow was funnelled down a cleft or chine near Ventnor straight on to the ship, water pouring in through the gun-ports; as Hopkins would imagine it:

> Now Carisbrook keep goes under in gloom;
> Now it overvaults Appledurcombe;
>   Now near by Ventnor town
> It hurls, hurls off Boniface Down.

(ll. 29–32)

The vessel sank within ten minutes, only the tops of the masts remaining visible to spectators on the cliff above, who included the four-year-old Winston Churchill. This maritime tragedy prompted a Kiplingesque poetic response from another writer trained by the Jesuits, in the form of a ballad subsequently included in Arthur Conan Doyle's *Songs of Action* (1898):

A grey swirl of snow with the squall at the back of it,
   Heeling her, reeling her, beating her down!
A gleam of her bends in the thick of the wrack of it,
   A flutter of white in the eddies of brown.

It broke in one moment of blizzard and blindness;
   The next, like a foul bat, it flapped on its way.
But our ship and our boys! Gracious lord, in your kindness,
   Give help to the mothers who need it today!

Give help to the women who wait by the water,
   Who stand on the Hard with their eyes past the Wight.
Ah! whisper it gently, you sister or daughter,
   'Our boys are all gathered at home for tonight.'[51]

By 2 April, Gerard Manley Hopkins, who had been posted to Mount St Mary's College, Chesterfield in Derbyshire, was sending Robert Bridges a draft of some verses on the wreck, 'The Loss of the Eurydice', modelled upon a Tennysonian metre – his first effort at poetry since his removal from St Beuno's College in North Wales. Whether or not Captain Marcus Hare was guilty of the 'stupidity' ascribed by the Astronomer Royal to master-mariners, he was posthumously cleared of blame for the loss of so many young lives. Hopkins aimed in this exercise at a greater simplicity of utterance than in the 'Deutschland' poem, but he takes the occasion of the wreck in both cases as a moment to reflect upon the religious state of England, producing as it were a Tractarian poetic document. A historically alert reading might also wish to ponder the imperial implications of a training ship returning from the waters around the sugar plantations of the Caribbean, where it had undertaken a prolonged demonstration of British naval power:

For did she pride her, freighted fully, on
Bounden bales or a hoard of bullion? –
   Precious passing measure,
Lads and men her lade and treasure.

                   (ll. 9–12)

Julia Saville pertinently identifies this image cluster as evoking both 'Britain's readiness to buy unlimited quantities of cotton from America's southern states prior to the Civil War, in spite of the complicity with slavery', and 'its readiness to buy newly discovered gold from California and Australia'.[52] But the ship, returning from its tour of duty in the West Indies with its 'Three hundred souls', might also conjure up subliminal memories of the slave-ships and their masters, the 'tight-packers' and 'loose-packers'. The 'Eurydice', that is to say, may be seen as playing a role, however minor, in the constitution of what Paul Gilroy has nominated 'the Black Atlantic' – a cultural and geographical zone in which 'ships were the living means by which the points within that Atlantic world were joined'. The ships, whether belonging to slave-traders, pirates or the British navy, 'were mobile elements that stood for the shifting spaces in between the fixed places that they connected'.[53] A reading of 'The Loss', in its depiction of the 'deadly-electric' storm, may thus aptly be framed by Marx's sense of the imminent approaching roar of 'the really *modern crises*, in which the contradiction of capital discharges itself in great thunderstorms'.[54] As Eric Williams has observed, the Caribbean plantation owners 'always pointed, in justification of their system, to their contribution to the naval supremacy of England'.[55] In a parodic reinstatement and reversal of the ships of the Middle Passage, with their densely packed human cargo, the 'Eurydice' returns from the colonised space with 'Three hundred souls' (l. 2), 'Lads and men her lade and treasure' (l. 12), to meet 'A beetling baldbright cloud thorough England/Riding' (ll. 25–6). As death begins 'teeming in by her portholes' (l. 39), the youthful crew is killed by the ship's suffocating maternal embrace: 'she who had housed them thither/ Was around them, bound them or wound them with her' (ll. 43–4).

The scene of death is, though, curiously eroticised, for Hopkins's vision of the individual sailor both nominates and evades the issue of sexual 'inversion':

> They say who saw one sea-corpse cold
> He was all of lovely manly mould,
>   Every inch a tar,
> Of the best we boast our sailors are.
>
> Look, foot to forelock, how all things suit! he
> Is strung by duty, is strained to beauty,
>   And brown-as-dawning-skinned
> With brine and shine and whirling wind.
>
>   (ll. 73–80)

The tentative and fleeting trace of sexuality here, condensed in the suggestive phraseology of 'foot to forelock', together with the racial hint of 'brown-as-dawning-skinned', may be located within Casarino's diagnosis of 'an emergent definition of sexual identity, as aboard ship one does become . . . an as yet unspecified, undefinable, unnamed something'.[56] Same-sex desire is, at this conjuncture, unrepresentable, and yet the poem gestures momentarily towards a homosexual subjectivity in a strategy which incorporates and problematises the role of the ship in the Victorian imagination.

In Casarino's account of sea-going narratives, whilst the place of the ship 'was being fatally put into question', the trope of the vessel 'turned into one of the most significant stages for the dramatisation of paradigm shifts in conceptions of sexuality'.[57] Hopkins's elegy for 'Men, boldboys soon to be men' (l. 14) hints at the question made explicit by Casarino: 'what new forms of being-in-common might arise when male bodies abandon themselves to each other?'[58]

John Schad postulates 'the unthinkability of *any* sexual encounter' in 'The Wreck',[59] but Hopkins verges upon the unthinkable in his second poem of shipwreck. His depiction of the young sailor's body may indeed be read as an elegy which simultaneously celebrates and cancels out an impe-rial 'muscular Christianity'. As Maureen Moran has argued, 'For the "muscular Christian", the Incarnation gave the body . . . a place of respect and honour', whilst for the Catholic, 'the body remained a receptacle of imperfection'.[60] Three years before the foundering of the *Eurydice*, Hopkins had asserted to Bridges that 'in a manner I am a Communist', and depicted late-Victorian England as 'in great measure founded on wrecking'.[61] The 'Red' letter may be framed by Casarino's thesis that 'the desire of commu-nism is corporeal, erotic, sexual', but simultaneously 'unrepresentable'.[62] In imagining a space of autonomy from capital, 'The Loss of the Eurydice' evinces its failure and daring by conjuring up and then dismissing unname-able desires in favour of a discourse of spiritual redemption, the naval brotherhood of the ship reimagined as the secret brotherhood of the Jesuit order. Both 'The Wreck' and 'The Loss', that is to say, conclude with what, in Casarino's argument are defining characteristics of modernity, in response to the permanent crisis of capital: 'inscrutable signs of a world stuck in a perpetual state of waiting for an eternally deferred event of redemption'.[63] The sinking of the 'Eurydice', however, with its occluded resonance of an empire founded in the slave-trade, problematises and undermines that very redemptive thinking offered by Hopkins's poem, his conclusion here offering what Gadamer, in his analysis of Paul Celan, has characterised as 'a theology of desperation':[64]

> But to Christ lord of thunder
> Crouch; lay knee by earth low under:
>   'Holiest, loveliest, bravest,
> Save my hero, O Hero savest.
>
> And the prayer thou hearst me making
> Have, at the awful overtaking,
>   Heard; have heard and granted
> Grace that day grace was wanted.'

> Not that hell knows redeeming,
> But for souls sunk in seeming
> Fresh, till doomfire burn all,
> Prayer shall fetch pity eternal.
>
> (ll. 109–20)

The Transcendental Ship

The waning of religious belief to which Hopkins's conflicted career and art paradoxically bore witness, tending finally towards his despairing diagnosis of his writing as so many 'ruins and wrecks',[65] led dialectically to a transcendental conception of a spiritual journey beyond the farthest horizon. As early as 1854, in *Walden*, Thoreau was ruminating that 'it is easier to sail many thousand miles through cold and storm . . . in a government ship . . . than it is to explore the private sea, the Atlantic and Pacific Ocean of one's being alone'.[66] As Gillian Beer observes, at this conjuncture the sea 'comes to represent the unconscious in which there is no narrative'.[67] This becomes a recurrent note later in the century as the diminution of Christian belief generated a variety of speculative experiments centred upon the chronotope of the ship. Richard Jefferies, for instance, concludes his 'spiritual autobiography', *The Story of My Heart* (1883), in this vein:

> Let me launch forth and sail over the rim of the sea, yonder, and when another rim arises over that, and again onwards into an ever-widening ocean of idea and life . . . with all the strength of the wave, and its succeeding wave, the depth and race of the tide, the clear definition of the sky; with all the subtle power of the great sea, there rises an equal desire.[68]

This gesture towards what Jefferies categorises as 'the Beyond' similarly informs some of Nietzsche's speculative thought. In *The Gay Science* (1887), for instance, under the sub-heading '*Horizon, infinity*', he declared, 'We have left the land and taken to our ship!' In this final venture of thought 'there is no longer any land': 'Send your ships out into uncharted seas!' Nietzsche exclaims: 'There is another new world to discover – and more than one! On board ship, philosophers!'[69] The poet of this impulse is Walt Whitman, whose work is so largely generated, as F. O. Matthiessen observed, by the 'sensuous amplitude' and 'mystery' of the shoreline, the 'unshored harbourless immensities' of ocean contrasted with 'the land's peaceful margin of safety'.[70] Matthiessen justly identifies a 'somnambulism' in Whitman's verse which enables him to be 'swept into the currents of the unconscious mind',[71] and this is classically the case in 'Passage to India' (1871), in which the opening of the Suez Canal becomes the occasion of a transcendental journey:

> Passage, immediate passage! The blood burns in my veins!
> Away O soul! hoist instantly the anchor!
> Cut the hawsers – haul out – shake out every sail!
> Have we not stood here like trees in the ground long enough?
> Have we not grovel'd here long enough, eating and drinking like mere
>   brutes?
> Have we not darken'd and dazed ourselves with books long enough?
>
> Sail forth – steer for the deep water only,
> Reckless O soul, exploring, I with thee, and thou with me,
> For we are bound where mariner has not yet dared to go,
> And we will risk the ship, ourselves and all.
>
> O my brave soul!
> O farther farther sail!
> O daring joy, but safe! Are they not all the seas of God?
> O farther, farther, farther sail!
>
> (ll. 242–55)[72]

This visionary afflatus, with its democratic and 'Uranian' undertones, centring upon the voyage towards unknown regions, elicited a wide response in late-Victorian and Edwardian culture epitomised musically, for instance, in Delius's *Sea-Drift* (1904) or Vaughan Williams's *A Sea Symphony* (1910). This type of sea-going rhetoric would not survive the ultimate crisis of monopoly capital embodied in the Great War: on the contrary, poetic language then undergoes a diminution, as Gadamer remarks of the Holocaust, moving towards 'the breathless stillness of muted silence in words which have become cryptic'.[73] Such attenuated utterance and premonition of cataclysm, the final moment of the poetic chronotope of the ship, was to be hauntingly sounded in 1912 by the loss of the ultimate 'ship of dreams':

> Well: while was fashioning
> This creature of cleaving wing,
> The Immanent Will that stirs and urges everything
>
> Prepared a sinister mate
> For her – so gaily great –
> A Shape of Ice, for the time far and dissociate.
>
> And as the smart ship grew
> In stature, grace, and hue,
> In shadowy silent distance grew the Iceberg too.

Alien they seemed to be:
No mortal eye could see
The intimate welding of their later history,

Or sign that they were bent
By paths coincident
On being anon twin halves of one august event,

Till the Spinner of the Years
Said 'Now!' And each one hears,
And consummation comes, and jars two hemispheres.[74]

CHAPTER 3

A Laodicean

Hardy and the Philosophy of Money

> I traced the Circus whose gray stones incline
> Where Rome and dim Etruria interjoin,
> Till came a child who showed an ancient coin
> That bore the image of a Constantine.
>
> She lightly passed; nor did she once opine
> How, better than all books, she had raised for me
> In swift perspective Europe's history
> Through the vast years of Caesar's sceptred line.
>
> For in my distant plot of English loam
> Twas but to delve, and straightway there to find
> Coins of like impress. As with one half blind
> Whom common simples cure, her act flashed home
> In that mute moment to my opened mind
> The power, the pride, the reach of perished Rome.
>
> 'In the Old Theatre, Fiesole'[1]

The Roman coin proffered to Thomas Hardy here serves, not in a system of exchange, but as an artefact redolent of imperial power and decline. Constantine was the first Christian emperor, and the poem may hint at Christ's allusion to the coins bearing the emperor's image. As Marx observed, 'a coin is a physical object which in this sense has no existence independent of men', and it is only transmuted into money when it 'forms an element within a definite set of social relationships'.[2] Hardy is always alert to this distinction, and nowhere more tellingly than in the incident in *The Mayor of Casterbridge* where the four ounce pennies left by Susan Henchard as weights for her eyelids after death are dug up by Christopher Coney, a 'cannibal deed' denounced by Mrs Cuxsom, but one which restores the coins to their exchange function. Money, both physical and metaphysical, is a defining concern for Hardy's fiction as it registers the transitions from an agrarian to an urban economy, and it is a theme which may be illuminated by reference to German sociological writing of the period.

It was Georg Simmel, writing at the turn of the century, who made a significant contribution to this debate, in a number of essays and in his massive study, *The Philosophy of Money*, first published in 1902. In his 1896 essay, 'Money and Modern Culture', Simmel discerns a contrast between a communal feudal society and a modernity that offers the individual unparalleled freedom whilst draining life of colour and personality. Thus he suggests that a medieval guild was a living community which absorbed the 'entire person', but the money economy offers an association based entirely upon 'spending and receiving money'. This process was to elicit what Simmel defines as 'impersonality and colourlessness'[3] – precisely the features complained of in early reviews of *A Laodicean* (1881), and a notable aspect of the change from the dominance of Henchard to that of Farfrae in *The Mayor*. Money, in Simmel's argument, brings into existence 'a community of action of those individuals and groups who stress their separation and reserve at all other points'.[4] Before we lament the alienating effects of monetary transactions, Simmel urges, we need to be reminded that money 'creates an extremely strong bond among members of an economic circle' because 'it refers people to others'.[5] The modern individual is therefore dependent upon a complex network of connections, and will perish, like Henchard, if she or he seeks isolation from this network. Paradoxically, money opens up 'a particularly wide scope to individuality and the feeling of personal independence',[6] a scope explored in radically dissimilar ways by both Paula Power and Michael Henchard. Modern culture elicits, at once in Simmel's sociology and in Hardy's fiction, two seemingly antipathetic tendencies: first, a tendency towards equalisation and 'levelling'; and secondly, a trend towards the elaboration of individuality. Simmel treats this development objectively, but in Hardy it contains the potential for satire (as in *A Laodicean*) or tragedy (as in *The Mayor*). Simmel observes: 'With money in our pocket, we are free, whereas previously, the object made us dependent on the conditions of its conservation and fructification. But how often does this very freedom simultaneously mean a vapidity of life and a loosening of its substance!'[7]

We may discern something of this modern 'vapidity' in many of the characters of *A Laodicean*. The innate qualities of the object are lost, and people begin to 'speed past the specific value of things', Simmel remarks, locating in this change the 'restlessness and dissatisfaction of our times'.[8] It is this very speeding up, the replacement of 'qualititative' with 'quantitative' values, that *A Laodicean* dramatises in its juxtaposition of ancient church and modern chapel, or medieval castle and railway, and its deployment of

photography and telegraphy as new modes of communication and representation. Indeed Hardy's novel may be said to trace a Simmelian process
of 'the growing spiritualisation of money',[9] in its paradoxical treatment of
the materiality of modern religion. The Baptist chapel which Somerset
stumbles upon in the opening scene is a 'monstrosity' of red brick, its 'white
regular joints of mortar' streaked in 'geometrical oppressiveness', with its
windows 'glazed with sheets of plate glass' and 'a temporary iron stove-pipe'
inserted into the slate roof.[10] This grossly concrete manifestation of the spiritual contrasts nicely with the metaphysical properties ascribed to money
by Hardy's characters. As Simmel expresses it, 'Only to the extent that the
material element recedes does money become real money'.[11] The money
economy generates what Simmel characterises as the 'blasé' attitude, as
individual sensibilities begin to atrophy. The individual in modern society
is motivated by the acquisition of money, and yet when this goal is attained,
'frequently deadly boredom and disappointment set in': money is 'only the
bridge to definitive values, and one cannot live on a bridge'[12] – a remark
that calls up memories of the two bridges in *The Mayor of Casterbridge* to
which all those 'who had failed in business, in love, in sobriety, in crime'
are drawn. Whilst the monetary system imposes new standards of punctu-
ality and exactness, it also tempts one into 'a certain laxity and
thoughtlessness of action'[13] in ways which Hardy explores not only in a
corrupt personality like that of William Dare but also more generally as an
ambivalently liberating and corrosive element in a modernising society. In
Georg Lukács's argument, which is curiously endorsed in the novel, the
capitalist process of reification 'both over-individualises man and objectifies him mechanically'. The division of labour 'makes men ossify in their
activity'; indeed, Lukács insists, 'it makes automata of them'.[14]

In *Fictions of State*, Patrick Brantlinger notes how the novel at this juncture registers 'both the substantiality of British power and prosperity and
its insubstantiality, its basis only in "credit"': thus, the Victorian novel operates through a metaphorical representation of a 'lack' of reality, fictionality,
that is parallel to the unreality of a money system founded in debt.[15] An
investment of belief in money, whether fiduciary, as notes and coins, or
scriptural, as book-keeping, is thus analogous to the credit extended to
works of fiction. In the period of decline in religious belief to which Hardy's
work bears witness, a form of capitalist 'religiosity' elicits what Brantlinger
defines as an imperially 'relentless pursuit of profits, territory, power, and
exotic theatricality'[16] – a pursuit which is a marked feature of the fictional
universe of *A Laodicean*, with its delineation of the clash between industrial
capital and the waning landed class, its 'exotic' outsiders William Dare and
Abner Power, and its plot dependence on amateur theatricals and erotic

gymnastics. Indeed, the diagnosis of capitalist development offered by the American economist Arthur MacEwan is cast in language which curiously reinflects Somerset's project of restoration at Stancy Castle. MacEwan suggests that the debt process is like building a tower:

> If we keep going higher and higher, at some point the whole structure will come tumbling down. There are, of course, ways to extend the limit. We can widen the base of the tower, for example, or construct some support structures. There comes a point, however, where we are devoting all our efforts and resources to shoring up the tower.[17]

Brantlinger's thesis that the era of realism coincided with the installation of debt as an unavoidable element of the modern economic system reveals the ways in which, like money, 'the novel is simultaneously a form of debt and of wealth, and a commodity in search of buyers'. It is also a commodity shadowed, as he notes, by 'the spectre of an empire founded in debt',[18] hence the dubious imperial exploits of both Abner Power and Sir William de Stancy. The thematic fictional concern with the dialectic of land and money that began with Jane Austen led inexorably to a cultural situation where narrative realism itself participated in an increasingly reified world-view. This came about, Brantlinger argues, since it is

> not just because novels are commodities written, manufactured, and marketed for profit but because the social realm depicted in them consists largely or wholly of commodities and commodified relations: of goods to be purchased and owned; of forms of property to be bought and sold, inherited or lost; and of characters who themselves behave like commodities or, if they are good, honest, and at least semi-heroic, struggle not to behave like commodities.[19]

In another fertile study of the relation between money and fiction, John Vernon argues that the realist novel suffers a 'failure of mimesis' because paper money is actually 'the absence of money', and he suggests that landed property becomes thought of 'in terms of the medium that passes from hand to hand', becoming simply 'another object for sale, with its price tag'.[20] This general analysis is germane to a reading of *A Laodicean*, where the plot turns upon the de Stancys' loss of the castle, the problematic heritage of the engineer John Power, and the pervasively commodified nature of social relations centring upon this contested property. As real estate, the castle stands in for England, a nation indebted for its hidden wealth to the occluded territories of empire. At the outset of the novel, when George Somerset is closing up his sketchbook, he sees a workman 'pulling down a rotten gate that bore on its battered lock the initials "W.De.S." and erecting a new one whose

ironmongery exhibited the letters "P.P."' (AL, 35). The hero then comes
across the 'mushroom modernism' of Sir William de Stancy's villa, and is
surprised by the ageing aristocrat's conversational obsession with the
'money market' and unstable 'fluctuations' in stocks and shares (AL, 36,
38). These opening encounters signal the symptomatic quality of the novel,
a quality aptly summed up in Marx's diagnosis of the English situation at
this time, which juxtaposed 'an archaic, timeworn and antiquated compro-
mise between the landed aristocracy, which *rules officially*, and the
bourgeoisie, which in fact *dominates* in all the various spheres of civil society,
but *not officially*'.[21] Kevin McLoughlin points out the double-bind whereby
money is both 'an ideal *and* a real thing', paper money specifically acquiring
its reality 'in *not appearing* as a substantial thing': 'unlike the substance of
the money commodity . . . the paper of paper money does not really exist
as a substance'. Money, that is to say, in a process shared by the characters
of *A Laodicean*, 'recedes as a substance'.[22] The commodity, in Catherine
Gallagher's analysis, 'is constantly on the brink of disappearing, being
replaced by a mere notation of value, such as money', and yet the uncertain
value of the literary text is mirrored in the 'dematerialisation and remate-
rialisation' which inhabits 'textuality itself'[23] – a flickering afterlife
curiously manifested in this particularly liminal Hardy text.

Thus Sir William, it is revealed, has squandered his fortune through
horse-racing and 'a visionary project of founding a watering-place', and has
'sunk thousands in a useless silver mine' (AL, 41–2). Illness has left him
'quite childish' as his brain has 'softened' (AL, 42). Similarly, his daughter
Charlotte is characterised in her simplicity as representing 'the second
childhood of her line' (AL, 78). The de Stancys are a living embodiment of
the way in which, according to Simmel's account in his seminal essay, 'The
Metropolis and Mental Life' (1903), money 'hollows out the core of
things'.[24] This tendency is neatly dramatised when, a little later, Somerset
falls down a 'hollow turret' at the castle and is temporarily incarcerated (AL,
64–6). The project of restoration gives Somerset a valued opportunity of
'playing with another person's money' (AL, 68), but his antiquarian role is
placed in question by the development of the railway system in which Paula
Power is 'one of the largest shareholders' (AL, 81). The technocratic nature
of the rail network masked a contradiction nicely traced by Mark Seltzer:

> Combining and adjusting the disciplines of organised movements, classes,
> time-tables, and classifications, on the one side, and the market principle of
> competitive agency in mobility, on the other, the railway journey and the
> railway system powerfully epitomise . . . the differences and rivalries
> between styles of competitive and disciplinary individualism.[25]

But the contrast here is not a straightforward one between antiquarianism and modernity: in the striking incident in the railway tunnel, 'a silent subterranean corridor' hidden beneath 'long grass, bushes, late summer flowers' (AL, 82), unbeknown to the panic-stricken Paula, Somerset evades the oncoming express train:

> In the middle of the speck of light before him appeared a speck of black; and then a shrill whistle, dulled by millions of tons of earth, reached his ears from thence. It was what he had been on his guard against all the time, – a passing train; and instead of taking the trouble to come out of the tunnel he stepped into a recess, till the train had rattled past, and vanished onward round a curve. (AL, 82)

Such a scene reinflects the melodramatic scenario of the 'railway rescue' which was a popular feature of both sensation theatre and fiction,[26] and endorses Walter Benjamin's notation of the way railways themselves 'entered into the world of dream and symbol':[27] in such moments technology comes to inhabit the realm of the unconscious. The combination of money and desire that the novel explores is tellingly exposed in William Dare's account of Paula at the dinner-party where, decked out in 'sapphires and opals', she 'carried as much as a thousand pounds upon her head and shoulders' (AL, 91), and in the later bank scene when, secretly observed by Somerset, she takes possession of the 'dazzling' necklace (AL, 190).

The amateur theatricals organised by the heroine expose the new ruling elite by 'a throwing open of fascinating social secrets not to be missed for money' (AL, 204), and her ensuing courtship by Captain William de Stancy is largely motivated by the search for funds. As Sir William remarks, '"My son has skill in gallantry, and now he is about to profitably exercise it"' (AL, 245). The predominance of the money economy is revealed by Hardy with reckless absurdity in the gymnasium scene, where William Dare arranges for his father, Captain de Stancy, to watch Paula's exercises, in order to counter the soldier's vow of fidelity to Dare's dead mother by inflaming his passion for the young woman and her castle. Through a gap in the walls, de Stancy watches a kind of 'optical poem' in which Paula, wearing a tight-fitting pink flannel costume, 'was bending, wheeling, undulating' in gyrations which expose her 'supple form' (AL, 152) – exercises which, in the more explicit serial version, 'showed to perfection every curve of her figure'.[28] The voyeuristic erotics of this scene have often been noted. Peter Widdowson, for example, justly remarks upon the staging of the male gaze as register of an 'overt sexuality', and also stresses the theatricality of the episode and its relation to Somerset's initial vision of Paula at the baptismal chapel ceremony.[29] In one sense this scene functions by transforming Paula into a commodity, an object fetishised by its would-be consumers. In Marxist theory human beings become dominated by their own products; they are, as one commentator phrases it, 'compelled by the power these products have over them'.[30] The commodity, like money itself, both conceals and reveals the social character of labour in a kind of economic striptease. Paula, characterised as a 'tantalising property' (AL, 244), unwittingly conforms to what Benjamin designates the 'participation of women in the nature of the commodity': dress (and in this case undress) registers as an attempt, as Benjamin expresses it, 'to lure sex into the world of matter'.[31] Hardy's mildly scandalous scene acts out the notion that, in Vernon's terms, 'money is an abstraction, a social power', or indeed, 'a sign of the appearances and illusions novelists are fond of stripping from their characters'. Sexuality, Vernon contends, is not shocking in itself, it only becomes shocking 'when placed on stage, when the private is made public, the tickets sold and purchased',[32] and this is the issue that links the gymnasium with the later theatrical scene when, to a packed audience, de Stancy appears to kiss a red-faced Paula. However, whilst Hardy's gymnasium scene stages the society of the spectacle demanded by capital, it also possesses a further range of significations. There is certainly a narcissistic element in Paula's desire to be observed: '"Now, Aunt, look at me – and you, Charlotte – is not that shocking to your weak nerves!"' (AL, 152). It is also notable that the men are excluded from Paula's domain and possess no control over her movements or over their own viewing pleasure; to that extent the gymnasium scene might be read as both deploying and refusing traditional gender roles. Both here and in the amateur theatricals, Paula strategically adopts the posture of masquerade, a manoeuvre through which, as Deborah Parsons has noted, 'women can subvert the superior possession of the male gaze by themselves controlling the image that it objectifies'. In this feminist scenario, a male observer such as the captain 'is denied possession of the woman because he is only presented with certain facades', 'fragments' of female identity 'put on display'. Thus, as Parsons observes, the woman transforms herself into an artist, one who presents herself 'as she wants to be seen'.[33]

Hardy's climactic scene may be productively interrogated by means of Jean Baudrillard's theory of fetishism, which proposes that in a capitalist economy bodily beauty functions within a generalised system of exchange in terms of a scenario of 'perfectionist vertigo and controlled narcissism'. Through this systematisation the human body becomes a 'perfect object': *'it is the artifact that is the object of desire'*.[34] The erotic transmutes into a sign system which renders the body invulnerable, 'yet offered up in the same turn as an idol, as the *perfect phallus for perverse desire*: that of others, and its own':[35]

> The white manilla ropes clung about the performer like snakes as she took
> her exercise, and the colour in her face deepened as she went on. Captain De
> Stancy felt that, much as he had seen in early life of beauty in woman, he
> had never seen beauty of such a real and living sort as this. (AL, 152)

Paula's corporeal display begins to take on a symptomatic quality in the
light of Baudrillard's analysis, since the modern 'rediscovery of the body'
which her exercise enacts 'is not innocently contemporary with monopoly
capitalism and the discoveries of psychoanalysis'. The body, that is to say,
functions by 'liquidating' the unconscious, producing under conditions of
monopoly capital a 'glorious agency', a body 'entirely positivised as the
capital of divine right' through which the 'subject of private property is
about to be restored'.[36] Such a restoration is promised by the 'fermentation'
this sight of Paula instigates in the disinherited captain, despite his previous
policy of 'incarcerating within himself all instincts towards the opposite
sex'; as he revealingly remarks to his sister, '"the castle and what it contains
have a keen interest for me now"' (AL, 157, 159).

The heroine's energetic affiliation with modernity is registered most
transparently through her innovative introduction of the telegraph wire
which vanishes 'through an arrow-slit into the interior' of the castle (AL,
17–18), and stands, the narrator asserts, as an emblem of 'cosmopolitan
views and the intellectual and moral kinship of all mankind' (AL, 18). This
uplifting thought is ironised by Charlotte's estimate that the telegraph has
cost 'six pounds a year for each mile' (AL, 29): the telegraph thus instanti-
ates a moment of nascent capital. Indeed, the most frenetic instance of
capitalist speculation, the gambling mania which afflicts several of the characters, was crucially expanded by the off-course betting on horse-racing
which the installation of the national telegraphic system afforded. John
Vernon has suggested that 'by the nineteenth century wealth had come to
be thought not in terms of the security of a landed estate, but in terms of
personal ambitions associated with expanding capital'.[37] But this person-
alisation went hand-in-hand with an increasing standardisation, human
conversation being replaced, as Iwan Morus notes, 'by standardised packets
of intelligence represented by the pulses of the electric fluid running
through the telegraph's wires'. Telegraphic communication thus 'violated
norms of privacy and notions of proper behaviour'.[38] The telegraph begins,
in the course of the novel, to take on a life of its own, possessing, the narrator
comments, 'almost the attributes of a human being at Stancy Castle'. When
the bell rings, people 'rushed' to attend to it and 'waited its pleasure' (AL,
43); in a familiar scenario, humanity becomes enslaved to the machine,
which connects 'extreme antiquity of environment to sheer modernism'

(AL, 186). In its inauguration of the immediate but disembodied message, Paula's machine also suggests the risky pleasures of telepathy, a phenomenon linked, Nicholas Royle suggests, 'to other nineteenth-century forms of communication from a distance', which in Royle's account significantly include 'the railway, telegraphy, photography'.[39] Indeed, it may be that the heroine's 'split and vacillating' character owes something to her investment in the paraphernalia of modernity: in a study of neurasthenia published in the same year as Hardy's novel, George Miller Beard attributed the 'rapid increase in nervousness' to 'steam-power, the periodical press, the telegraph, the sciences, and the mental activity of women'.[40] *A Laodicean* was composed during a period of serious illness, and Emma Hardy's role in acting as the sick author's amanuensis, taking down substantial portions of the novel from her husband's dictation, refracts the issues of telecommunication highlighted by the novel's plot.[41] Joe Fisher, in his analysis of the gap between 'traded' and 'narrated' texts in Hardy, intriguingly suggests that this act of dictation 'implies a surrender of narrative control' on Hardy's part. Narrative authority, he argues, is thus greatly reduced, with the consequence that Hardy 'is less well protected here than in any other text because the gap between trader and narrator is in danger of being eroded'. As a result, *A Laodicean* 'is a Hardy text which is only partly narrated by Hardy'.[42]

The ubiquity of the market registered by the telegraph is also embodied in the castle clock which Paula has introduced, 'new and shining, and bearing the name of a recent maker' (AL, 20). The old clock, Charlotte informs Somerset, 'was quite worn out' – a verdict also applicable to her own family – but the new clock, significantly, 'tells the seconds', time now being so valuable it 'must of course be cut up into smaller pieces' (AL, 29). E. P. Thompson observed in a discussion of time and capital that the transition to a mature industrial society entailed profound changes in 'the inward notation of time': thus, an internalisation of the Puritan ethic meant that 'all time must be consumed, marketed, put to *use*', since without time-discipline 'we could not have the insistent energies of industrial men' (such as John Power).[43] The new clock at Stancy Castle in effect functions like the clocks installed at the great railway termini. The ramifications of electro-technology, here paradoxically focused upon a medieval edifice, were to be massive, as Peter Galison observes in his discussion of the origins of Einstein's theory of relativity: 'The Euro-American world was criss-crossed with overlapping networks of co-ordination: webs of train-tracks, telegraph lines, metereological networks, longitude surveys under the watchful, increasingly universal, clock system'.[44]

In *The Philosophy of Money*, Simmel argues that the 'projection of mere relations into particular objects is one of the great accomplishments of the mind', and he cites the 'telegraph wires that connect different countries' as objects which possess no significance for the individual, 'but only with reference to the relations between men and between human groups'. The supreme example of such a symbolic object is money, which is 'nothing but the pure form of exchangeability'.[45] Yet the end-means rationality presupposed by clock and telegraph, and indicated by the heroine's paternity, is to some extent cancelled out by her own natural Laodicean ambivalence and partiality for flirtation. Paula's credentials as an emergent New Woman, firmly established by her adoption of the telegraph and devotion to a regime of physical fitness, are compromised by the narratorial insistence upon her instabilities of character. Jane Thomas has provided an astute account of the ways in which Paula's personality and her desire for self-expression are manipulated in accordance with essentially patriarchal social norms, and she justly notes the ways in which successful social 'performance' 'requires [Paula] to subsume her desires beneath the illusion of a stable and integrated mask'.[46] The narrator remarks patronisingly upon the 'illimitable caprice of a woman's mind' (AL, 14), and such caprice, Somerset reflects after the débâcle at the chapel, 'was not foreign to her composition' (AL, 16). Later in the narrative, as the lovers place their hands over the stone carving, he concludes that 'coquetry was no great sin' (AL, 78), yet her sudden appearance at the railway cutting seems to reveal her as 'a finished coquette and dissembler', and her discussion of the Greek court design is marked by a 'suave sauciness' (AL, 81, 91). The bogus newspaper advertisement of her engagement to de Stancy does not, in fact, prove her the 'arrant coquette' Somerset first believes her to be (AL, 222), but the original magazine version of the novel went a good deal further in this misogynist vein, its vocabulary of 'flirtation, theatricals, polka-mazurka, true-lover's knot'[47] serving to point up the sexual and material connotations of this discourse. More generally, Hardy's heroine may be taken, both in her psychological vacillation and in her physical wanderings, as type or figure of the female artist.

Alison Chapman perceptively comments upon the Victorian poet Mary Coleridge being dispossessed of name and place, her 'waywardness' attributable to the dominance of her great-uncle, the poet, and to powerful male gatekeepers of culture such as Henry Newbolt and Robert Bridges. This process of dispossession, Chapman suggests, generates the 'Wanderers, ghosts and outcasts' who populate Coleridge's poetry to the extent that she becomes a 'wandering signifier', one with 'no place and no name'.[48] Such an analysis illuminates the predicament of Paula Power in her subordinated relations with her engineer father, her enigmatic uncle and her two unsatisfactory lovers, and in her perfunctory journeyings across Europe. Paula's Laodicean qualities are the condition of living between irreconcilable polarities: both the landed aristocrat (de Stancy) and the technocrat (Somerset) claim her allegiance and, after the final conflagration, this divided loyalty prompts her declaration to her husband, "'I wish my castle wasn't burnt; and I wish you were a De Stancy'" (AL, 379). The castle, the grounds and the portraits are possessions which signal dispossession, her unfathered status notated textually through a contestation of language registers that echo and reinflect contests over property and money in which the heroine functions as something of a pawn. Paula's freedom as a woman stands revealed as a compulsion to accede to male authority, the only alternative imaginable to the novel being Charlotte de Stancy's belated incarceration in one of the newly established Anglican sisterhoods.

Whilst the plot of *A Laodicean* turns upon the rivalry between Somerset and Captain de Stancy for possession of Paula Power and her estate, her true alter ego is the illegitimate de Stancy, William Dare, whose feckless career in its excess doubles and shadows the conformity exacted of the heroine. Dare's origins are mystified and deracinated: when Somerset surmises that he is 'not an Englishman', Dare replies, "'I have lived mostly in India, Malta, Gibraltar, the Ionian Islands and Canada'" (AL, 46). For Somerset he is Canadian; for Paula, East Indian; whilst Charlotte identifies 'Italian blood'. As Somerset concludes, "'he is a being of no age, no nationality, and no behaviour'" (AL, 63). Dare, indeed, is permanently at a loose end, 'humming the latest air from Offenbach' (AL, 120), illicitly copying Somerset's designs to aid the rival architect, and carrying the secret of his birth tattooed on his chest as signifier of his disinherited status. Whilst he is instrumental in igniting both Captain de Stancy's passion for Paula and Stancy Castle, he is essentially, as he remarks, 'a mere spectator' (AL, 320), an uninvolved 'cosmopolite' (AL, 63) circulating around Europe with the enervated logic of the classic *flâneur*. Indeed, at his first appearance, Dare possesses the hallmarks of the Baudelairean dandy combined with the androgynous hairstyle anticipative of Aubrey Beardsley:

> He had a broad forehead, vertical as the face of a bastion, and his hair, which was parted in the middle, hung as a fringe or valance above, in the fashion sometimes affected by the other sex. He wore a heavy ring, of which the gold seemed good, the diamond questionable, and the taste indifferent. There were the remains of a swagger in his body and limbs as he came forward. . . . (AL, 45)

In his analysis of this cultural matrix, David Frisby stresses the proximity of the two types, arguing that 'the figure of the *flâneur* is close to that of the dandy as a downwardly mobile aristocratic and gentry figure'.[49] If the stroller shadows the role of the author who puts himself on the market, he is also supremely adaptable to changing social conditions, one who participates readily in an expanding spatialisation which takes in new economic circuits, rapidly changing commodity prices and encounters with alien cultures. But Hardy's representation of Dare intriguingly conflates the sexually ambivalent figure of the *flâneur* with that of the stranger, as defined by Simmel. As Rob Shields demonstrates, the stranger adopts the role of 'an insider who nonetheless maintains an outsider status', becoming someone who violates 'the division of near and far': *'The Stranger is thus a foreigner who becomes like a native, whereas the flâneur is the inverse, a native who becomes like a foreigner'.*[50] The key to Dare's personality is his devotion to his 'Book of Chances' that sets out the 'doctrine of expectations' (AL, 121) by which he lives, a doctrine dramatically explored in the bizarre scene in which he gambles at cards with his father in the village churchyard. The social implications of that scene are fully exposed in the later episode at the Monte Carlo casino,[51] in which humanity takes on the air of 'a heated phantasmagoria of tainted splendour' so that even the strait-laced Somerset gets caught up in its 'suggestive charm' (AL, 250). The devotees of the gaming-tables, according to the narrator, demonstrate 'the powerlessness of logic when confronted with imagination', and in the excitement Dare's face turns 'as rigid and dry as if it had been encrusted with plaster' in his 'intolerably overpowering mania for more money' (AL, 250, 251). This mania has also afflicted the youth's grandfather, who, in the serial version, is described as gambling 'to the tune of forty thousand at a sitting',[52] and his 'illegitimate' father who, on the revelation to Paula of his relation to Dare, adopts the mood of 'the gambler seasoned in ill-luck' (AL, 343). Gambling is thus symptomatic of a society gripped by the new monetary system, but it is also, as Gillian Beer has shown, a pursuit intimately related to story-telling. The speculation demanded by gambling, she points out, 'includes the idea of hypothesising, surveying, watching, risking goods against future events'.[53] Gambling scenes, such as those which determine the plots of *A Laodicean, The Return of the Native* and *The Mayor of Casterbridge*, take the form of religious or erotic rituals that, in Beer's phrase, seek 'to discover more and more spontaneous possibilities within a narrowly determined field'. These scenes, Beer argues, enact the readerly relation with story, bestowing on the reader 'power moment by moment to amplify the text with multiple alternative outcomes'. Beer, though, also identifies a countervailing desire, notable here in the curiously asexual William Dare, 'to spend, to be expended, to lose everything'.[54] The progressive disinheritance and consequent plotting of the de Stancys is an instance of the way, as Beer suggests, the institution of the family 'proves to be a form of extended gambling'.[55] John Vernon argues that 'frenetic time' as represented here by the telegraph or railway, 'finds its fullest expression in the image of gambling', and he pertinently observes that the gambler's project is 'a special case of the project of the plotter, who must manipulate reality by getting others to do his bidding'.[56] The true gambler is thus Thomas Hardy.

We may note, however, in this connection how Georg Simmel, defining the 'blasé' attitude, precisely delineates the role and personality of William Dare: 'A life in boundless pursuit of pleasure makes one blasé because it agitates the nerves to their strongest reactivity for such a long time that they finally cease to react at all'. This attitude is therefore 'the faithful subjective reflection of the completely internalised money economy'.[57] As principal plot-maker, William Dare thus shadows the role of his creator; as Simmel remarks, the gambler is one who 'has abandoned himself to the meaninglessness of chance', and yet servitude to chance 'makes sense and contains some necessary meaning'. The addictive pursuit of money which reaches its climax in the gambling mania gives a sharp focus to the way money's 'lack of qualities brings in its wake the lack of qualities among people as payers and receivers of money'.[58] The progressive draining away of personality in this novel, which is a notable feature of its curiously banal European scenes, aptly mirrors the process whereby, according to Simmel, 'no person is worth anything' and 'only money has worth'.[59] In the casino, Dare feverishly expounds his system to Somerset, claiming that '"the certainty that I must win is almost mathematical"':

> I have staked and lost two hundred and thirty-three times. Allowing out of that one chance in every thirty-six (which is the average of zero being marked), and two hundred and four times for the backers of the other numbers, I have the mathematical expectation of six times at least, which would nearly recoup me. (AL, 252–3)

The implications of this scene are clarified by Walter Benjamin's note, in the arcades project, that a bet is 'a means of conferring shock value on events, of loosing them from the contexts of experience'. This unsettling cultivation of shock is shared by the gambler and the narrator alike, both moving towards inevitable climax: 'The ideal of the shock-engendered experience is the catastrophe. This becomes very clear in gambling: by constantly raising the stakes, in hopes of getting what is lost, the gambler steers toward absolute ruin'. The inexorability of William Dare's progress from gambler and forger to arsonist, and the final scene of 'absolute ruin' as Stancy Castle burns, clarifies the link between wager and story. The key to

Dare's enigmatic sexual identity and parasitic relation to the captain is also furnished by Benjamin's speculation that the 'insatiable greed' of the gambler arises 'from the narcissistic compulsion to fertilise and give birth to oneself in an anal birth fantasy, surpassing and replacing one's own father'.[60] The vogue for gambling affects the tone of the entire novel, along the lines indicated by Benjamin's citation from an essay by Paul Lafargue:

> Modern economic development as a whole tends more and more to trans-
> form capitalist society into a giant international gambling house, where the
> bourgeois wins and loses capital in consequence of events which remain
> unknown to him . . . The 'inexplicable' is enthroned in bourgeois society as
> in a gambling hall . . . Successes and failures, thus arising from causes that
> are unanticipated, generally unintelligible, and seemingly dependent on
> chance, predispose the bourgeois to the gambler's frame of mind.[61]

Thus it comes about that in the frantic world of *A Laodicean* the castle is lost and won by chance, Somerset loses and then gains the heroine through the 'unknown' forging of his photograph, Abner Power manufactures bombs for European anarchists, and William Dare sets fire to his ancestral home.

When Havill, the rival architect, characterises Dare as 'artist, archaeologist, Gothic photographer', the youth is quick also to claim a professorial title (AL, 112). The elusive nature of Hardy's villain, however, is best indicated by a proposed definition of the nineteenth-century *flâneur*: 'He is the "dandy", protesting with his sometimes feigned idleness the bourgeois work ethic and clinging to the remnants of an aristocratic aura, but now forced to go on the market. He is the genius, whose spirit has been capitalised'.[62] In this respect Dare's role as photographer parodies the role of his creator: he is the dark double of an author of humble origins but aristocratic pretensions who found himself compromised by his entry into the field of popular fiction. In a novel dominated by the visual, as Mark Durden has noted, 'exchanges of looks now pivot round the photographer', a 'diabolical' figure who 'instigates acts of voyeurism'.[63] The narrator sets up a dialectic between the de Stancy portraits and the new techniques of photography. The family pictures are resonant of aristocratic decline, their frames 'dropping apart', and colours so dim 'they might have been painted in an eclipse' – a state of 'singular dilapidation' so advanced that Charlotte de Stancy's physiognomy now resembles, to Somerset's gaze, 'a defective reprint' of the family face (AL, 20, 21, 23). The decaying portrait gallery stands in distinct contrast to William Dare's up-to-date 'photographic apparatus' and his reputation in Markton as 'a maker of negatives', a reputation confirmed by his fraudulent copying of Somerset's architectural design for what the narrator designates the hero's 'new erection' (AL, 62, 122). Captain de Stancy's hasty concealment of the photo of Dare from the chief constable hints at the developing significance of photography in criminal investigations at this juncture, and his employment of his son's 'patent photographic process' (AL, 171) to make copies of the family portraits gestures towards the Benjaminian loss of the 'aura' of the work of art through mechanical reproduction, a loss neatly mirrored in the 'counterfeit' kiss he bestows on Paula during the performance of *Love's Labour's Lost* (AL, 208). Benjamin viewed 'the photographic reproduction of artworks as a phase in the struggle between photography and painting',[64] a conflict neatly resolved here by Dare's act of torching the family pictures. The plot turns crucially upon the touched-up photograph depicting Somerset with 'the distorted features and wild attitude of a man advanced in intoxication' (AL, 281), which combined with the bogus telegram complaining to Paula of gambling debts serves to discredit the hero. The act of 'photographic distortion', however, is comically endorsed by one of the rustics, who advocates a similar policy of alteration for the family portraits (AL, 335, 370).

Dare's photographic activities may be read meta-textually as a reflection on the claims to realism of the nineteenth-century novel, and Nancy Armstrong has pertinently traced the ways, in this period, that 'fiction and photography produced a spatial classification system specific to their mutual moment and class of consumers'. As Armstrong explains, this system 'contained the bodies, possessions, and practices in relation to those whom the Victorian readership considered outside the boundaries of self, home, class, and nation'.[65] Through the containment of Paula's body and possessions, the exclusion of outsiders like Abner Power and William Dare, and the manipulations of Somerset's design and picture, *A Laodicean* dramatises what Benjamin designated the 'extension of the commodity world through the photo'.[66] Armstrong describes the vogue for photography which swept Britain from the 1860s onwards, noting that there were over six thousand professional photographers by 1881, the year of the novel's appearance. She remarks appositely that the advent of the camera 'made viewers yearn for the very things that photos were displacing', those 'remnants of an earlier England that had crumbled'[67] – like Stancy Castle, Dare's ancestral home. The Gothic novel, it has been postulated, 'usually says that the castle contains some family secret', to the extent that the building becomes 'the core for fantasies based on a childish desire that adulthood be an exactly defined secret one can discover'.[68] The classificatory use of the new invention by eugenicists such as Francis Galton was, Nancy Armstrong observes, often compromised by doctored evidence and trick photography, practices that placed in question photography's ability

Hardy and the Philosophy of Money   **57**

to capture 'the essential features of the original'.[69] Benjamin's notation of the photograph as 'the earliest image of the encounter of machine and man'[70] adumbrates a central concern of *A Laodicean*. Indeed, the late-Victorian vogue for the studio portrait and the *carte-de-visite,* together with the introduction of the hand-held camera, demonstrates how photography catered for needs which were 'alternatively manufactured and satisfied by an unlimited flow of commodities'.[71] And yet, whilst photography offered a classic model of capitalist growth, it continued to be denigrated as an art-form and subordinated to painting in ways which echo Hardy's own valuation of poetry over fiction. Furthermore, it may be the case, as Durden suggests, that photography, like the telegraph, 'while showing the onset of modernity', 'also hints at a certain value of authenticity in hand-written and hand-drawn, a value lost with mechanical reproduction and communication'.[72]

At the end of the novel, as Somerset and Paula return from their continental honeymoon, a figure is discerned 'flitting in and about those draughty apartments' in the castle (AL, 373), piling up the family portraits into a heap. It is William Dare's final act, a 'catastrophe' that leaves the castle in ruins. John Schad has pointed out the relation between photography and writing, arguing that the 'sheer unreliability of writing' is what photography 'serves to foreground'. Thus, he suggests, 'Dare's photography represents a shadow of not only architecture but writing, not only Somerset's pursuits but Hardy's' (AL, xxiv). But if this is so, then Dare's pyromania seems to hint at a self-destructive vein at the heart of Hardy's writing project, a secret desire to consign what he has written to the flames, anticipative of his action in burning the manuscript of this novel in annoyance at his wife's claims to authorship, and of the bonfires of recriminatory personal documents destroyed after Emma's death. Hardy's literary output, indeed, is significantly punctuated with conflagrations – we may recall, for instance, the fire that destroys the inn in *Desperate Remedies*, the sexually compromising blaze depicted in 'The Bride-Night Fire', the Venetian theatre fire that ruins Willowes's physiognomy in 'Barbara of the House of Grebe', or Pierston's burning of the love-letters in the opening scene of *The Well-Beloved.* The conjunction of photography, the erotics of writing, and a refining fire which comes to a head in Dare's possible self-immolation also motivates a notable poem, 'The Photograph', in which the poet consigns the photo of a woman he knew to the flames:

> The flame crept up the portrait line by line
> As it lay on the coals in the silence of night's profound,
>   And over the arm's incline,

And along the marge of the silkwork superfine,
And gnawed at the delicate bosom's defenceless round.

Then I vented a cry of hurt, and averted my eyes;
The spectacle was one that I could not bear,
     To my deep and sad surprise;
But, compelled to heed, I again looked furtivewise
Till the flame had eaten her breasts, and mouth, and hair.[73]

Tim Armstrong tellingly cites this text as an instance of 'the way in which forms of materialism and positivism seem haunted': the poet is overtaken by a 'fascinated voyeurism' as the image of the female body is reduced to the 'ashen ghost of the card it had figured on'. The cult of 'spirit photos' at this juncture, produced by differential exposure times, Armstrong suggests, exemplifies the way technology 'enables the "materialisation" of doubles and ghosts'.[74]

Precisely such a trajectory from the grossly materialist spirituality of the initial Baptist service to the psychologically compelling pursuit of beauty and property marks the plot of A Laodicean; this plot enacts, in its veering away from chapel and castle to casino and hotel, a process whereby, as John Vernon observes, 'money becomes an ironic substitute for that discredited spiritual world displaced by matter'.[75] A commodified culture produces a society of ghosts: thus we have Somerset's 'spectral smile', and the remarks on familial 'ghosts of our dead' by William Dare, a *chevalier d'industrie* by whom the captain is 'perpetually haunted' (AL, 200, 320, 324). Indeed, Geoffrey Batchen has argued that, because the 'photographic moment' memorialises a relation between two binary opposites, it functions through 'a logic that continually returns to haunt itself', carrying within it ghostly traces of a 'perennial alterity'.[76] But it is Paula's phlegmatic uncle, Abner Power, who registers as most entirely 'ghoul-like', in a characterisation that gestures towards an examination of the return to the metropolis of the secrets of empire. Abner's pock-marked physiognomy offers a registration of suffering and evil, his face 'the plaything of strange fires or pestilences', denoting one who was 'victim of some terrible necessity'. Power's invention of the explosive device utilised by European anarchists literally blows up in his face and leads him to seek his fortune in the guano trade of Peru. Like the monetary system he embodies, Abner circulates mysteriously: known as a 'great traveller', he is 'wanted by certain European governments' (AL, 329, 208, 327). The intervention of this enigmatic individual makes explicit the occluded links between Englishness and empire – Peru, for instance, being specifically cited by Marx as an instance of a developed economy held back by the absence of a monetary system.[77]

It is only the final conflagration at Stancy Castle that enables the symbolically significant building of a 'mansion of independent construction' which will be 'unencumbered with the ghosts of an unfortunate line' (AL, 378). But the resonance of this ultimate scene suggests an ambivalent response to the pressures of modernity. William Dare's possibly suicidal action in piling up the portraits, tapestries, cushions and wood-shavings may be read as an allegory of the way that, in a paper-money economy, as John Vernon argues, 'metal currency became reduced to the state of leftover matter': 'objects, clothing, houses, furniture and flesh all take on a common physical status, all are pieces or fragments of leftover matter, signs of a partial and quantified world'. Dare's actions leave the 'edifice in ruins' (AL, 378), a fitting final emblem of what Vernon terms 'a material world emptied of value and becoming an image of itself, a shell'.[78]

And yet there remains a margin of undecidability surrounding the representation of Stancy Castle as 'half ruin, half residence'. 'Irregular, dilapidated, and muffled in creepers', this edifice is dominated by 'a square solid tower', and entered via a modern arch spanning the ditch. On his first visit, Somerset, one of the class of 'belated travellers', discovers that the 'large door under the porter's archway was closed and locked' (AL, 17), though later he gains access to the 'inner buildings' with their staircases and gallery, and becomes temporarily trapped in the turret. The building's signification is riddled with ambiguities, suggesting both 'hard distinctions in blood and race' and 'deadly mistrust of one's neighbour', as well as what the narrator designates the 'fairer side of feudalism – leisure, lighthearted generosity, intense friendships, hawks, hounds, revels, healthy complexions' (AL, 18). Although he studies the location of the castle on the map, Somerset has significantly 'never understood its position in the county' (AL, 19). With its 'lower storey' and 'crypt-like hall' (AL, 24), Stancy Castle may stand as a female emblem which the male protagonists attempt to penetrate, just as the telegraph wire enters 'through an arrow-slit into the interior' (AL, 17–18). In the absence of the usurping patriarch, John Power, both Somerset and Captain de Stancy seek, like Kafka's protagonist K, to possess the castle, in the process becoming embroiled in a plot whose absurdities shadow forth modernist existential crisis. The comedy of errors arising from acts of misinterpretation and forgery suggests that the architect's attempts to approach and comprehend village and castle are as doomed as those of Kafka's land-surveyor. Maurice Blanchot has observed of *The Castle* that the text proffers 'a truth that seems always to say of itself more than anything one could say about it', and he goes on, in terms which might also apply to *A Laodicean*, to note how both reader and narrator are engaged 'in the torment of an endless commentary'.[79] Both written and visual texts – letters, diagrams, photographs, portraits, telegrams – as often in Hardy become sources of confusion, misprision and delay. In the end the true ambivalence of the titular Laodicean is that of the reader, who is denied any stable interpretative position. Captain de Stancy, at the crisis of the plot, declares himself a 'homeless wanderer', and espouses the Oedipal wish that he and his sister 'were behind the iron door of our old vault' (AL, 317).

Whilst the vapidity of Somerset's character protects him from the ontological insecurities which are visited upon Kafka's hero,[80] some of the architect's experiences gesture towards an undeclared existential crisis. In descending to the 'lower storey', he is confronted with a 'crypt-like hall' whose central pillar exhibits 'some of the most hideous grotesques in England', but discovers that his 'ingress' is barred by a locked door (AL, 24). He is then confounded by the sight of a large map which 'showed streets and open spaces corresponding with nothing he had seen in the county', and discovers that the town 'is not anywhere but in Paula's brain' (AL, 29, 30). The architect's bafflement reaches its climax when, 'with a vague consciousness that he was going to do something up there', he returns to the top of the great tower, and, relinquishing 'rule and compass', enters one of the turrets opening onto the roof. He falls into the hollow of the turret, realises he has become 'a prisoner', and faced with a 'mass of masonry', 'his heart failed him for a moment'. He observes the enigmatic inscriptions, 'De Stancy' and 'W. Dare', cut into the stonework, and a 'dry bone' reminds him of 'other cribbed and confined wretches'. Somerset fantasises about being rescued by Paula, but it is 'a dreary footman' who eventually brings the ladder to his aid (AL, 64, 65, 66). Despite this release from his 'dismal dungeon', the episode of Somerset's temporary entrapment, marked as it is by that blankness and mild incomprehensibility that characterises the entire action, remains a haunting one for the reader in ways which bear no relation to the plot. In such a scene, Hardy diligently assembles the paraphernalia of the Gothic – medieval castle, vaults, locked doors, secret passageways, incarceration – only to thwart and divert readerly expectations. Somerset's entrapment clearly reduplicates that of Emily St Aubert in Ann Radcliffe's *Mysteries of Udolpho* (1794), but in place of the Gothic emphasis upon feeling and affect, Somerset responds with a bland imperviousness. The architect's predicament thus gestures towards an existential 'limit-situation', calling up Heidegger's proposition that Being or *Dasein* 'is dying as long as it exists, but proximally and for the most part, it does so by way of *falling*'. The idle talk of others, what Heidegger categorises as 'the they', '*does not permit us the courage for anxiety in the face of death*', but through the kind of anxiety elicited by the tower adventure, Being 'is brought face to face with itself'. Heidegger goes on: 'temptation, tranquillisation, and alienation are distinguishing marks of the kind of Being called *falling*. As falling, everyday being-towards-death is a constant *fleeing in the face of death'*. In this account, the anxiety proper to Being is transmuted by public opinion into mundane fear, and the trope of falling takes the form of 'an evasion *in the face of death'*.[81] It is this 'tranquillisation' that is registered unmistakably as the key to Somerset's responses in the turret. The appearance of the footman is only one of a number of instances where Somerset is attended by enigmatic officials, but most baffling are his trio of shadowy architectural deputies, Knowles, Bowles and Cockton, who exist in the margins of the text, and the castle, only to reappear decisively at the abbey in Caen. Somerset's relations with this trio curiously anticipates K's tribulations with his pair of manically identical assistants in *The Castle*. The simultaneously liberating and imprisoning effects of the monetary system are thus deeply embodied in the architectural features of Hardy's castle, as Georg Simmel would assert in his ruminations on modernity: 'the bridge indicates how humankind unifies the separatedness of merely natural being, and the door how it separates the uniform, continuous unity of natural being'.[82]

In postulating a link between the ostensibly different writing projects of Hardy and Simmel, it is germane to note how, in Zygmunt Bauman's account of the sociologist's analysis, reality 'fell apart and refused to be patched together again by the unifying impact of church, the state or the *Völksgeist'*. In relation to both the schemes of the engineer John Power and the architects George Somerset and Thomas Hardy, and to the piecemeal structure of *A Laodicean*, it is pertinent to recall Bauman's diagnosis of a Simmelian sociology that traces 'the debris of failed engineering dreams in all its splintered, fragmentary, episodic truth'. Scanning the human condition 'from the perspective of a lonely wanderer', Simmel perceived 'episodes without cause and consequence'. As Bauman sees it, this is a sociology 'about the art of building – rather than grand, harmony-conscious architectural designs'.[83]

In a similar vein, George Steiner speaks of man, in Heideggerian thought, 'dwelling in a house of which he is, at his rare best, a custodian, but never architect or proprietor',[84] and the ending of the novel, where Somerset declares to Paula, '"We will build a new house from the ground"' (AL, 378), appears to endorse Heidegger's definition of building as 'a distinctive letting-dwell': despite the 'warp' given to the heroine's mind by the castle's medievalism, she half-heartedly endorses the architect's project of becoming 'a perfect representative of "the modern spirit"' (AL, 379). Heidegger's thought alerts us to the hidden links between Somerset and John Power, castle and railway, since, as he argues, 'the essence of the erecting of buildings cannot be understood adequately in terms either of architecture or of engineering construction': *'Only if we are capable of dwelling, only then can we build'*. Hardy, architect turned writer, moves tentatively in his final scene towards a Heideggerian sense that 'the essence of building is letting dwell'. In the existential thought adumbrated by both writers, 'mortals ever search anew for the essence of dwelling, that they *must ever learn to dwell'*.[85]

CHAPTER **4**

Sensations of Earth

Thomas Hardy and Richard Jefferies

The unhomely being homely of human beings upon the earth is 'poetic'.
Martin Heidegger[1]

This conjunction of writers is a shorthand way of signalling the strategy of interference through which a group of texts may be read – in this case a process through which philosophy may be read as literature and vice versa in order to produce that which, as Deleuze and Guattari put it, 'cannot be thought and yet must be thought'.[2]

Nietszche speaks, in *Ecce Homo*, of his feeling of weakness and 'susceptibility of the skin to pinpricks' after the completion of a major work, and goes on to identify a seminal moment of heightened sensory awareness:

> While in such a condition I once sensed the proximity of a herd of cows even before I saw them through the return of milder, more philanthropic thoughts: *that* had warmth in it.[3]

This bovine encounter might be termed the sign or manifestation of a philosophical swerve – the turn to a phenomenological reading of existence – that also marks the scenes to be examined below in Hardy and Jefferies. Earlier in his argument, Nietzsche proposes that the 'little things' – 'nutriment, place, climate, recreation . . . are beyond all conception of greater importance than anything that has been considered of importance hitherto', and he adds:

> Those things which mankind has hitherto pondered seriously are not even realities, merely imaginings, more strictly speaking lies from the bad instincts of the sick, in the profoundest sense injurious natures – the concepts 'God', 'soul', 'virtue', 'sin', 'the Beyond', 'truth', 'eternal life'.[4]

In *The Gay Science*, Nietzsche ponders these issues further, insisting that what he terms 'conscious thinking' is the most 'superficial' part of human reflection. It is, he argues, 'not only language which serves as a bridge between man and man', but also 'the glance, the clasp, the bearing': 'our becoming-conscious of our own sense-impressions, the power of fixing them and, as it were, setting them outside ourselves, has increased in the measure that the constraint grew to transmit them *to others* by signs'. In this process of acculturation, the world is transmuted into what is 'only a surface- and sign-world, a world made universal and common'; it is against this tendency towards a state in which life 'becomes shallow, thin, relatively stupid, general, sign' that the Nietzschean transvaluation of values is projected.[5]

In one of his notebooks, Thomas Hardy copied down an observation of Leslie Stephen's to the effect that 'history depends upon the relation between the organism & the environment'.[6] The furze-cutting scene of Clym Yeobright on the heath, in *The Return of the Native* (1878), depicting a man in 'the full swing of labour' (RN, 253),[7] dramatises the problematics of the relation between *Homo sapiens* and nature and is crucially predicated upon issues of perception. Because of his impaired sight, Clym's seeing is of a 'curious microscopic sort' (RN, 253) as he attains a visionary closeness to the creatures around him:

> His daily life was of a curious microscopic sort, his whole world being limited to a circuit of a few feet from his person. His familiars were creeping and winged things, and they seemed to enrol them in their band. Bees hummed around his ears with an intimate air, and tugged at the heath and furze-flowers at his side in such numbers as to weigh them down to the sod. The strange amber-coloured butterflies which Egdon produced . . . quivered in the breath of his lips, alighted upon his bowed back, and sported with the glittering point of his hook as he flourished it up and down. (RN, 253–4)

The abundance of creaturely life here, the 'emerald-green grasshoppers', the 'huge flies', the snakes and rabbits whose ears are pierced to a 'blood-red transparency' by the sun, serves to create an investment in the sensuous richness of nature which appears to bridge the gulf between subject and object. This writing explores the sense in which, in the argument propounded by Adorno and Horkheimer, the subject 'creates the world outside himself from the traces which it leaves in his senses'. The 'depth of the subject', they argue, 'consists in nothing other than the delicacy and wealth of the external world of perceptions'. It is only by a process of 'mediation' in which 'thought abandons itself without reservation to the predominant impression' that what Adorno and Horkheimer define as 'that pathological loneliness which characterises the whole of nature' is overcome.[8] This is pertinent to the case of Clym Yeobright, whose 'well-shaped' face is marked by the impress of thinking, being 'a mere waste tablet', and whose good looks, when first glimpsed by Eustacia at the mumming-scene, become 'ruthlessly overrun by its parasite thought' to produce a countenance 'overlaid with legible meanings' (RN, 138). More generally, Horkheimer and Adorno's point, that 'Men have always had to choose between their subjection to nature or the subjection of nature to the Self',[9] hints at the possibility of a theorised reading of these two passages.

The densely written scene of Clym's furze-cutting raises seminal issues of perception and labour which may be interrogated further. An empirical account of perception, as Merleau-Ponty has argued, 'falsifies the natural world by reducing it to stimuli'. Phenomenology insists rather that 'Seeing is *vital* and rich': in Merleau-Ponty's account 'there is a "phenomenal field", an "ambiguous domain" in which perspectival subjects are situated'.[10] Such a phenomenological reading permits a reinflected account of the famous opening evocation of Egdon Heath as a 'pallid screen' stretching to the 'distant rim of the world' (RN, 3). In the furze-cutting scene Clym exists as both subject and object: as subject he perceives the life of his 'familiars', the 'creeping and winged things' around him (RN, 253), the bees, butterflies, grasshoppers, flies, snakes and rabbits cohabiting in a communality of creaturely being. However, 'disguised by his leather accoutrements', Clym is also, from a different but characteristically Hardyan perspective, an object in the landscape, 'a brown spot in the midst of an expanse of olive-green gorse, and nothing more' (RN, 253). The scene is one of profound silence, broken eventually by Clym's French song which brings Eustacia to 'sick despair' (RN, 255). Such a lack of utterance may be illuminated by Walter Benjamin's thesis that after the fall of man, 'when God's word curses the ground', the appearance of nature 'is deeply changed': in this state, human language descends into multiplicity, losing its access to the divine names for things in a process which silences nature:

> Now begins its other muteness, by which we mean the deep sadness of nature. It is a metaphysical fact that all nature would begin to lament if it were endowed with language . . . She would lament language itself.

What Benjamin designates the 'great sorrow of nature' is its 'speechlessness': 'Because she is mute, nature mourns'; but this proposition may also be inverted so that 'the sadness of nature makes her mute'.[11] Alexander Düttmann glosses this, postulating that 'Mutism is at once the decisive trait of the language of things, of the thing which receives the name corresponding to it, and the effect of melancholy'.[12] The pair of goggles which Clym is 'obliged to wear over his eyes' (RN, 253) is a form of disguise such that, as Hardy records in a phrase which echoes the parable of the Good

Samaritan, 'his closest friend might have passed by without recognising him' (RN, 253). There is a scrupulous registration of class operating here: whilst spectacles offer a middle-class denotation of learning, in the working class, as Regenia Gagnier observes, 'glasses signified that a man was too old to work and ensured that he would be fired'.[13] But Clym's loss of sight, like Oedipus' blinding, signals an access of knowledge. Indeed, the scene is framed by the reminder of 'his mother's estrangement' (RN, 253): thus Clym's labour takes the form of what Jean Baudrillard designates 'the genital combination of labour-father and earth-mother' in a theoretical scenario curiously mirroring that on Egdon Heath:

> Nature is carnal, a carnal arrangement on a horizontal plane, on a ground or a table . . . It is always underscored by the horizontal.[14]

This Baudrillardian insistence on the carnality and horizontality of nature is memorably dramatised at the end of an intense encounter between Clym and Eustacia prior to their clandestine marriage. Hearing the 'rustle of her dress over the sprouting sedge' as she moves away,[15] Clym is 'overpowered' by 'the dead flat of the scenery':

> There was something in its oppressive horizontality which too much reminded him of the arena of life: it gave him a sense of bare equality with and no superiority to a single thing living under the sun. (RN, 209)

Hardy's furze-cutting scene is a site of perception, but also of hand-work: 'when in the full swing of labour', the narrator notes, Clym was 'cheerfully disposed and calm' (RN, 253); the 'monotony of his occupation soothed him, and was itself a pleasure' (RN, 254), though Eustacia, when she approaches, constructs her husband as 'a poor afflicted man, earning money by the sweat of his brow' (RN, 254). The return of the native thus takes the scandalous form of a willed and desired social descent, Clym voluntarily placing himself on a level with the local furze-cutters in a temporary gesture of solidarity which his wife classifies as 'social failure' (RN, 255). In imploring her husband to 'leave off this shameful labour' (RN, 255), Eustacia registers the distinction between Clym's gentlemanly, Tolstoyan espousal of agricultural work and the economic necessity which drives the workers on Egdon, the foresters in *The Woodlanders* or the swede-cutters in *Tess*. Significantly, in his notebooks Hardy interpreted Tolstoy's message as urging that 'the link between man and nature shall not be broken'.[16]

It is in *The Return of the Native* that Hardy begins to focus precisely upon those issues – forces of production, class consciousness, base and super-structure – which also inform the Marxist analysis of capital, and the furze-cutting scene may be productively brought into conjunction with some of Marx's reflections in the *Economic and Philosophic Manuscripts* of 1844. In Marx's terms, Clym's somewhat playful adoption of the mask of the labourer protects him from the '*alienation* of the worker in his product' in a process through which 'his labour becomes an object, an *external* existence' which 'exists *outside him*, independently, as something alien to him', transforming his life into 'something hostile and alien'.[17] It is precisely this alienation which leads dialectically in the novel to the stress upon those moments of carnival – the bonfires, the mumming play, the songs, the country dancing, the Maypole revels – which punctuate and alleviate the quotidian tedium of labour. In the furze-cutting scene Hardy reflects upon the issues surrounding human labour, and the relation to and transformation of nature which that labour necessitates. By 'chopping away at the furze' to produce 'a long row of faggots' (RN, 254) Clym utilises nature for his own ends. The scene thus paradoxically celebrates the free life of the natural world and its transformation through labour. As Marx claims, the worker 'can create nothing without *nature*, without the *sensuous external world*' which is 'the material on which his labour is realised'. But there is a contradiction inherent in this procedure, because 'the more the worker by his labour *appropriates* the external world, sensuous nature, the more he deprives himself of *means of life*', to the extent that in the end 'the worker becomes a servant of his object'[18] – this is the danger to which Eustacia is alert.

Marx observes that labour produces 'wonderful things for the rich' (such as the jewellery which Clym has purveyed in Paris), 'but for the worker it produces privation', condemning him or her to the 'hovels', 'deformity', 'stupidity' and 'cretinism' which Hardy patronisingly treats in the comic instance of Christian Cantle.[19] Man exists on Egdon as what Marx terms a 'species being', viewing himself, as Clym does here and in his programme for rustic enlightenment, 'as a *universal* and therefore a free being', and this species being situates man ineluctably within 'the sphere of inorganic nature on which he lives', so that 'plants, animals, stones, air, light' become 'a part of human consciousness' and partly 'objects of art'.[20] Nature, Marx goes on, is 'man's *inorganic body* – nature, that is, insofar as it is not itself human body',[21] and it is the implications of this thesis that both Hardy and Jefferies explore – indeed, Clym is so close to the heath that 'he might be said to be its product' (RN, 175). The animal, like the creatures surrounding Clym on the heath, 'is immediately one with its life activity', whereas man 'makes his life activity itself the object of his will'[22] – an act of incorporation exemplified by Clym's decision to abjure academic study and take up physical labour. Men work upon nature to create '*a world of objects*', such as 'the long row of faggots representing the labour of the day' (RN, 254). In the course of her final doom-laden walk across the heath Mrs Yeobright enjoys a memorable vision of a colony of ants, 'a never-ending and heavy-laden throng' (RN, 291), which may be contextualised by Marx's concession that 'animals also produce': 'They build themselves nests, dwellings, like the bees, beavers, ants, etc.'.[23] Earlier in her heated traversal of the heath, however, Mrs Yeobright has observed 'independent worlds of ephemerons . . . passing their time in mad carousal', and 'maggoty shapes of innumerable obscene creatures . . . heaving and wallowing with enjoy-ment' in short-lived 'happiness' (RN, 278). The distinction between animal and human worlds, for Hardy as for Marx, is crucially one of consciousness; in words which conjure memories of Hardy's original career, Marx observes that 'what distinguishes the worst architect from the best of bees is that the architect builds the cell in his mind before he constructs it in wax'.[24] For both writers, in contradistinction to Jefferies or Ruskin, the framing vision is essentially Darwinian. In looking at nature, Marx writes, men could see 'the bitterest competition among plants and animals' such that the 'tall and stately oaks' are perceived as 'tall and stately capitalists', whilst the minutest creatures, such as the 'parasites' observed by Mrs Yeobright, function as 'the ideologists of the vegetable world'.[25] What Clym is seeking here is a similar return to species-being, a state in which 'work upon the objective world' makes nature '*his* work and his reality'. He turns away from the 'estranged labour' of capital embodied in the Parisian jewellery trade, seeking instead something akin to Marx's 'spontaneous, free activity'.[26]

Both Hardy and Jefferies offer the reader a type of 'psychotopographic' literary experience in which inner processes are projected onto an exterior landscape, but for Hardy, as for Marx, nature is primarily to be seen as the 'source of all instruments and objects of labour'; indeed, Marx sanctions the insight, in terms which are reduplicated in Eustacia's dissatisfaction with the heath, that nature is '*rigidly* separated from man, is *nothing* for man'.[27] Anson Rabinbach has postulated that 'the early Marx viewed nature as man's "inorganic body", mediated through society as society is mediated through nature', and he adds that in this argument the 'metabolism between man and nature is the framework for Marx's view of labour as the paradigm of nature and this led him to characterise this relation as a process of exchange'.[28] In his later thought, embodied in the first volume of *Capital*, Marx would argue that

> Labour is, first of all, a process between men and nature, a process by which man, through his own actions, mediates, regulates and controls the metab-olism between himself and nature. He confronts the materials of nature as a force of nature.[29]

Marx in this final theorisation postulates, in terms applicable to Clym Yeobright, that man 'acts upon external nature and changes it, and in this way he simultaneously changes his own nature'.[30] Equipped with the borrowed accoutrements of his labour, Clym enacts Marx's thesis that 'nature becomes one of the organs of [man's] activity, which he annexes to his own bodily organs'.[31]

The crucial distinction to be drawn between Hardy and Jefferies lies in their differing conceptualisation of history. For Jefferies, as will be seen, nature represents a kind of exit from the historical process, or rather, as Adorno puts it, 'Natural beauty is suspended history, a moment of becoming at a standstill'.[32] Hardy's depiction of the heath-dwellers and of Clym's project of enlightenment for such as Grandfer Cantle and Timothy Fairway takes him much closer to Marx's thesis that nature is merged in history, a history 'only differentiated from natural history as the evolutionary process of self-conscious organisms'.[33] In the monotonous labour of Clym and his fellow furze-cutters, as in the more dramatic depiction of the steam-threshing machine in *Tess of the d'Urbervilles*, man and woman form the link between the instrument of labour and its object: nature, that is to say, is here the subject/object of labour, human productive forces stamping their impress upon the face of nature even in the imperviosity of Egdon Heath. The furze-cutting scene delineates a direct transaction between the human and nature when exchange-value is introduced, as for example in the sale of furze as cooking fuel, in a structure which inaugurates the process of man's alienation from his environment. In a scene of immediate reciprocity, the earth is located as the basis of community: the furze-cutters exemplify Marx's designation of this relation as 'naïve'; the rustic group – Timothy Fairway, Humphrey, Olly Dowden, Christian and Grandfer Cantle – regard themselves, in Marxian terminology, as *communal proprietors* of the heath, 'members of the community which produces and reproduces itself by living labour'.[34] In the *Grundrisse*, Marx notes how money *represents* the price of one commodity as against all other commodities', so that 'it is not only the *representative* of commodity prices, but the *symbol* of itself'. In terms which are curiously mirrored in the Egdon gambling-scene for the spade-guineas, Marx contends that 'in the act of circulation', the material constituent of money, 'its gold or silver, is irrelevant'.[35] The sense of communality of ownership on the heath is evaporating under the impress of modernity, hence the ineffectual nature of Clym's virtually posthumous Saint-Simonian sermons at the close of the novel, which 'some believed' and 'some believed not', his words being found 'commonplace' and lacking in 'spiritual doctrine' – the final career of a man 'who could not see to do anything else' (RN, 412). The hero's final predicament may be framed by Heidegger's conception of that 'decline of the truth of beings' which 'occurs through the collapse of the world characterised by metaphysics' but also 'through the desolation of the earth', a crisis which eventuates in a scenario curiously mirroring that of Clym Yeobright, a blinded instance of 'metaphysical man':

> Collapse and desolation find their adequate occurrence in the fact that meta-physical man, the *animal rationale*, gets fixed as the labouring animal. This rigidification confirms the most extreme blindness to the oblivion of Being.[36]

In opening the autobiography which he published five years after Hardy's novel, *The Story of My Heart* (1883), Richard Jefferies consciously repudiates that 'dual emphasis on family and *literary* lineage' which, as Regenia Gagnier has shown, characterises 'canonical literary autobiographies' at this juncture.[37] It is rather the issue of perception which is central to Jefferies in his ascent of the Wiltshire Downs. Climbing towards 'the summit' he casts aside 'the petty circumstances and the annoyances of existence': 'I felt myself, myself' (SH, 18).[38] Here he attains 'the view over a broad plain . . . inclosed by a perfect amphitheatre of green hills', and he takes the decisive step in projecting himself towards the earth:

> I was utterly alone with the sun and the earth. Lying down on the grass, I spoke in my soul to the earth, the sun, the air, and the distant sea far beyond sight. I thought of the earth's firmness – I felt it bear me up; through the grassy couch there came an influence as if I could feel the great earth speaking to me . . . Then I addressed the sun, desiring the soul equivalent of his light and brilliance, his endurance and unwearied race. I turned to the blue heaven over, gazing into its depth, inhaling its exquisite colour and sweetness. The rich blue of the unattainable flower of the sky drew my soul towards it, and there it rested, for pure colour is rest of heart. By all these I prayed; I felt an emotion of the soul beyond all definition; prayer is a puny thing to it, and the word is a rude sign to the feeling, but I know no other. (SH, 18–19)

There is a curious juxtaposition here of the transcendental – the response to earth, sun and ocean – and the quotidian – that 'dry chalky earth' he lets fall through his fingers, and it is this heady combination which leads to the spiritual afflatus, the mystical union, attained as Jefferies hides his face in the grass (SH, 18–20). Later in the book, in Sussex, he discovers 'a deep hollow on the side of a great hill, a green concave opening to the sea': 'Silence and sunshine, sea and hill gradually brought my mind into the condition of intense prayer' (SH, 31):

> Behind me were furze bushes dried by the heat; immediately in front
> dropped the steep descent of the bowl-like hollow which received and
> brought up to me the faint sound of the summer waves. Yonder lay the
> immense plain of the sea, the palest green under the continued sunshine, as
> though the heat had evaporated the colour from it; there was no distinct
> horizon, a heat-mist inclosed it and looked farther away than the horizon
> would have done. Silence and sunshine, sea and hill gradually brought my
> mind into the condition of intense prayer. (SH, 31)

These experiences lead to the annihilation of time in which Jefferies can
affirm, 'Now is eternity; now is the immortal life' (SH, 39). Such writing,
with its transcendental resonance, is difficult to analyse or frame, posited as
it is in a mystical sense of communion with nature which is virtually inex-
pressible. The thinker in such a scenario, as Hannah Arendt suggests, 'has
drawn every appearance inside himself, and his "consciousness" becomes a
full substitute for the outside world presented as impression or image'. In
this transaction, she argues, consciousness 'undergoes a decisive change'
through which 'I myself, as sheer consciousness, emerge as an entirely new
entity'.[39]

The distinction between Hardy and Jefferies here lies in the definition
of art which is presupposed: for Hardy the function of writing is represen-
tational and historical, for Jefferies in *The Story of My Heart* (though not
always in his radical novel, *The Dewy Morn* or the sociological essays) it is
defamiliarising and transcendental, a revelation of being.[40] Narrative is
founded in the principle of repetition, whilst the experience recounted in
The Story is literally unrepeatable. As James Phillips glosses Heidegger, 'The
home of *Dasein* is a secret because it is too private (*heimlich*) to ecstatic
temporality for it to assume the cast of a repeatable entity'.[41] Jefferies'
posture here, indeed, is Transcendental in the technical sense, surely
drawing upon the New England doctrine of the 'universal mind' or
'Oversoul', and the desire, as Emerson put it, to do away with 'the prepos-
terous There and Then and introduce in its place the Here and Now'.[42] In
his seminal essay, 'Nature', Emerson adumbrates many of the concerns of
Jefferies' autobiography:

> Standing on the bare ground, – my head bathed by the blithe air, and
> uplifted into infinite space, – all mean egotism vanishes. I become a trans-
> parent eye-ball; I am nothing; I see all; the currents of the Universal Being
> circulate through me; I am part or parcel of God. [43]

These moments in Jefferies may be traced back to Romanticism, and specifically to those Wordsworthian 'spots of time' defined by Saree Makdisi as
'self-enclosed and self-referential enclaves of the anti-modern'.[44] Martin

Heidegger expounded his philosophical project as a wish 'to open up to the vastness and at the same time be rooted in the dark of the earth',[45] and it is his thought, especially the 1936 essay 'On the Origin of the Work of Art', which may provide a productive framework for Jefferies' writing. This is a mode of writing, in the Heideggerian definition, that is created out of nothing:

> Truth is never gathered from things at hand, never from the ordinary. Rather, the opening up of the open region, and the clearing of beings, happens only when the openness that makes its advent in thrownness is projected. [46]

If the 'Being of beings comes into the steadiness of its shining', then it is 'Upon the earth and in it' that 'historical man grounds his dwelling in the world'.[47] Hardy occupies what Heidegger designates 'world', a space 'to which we are subject as long as paths of birth and death, blessing and curse keep us transported into Being'.[48] Jefferies in contrast seeks the clarification of 'earth', his ascent up to the Downs bestowing access to Heidegger's famous 'clearing', an 'open centre' 'not surrounded by beings': 'rather, the clearing centre itself encircles all that is', and beings 'stand within and stand out within what is cleared in this clearing'. 'In the midst of beings as a whole an open place occurs. There is a clearing'.[49] Indeed, Heidegger affirms what Jefferies gestures towards: 'At bottom, the ordinary is not ordinary; it is extraordinary' and the 'truth' is arrived at through a 'clearing of the paths of the essential guiding directions with which all decision complies', to the extent that, as Heidegger expresses it, 'Earth juts through the world and world grounds itself on the earth'.[50] As Jefferies sinks to the ground, so Heidegger ponders the weight of the stone in its heaviness, and the way earth 'shatters every attempt to penetrate it', as the work of art 'sets this world back again on the earth'. All art is '*in essence, poetry*', taking place in 'the open region which poetry lets happen', such that beings 'shine and ring out'.[51] The ground in which man 'bases his dwelling' Heidegger designates 'the *earth*', an open region in which 'The Being of beings comes into the steadiness of its shining'.[52] In the *Contributions to Philosophy* of 1938, published posthumously, Heidegger notably associated the thinker with the agricultural field-worker who, 'with his heavy, halting, ever composed step walks along the furrows and with the cast of his arm measures and shapes the space of all growth and ripening'.[53]

Heidegger counters the theory of language as communication, to claim, with Jefferies, that poetry 'is the saying of the unconcealment of beings', and that 'language is not only and not primarily an audible and written expression of what is to be communicated'.[54] Unlike the primarily verbal Clym Yeobright, Jefferies here espouses a profound silence, a Heideggerian silence denominated, in 'The Way to Language' (1959), as one which 'corresponds to the noiseless ringing of stillness, the stillness of the saying that propriates and shows'.[55] Jefferies' vantage points on the downland heights are saturated with a sense of sun and light. In this writing, as Heidegger puts it in 'The End of Philosophy' (1969), 'Light can stream into the clearing, into its openness', but he goes on to insist that 'light never first creates the clearing': 'Rather, light presupposes it'.[56] And Heidegger's citation from Goethe here is apposite to Jefferies' project: 'Look for nothing behind phenomena', writes Goethe, 'they themselves are what is to be learned'.[57] In *The Story*, Jefferies strives towards Heidegger's postulate that the clearing, in its 'free openness', will ultimately bestow 'pure space and ecstatic time'. There is 'No outward appearance without light', and 'no brightness without the clearing'. It is in that clearing that 'possible radiance' is to be found, 'that is, the possible presencing of presence itself'.[58] It is this insistence on presence that binds the two thinkers together, sharing as they do the sense that 'the clearing grants first of all the possibility of the path to presence, and grants the possibility of that presence itself'.[59] Jefferies and Heidegger are both attentive to what the philosopher designates 'the destiny of a historical people',[60] but this destiny is effected through language. We may read off *The Story of My Heart* as a work which 'sets forth' the earth. This strange spiritual autobiography *'lets the earth be an earth'* in the sense that this writing compels us by the obscure and resistant weight of its language, its excess of words over sense. Heidegger thus shares with Jefferies a sense of the earth not as a resource but as a dwelling-place which is 'sheltering and concealing', because 'The world grounds itself on the earth'.[61] Both writers seek out the 'clearing' in a movement antithetical to Hardy or Marx, the attainment of the 'lighting centre' which 'encircles all that is and which enables beings to be unconcealed'. As in Heideggerian thought, *The Story of My Heart* premises a series of new attempts to locate this clearing in the concealment of earth: the truth of being is located for both thinkers in a dialectic between openness and concealment; as one of Heidegger's commentators puts it, 'the work of art keeps the earth in the open of the world, thereby allowing the earth to be earth'.[62] According to Paul de Man, 'Earth is precisely the going beyond the obstacle of sense perception toward being', yet this 'going beyond' remains 'rigorously enclosed within the limits of the mediated' to the extent that 'it designates the ontological priority of *consciousness* over the object'[63] – a priority which Jefferies, at least in his late essays and notebooks, would endorse.

Language for both writers is in essence poetic, and the implications of this are particularly explored in the second passage from *The Story*, where

Jefferies proclaims, 'Now is eternity; now is the immortal life' (SH, 39).
This moment of being is predicated upon the suspension of time in a movement fruitfully theorised by Jacques Derrida's enquiry, 'how is it to be
thought that time is what is not?' Time, he argues, is temporal 'only in
becoming temporal, that is, in ceasing to be, in passing over to nothingness
in the form of being past or being future'. Thus, Derrida argues in terms
which echo Jefferies, 'to participate in beingness . . . is to participate in
being-present, in the presence of the present': 'Beings are what *is*'.[64]
Jefferies' late essays are deeply inflected with this concern for being to
produce a set of pieces in which, as W. J. Keith remarks, the 'factual preci-
sion of the earlier writing blends with the idealistic thinking of *The Story of
My Heart*'.[65] The 1883 essay, 'On the Downs', aptly encompasses that
ecstatic, celebratory mode which Hardy generally eschewed. Here Jefferies
is aiming to trace the effects of light on the sea and hillside, and he dismisses
metaphysics as incapable of satisfying 'the well of thought'; indeed the
writing here is posited upon what Jefferies terms the 'fullness of Nature and
the vacancy of mental existence'. The mind, he insists in anticipation of
phenomenology, must allow itself to 'rest on every blade of grass and leaf".[66]
He goes on, in a seminal passage:

> *Stoop and touch the earth*, and receive its influence; touch the flower, and feel
> its life; face the wind, and have its meaning; let the sunlight fall on the open
> hand as if you could hold it. Something may be grasped from them all, invis-
> ible yet strong. It is the sense of a wider existence – wider and higher.

This sense of 'absorbing something from the earth' is 'like hovering on the
verge of a great truth'.[67] Four years later, while in his final illness, Jefferies
still seeks in his notebooks what he terms 'the Beyond', 'Soul-Life' or 'Sun-
Life', again adumbrating a phenomenological world-view:

> No theory, philosophy, religion, meets the labourer rough and red, the
> woman to the draw-well, the invalid on his bed, the omnibus driver: all spec-
> ulation, they do not touch the real.[68]

Yet the quotidian is ineluctably linked, in these moving final ruminations,
with transcendence, 'the sun in silence rising over the sea' linking Jefferies
with 'a sense and sympathy with some larger life'. This gives what he terms
a 'great view of the greater earth – *putting soul – thought into the greater sphere*'.
Although in these reflections he feels 'utterly abandoned', it is the 'intense
beauty and love of nature – every grain of sand',[69] which dominates the late
meditations:

> I fetish Nature. Sea, sunshine, clear water, leaves. If I can see why not – if

they cannot see I cannot help that – I see the sands and the stars, and the subtle cosmical material far up, and feel through, and the more I touch these the greater grows my soul life and soul touch.[70]

In his final note Jefferies offers a summation of his philosophical journey: there is, he argues, 'Nothing for Man. Unless he has the Beyond', and he concludes, '*I dream of Ideality*'.[71]

In *The Story of My Heart* and elsewhere Richard Jefferies might be described as a Heideggerian 'shepherd of Being', one who, according to the 1947 'Letter on Humanism', propounds 'ecstatic dwelling in the nearness of Being'.[72] As he climbs the downs towards his 'perfect amphitheatre of green hills', Jefferies reflects that words are 'clumsy' once 'the wooden stage of commonplace life is left' (SH, 18), just as Heidegger would propose that 'language requires much less precipitate expression than proper silence'.[73] Jefferies' Wiltshire amphitheatre and his 'green concave opening to the sun' in Sussex (SH, 31) afford a platform in which he 'stands out in the openness of Being', arenas for that Heideggerian 'clearing of Being' into which man is 'thrown'.[74] 'This being in the midst of', Heidegger writes in 1929, 'belongs to transcendence', an afflatus 'rooted in the essence of time, i.e., in its ecstatic-horizontal constitution'.[75] However, Heidegger's argument in the 'Letter', in particular his admonition as to the 'malignancy' which threatens 'if the open region of Being is not cleared',[76] may alert us to a more ominous dimension in this line of thinking. In his 1942 lectures on Hölderlin, Heidegger argued that 'Whatever is of the fatherland is itself at home with mother earth': 'This *coming to be* at home in one's own', he added, 'in itself entails that human beings are initially, and for a long time, and sometimes forever, not at home'.[77] It is impossible to overlook the crypto-fascist hints in *The Story*, as for instance in Jefferies' cult of Julius Caesar, the one man 'truly great of all history' who attained 'the ideal of a design-power arranging the affairs of the world for good' (SH, 65–6). Later, Jefferies longs for 'an iron mace' with which he might 'crush the savage beast and hammer him down' (SH, 80). In such instances the quest for a 'fullness of physical life', leading to 'a deeper desire of soul-life' (SH, 81), acquires an alarming resonance when framed by the record of Heidegger's naïve yet duplicitous investment, as Rector of Freiburg University, in National Socialism. Simon Grimble justly discerns 'a rhetoric of violence and a post-apocalyptic landscape' in parts of *The Story*, and argues that the source of this is Jefferies' lack of a 'strong and conscious sense of cultural life as battleground'.[78] It may be suggested that the longing for a return to nature took the form of a justified response to the bourgeois experience of alien-

ation and domination in a mass society, but the reactionary possibilities of
such a return were persuasively laid bare in a 1937 essay on the Norwegian
nature-novelist, Knut Hamsun, by a member of the Frankfurt School, Leo
Löwenthal. Drawing upon Ibsen, Löwenthal demonstrates how the 'path
to nature' took the form, not of a flight from reality, but rather of a movement towards liberation.[79] However, in the late-nineteenth-century
development of which Hamsun is an exemplar, Löwenthal argues that
'this new type of submission to nature is closely related to political submission', with the ominous result that 'communion with nature is
transformed from sentiment into sentimentality, and then into brutality'.[80] In bourgeois liberalism, nature had been transformed 'by organised
societal enterprise', becoming 'an object for scientific and practical control', whereas in the new nature-mysticism embodied by Hamsun, the
individual 'consecrates his life in rapt surrender and even in mystical identification'[81] to generate 'a jumble of mawkish sympathies for both natural
objects and spiritual difficulties', such that Hamsun's world, in
Löwenthal's critique, 'foreshadows the affinity of brutality and sentimentality' which would become so marked a feature of Nazism.[82] But whilst
certainly the heroisation of the figure of the peasant in Hamsun's fiction
might justly be applied to features of Heidegger's thought, Löwenthal's
diagnosis of nature-mysticism as an 'exodus from social reality'[83] is of
questionable application to the case of Richard Jefferies. The nuanced
reading propounded by Edward Thomas's 1909 study of Jefferies notes
how, in the trajectory of his embattled career, the mood and vocabulary of
early books such as *The Gamekeeper at Home*, *The Amateur Poacher* or *Hodge
and His Masters* militated against 'the revelation of which he was in
search'.[84] It was only at the age of thirty-four, already fatally ill, that
Jefferies felt able to speak in his own persona, making *The Story* 'the
unflinchingly true revelation of a human spirit'.[85] Thomas reads the book
as a poem, an almost musical structure attaining an 'absolute, more than
logical, unity',[86] and as Keith notes, 'the imagery is not merely a literary
device but an essential element in the intellectual scheme'.[87] It is thus as
an authentic statement of 'a personal rather than a public philosophy'[88]
that *The Story of My Heart* makes its impact.

Furthermore, any juxtaposition of a liberal Hardy and a reactionary
Jefferies would be tendentious. Both passages might be characterised as
expressions of self-emancipation, predicating the arrival of a socialist or non-
antagonistic society emerging out of the pressures of modernity – Hardy
and Jefferies, that is to say, are led by a necessary dialectic from the intense
observation of what exists to the utopian desire for a new society. In postulating links, connections and differences between Hardy and Jefferies, it is

valuable to recall Heidegger's postulate that 'even Nature is historical . . .
as a countryside, as an area that has been colonised or exploited'.[89] In exam-
ining the possibilities of nature for exploitation or renewal, the writing of
Hardy and Jefferies struggles to prefigure a social order beyond capital, and
this social order is registered through concrete natural imagery rather than
through the abstract philosophical or positivist concepts of Clym
Yeobright's final sermons. Whilst Clym's experience as a furze-cutter on
Egdon adumbrates the beginnings of the exchange principle that Marx saw
as the engine of capital, converting concrete acts of human labour into
abstract units of labour time, in Jefferies' spiritual autobiography writing
as a conjunction of sensuous and conceptual truth foreshadows a new social
order through a mimesis based in the beauty of the natural world. Here
Jefferies affirms what Merleau-Ponty designates 'another nature, the
domain of an "originary presence"' which calls up 'the total response of a
single embodied subject'.[90] Both writers meditate with different emphases
upon what has been termed 'species imperialism'. John Lucas, in a reading
of Wordsworth, has remarked how 'landscape is to be read – marked – in
terms of work, love and aspiration', and he notes the way in which 'the loss
of a dwelling is the loss of a word and the loss of the values embodied in that
word'.[91] For both Hardy and Jefferies writing took the form of a social
labour, the conversion of commodified literary labour into capital, cultural
or otherwise, but it may be that Jefferies' relative failure in the literary field
partially released him from the bonds of this commodification. However
that may be, both writers here meditate upon the concept of dwelling upon
the earth, and the implications of their writing are borne out in Heidegger's
final message: 'there is need for contemplation whether and how in the age
of a uniform technological world civilisation, there can still be such a thing
as home'.[92]

Hardy and Jefferies represent differential responses to this conjuncture
– that loss of home or dwelling which marks the epistemological moment
of modernity, a moment compromised and energised by the bourgeois
domination of nature. The question they both pose, but answer in diamet-
rically opposed ways, is whether it is possible to comprehend nature
through history. This crisis generates in the one case narrative realism, in
the other a stress upon authenticity which undermines narrative coherence.
In other terminology, these writers deploy a negative and a positive
hermeneutic, Hardy pursuing what Fredric Jameson, in his discussion of
Bloch, terms 'the hermeneutics of suspicion', whilst Jefferies' writing here
is marked by 'the hermeneutics of a restoration of some original, forgotten
meaning'.[93] For Hardy, Clym's predicament enacts, in its unresolved
tensions, the imperatives and impossibilities of a return to nature; for

Jefferies such a return offers possibilities of ecstatic renewal or 'moments of vision' that transcend quotidian reality. Whilst Clym's adoption of the role and technique of furze-cutter problematises the class distinction between intellectual and manual labour, Jefferies' inscription of material practice takes the form of an overcoming of 'false consciousness' in terms of a literal return to earth. Raymond Williams has scrupulously noted the creative contradictions inherent in Jefferies' position:

> There is the intensity, a lonely intensity, of his feelings for the natural world: the green language that connects him with Clare and Lawrence. But the working rural world, where the physical experiences are most commonly found, is decisively altering. The labourers' options are very firmly for change. A fault can then occur, in the whole ordering of a mind.[94]

This is just in relation to Jefferies' whole *oeuvre*, perhaps, but in the last analysis both Hardy and Jefferies, in these instances, are committed to recuperating a Marxian sense of 'species-being', and might be read in light of Marx's contention that

> Man lives from nature, ie. nature is his body, and he must remain in a continuous process with it if he is not to die. To say that man's physical and mental life is linked to nature simply means that nature is linked to itself, for man is a part of nature.[95]

For Marx, man is a natural being dependent upon other objective natural beings, but is also a thinking being, and it is this dichotomy, according to Kostas Axelos, which means that Marx 'turns his back to Nature', concerning himself 'only with the process of the transformation of nature into History': 'Nature *is* only to the extent that man and his technique take hold of it'.[96] This dual concept illuminates the position adopted by Clym Yeobright and Richard Jefferies in differentially conceptualising the otherness of the natural world. The distinction between the two may be defined as linguistic, Jefferies' practice highlighting the metaphoric, polysemic and speculative functions of language, its mimetic potential, whilst Hardy stresses language as communicative action. In *The Return of the Native*, as in Hardy's fiction generally, history is conceived as a longitudinal totality. Jefferies is concerned, in *The Story*, to challenge that concept, but both authorial procedures might be explicated by an observation of Michel Foucault, who argues that, whilst 'the nineteenth century is commonly thought to have discovered the historical dimension', it did so 'only on the basis of the *circle*, the spatial form which negates time' through which 'men manifest their *return to their native ground* of finitude'.[97] There is, in short, a profound element of deconstructive/irrational naturalness in the textuality of *The Story of My Heart* which enables us to conceive the id as a source of infinitely deferred desire modelled upon the gap between signified and signifier.

The juxtaposition of these passages thus enables us to confront a crucial debate in current linguistic theory whilst remaining duly attentive to the period inflections of both texts. Jefferies is indisputably the more utopian writer here, if we define the concept of utopia as the negation in art of existing conditions, and the imagining of a different social dispensation, even where that futurity cannot be described. This visionary element, which is largely absent from Hardy's work, reconfigures history to reveal a structure, in Walter Benjamin's terms, 'whose site is not homogeneous, empty time, but time filled by the presence of the now'. Richard Jefferies here projects a Benjaminian 'cessation of happening', a seizing of the time of the now which may offer 'a revolutionary chance in the fight for an oppressed past'.[98] The discomfiting raptures of *The Story of My Heart* are precisely untimely in their projection of an unhistorical time of potentiality.

Edward Thomas's close friend Eleanor Farjeon tells the story of how, in the second year of the Great War, the poet stooped towards the earth in a haunting gesture reminiscent of the posture of Clym Yeobright and Richard Jefferies:

> It might have been next year when we were walking in the country that I asked him the question his friends had asked him when he joined up, but I put it differently. "Do you know what you are fighting for?" He stopped, and picked up a pinch of earth. "Literally, for this." He crumbled it between finger and thumb, and let it fall.[99]

In disavowing metaphysics and the ideologies of patriotism, Thomas seized upon the earth itself in a gestural moment that was not only personal but also aesthetic in its implications. His response was both materialist and poetic in its espousal of what Heidegger designates 'the thingly aspect of the artwork'. 'The stone in the ground is a thing', Heidegger observes, 'as is the clod in the field', whilst, he adds, a man 'is not a thing'.[100] Thomas's act in bending to the earth, reinscribing the gestures of Clym Yeobright and Richard Jefferies, is a moment of re-cognition, acknowledging the 'constancy and pith', the 'particular mode of sensuous pressure' that constitutes the clod of earth, but also seeking to transform that 'thing-concept' into the work of art, the poem. Thomas contrives here, as Heidegger puts it, to keep 'at a distance all the preconceptions and assaults' of predetermined thought, recognising that the 'unpretentious thing evades thought most stubbornly'.[101] As Thomas expresses it in 'Digging', 'It is enough/ To smell, to crumble the dark earth'. The work of art, in Heidegger's formulation, partakes of 'an earthy character', as the earth 'juts up within the work':[102] it is, in both writings, the everyday that is made strange and invites meditation on its familiar outlook.

Thomas's poem 'Tall Nettles' delivers us up to one his 'epiphanies of melancholy', delineating a 'momentary experience with subjective and objective components' – a sense of mystery and intensity characteristically linked with the everyday and quotidian:[103]

> Tall nettles cover up, as they have done
> These many springs, the rusty harrow, the plough
> Long worn out, and the roller made of stone:
> Only the elm butt tops the nettles now.
>
> This corner of the farmyard I like most:
> As well as any bloom upon a flower
> I like the dust on the nettles, never lost
> Except to prove the sweetness of a shower.[104]

The poem places at issue the question of voice, the first stanza offering a quasi-impersonal description, the second introducing the personality of the poet with his celebration of the nettles. Yet the 'dust' also gestures towards that final silencing of the poet's voice by a German shell, the poem moving from a communally experienced record of that agricultural decline recorded by Jefferies and Hardy, a decline registered in the heavily stressed syllables of the fourth line, into a more personalised, tentative response embodied in the half-rhymes, done/stone, most/lost, and in the smoothed-out rhythm of the final line. The rhythmic representation of the human voice also acts out that voice's ultimate diminution and silencing. After leaving England for the Western Front, Thomas wrote no further poems, instead composing a diary in which he recorded both the virtually posthumous vivacity of the natural world, the very 'South Country' he inherited from Borrow, Hardy and Jefferies, and the ultimate transfiguration and degradation of that landscape into a theatre of death:

> No Man's Land like Goodwood racecourse, with engineers swarming over it and making a road between shell holes full of blood-stained water and beer bottles among barbed wire. Larks singing as they did when we went up in dark and were shelled. Now I hardly felt as if a shell could hurt, though several were thrown about near working parties.[105]

CHAPTER 5

The Guilty River
Wilkie Collins's Gothic Deafness

---

*Origin is an eddy in the stream of becoming, and in its current
it swallows the material involved in the process of genesis.*
Walter Benjamin[1]

Wilkie Collins's late novella, *The Guilty River* (1886), intuitively blends
Gothic and modernist elements to produce a narrative which is simultaneously baffling, banal and complex, addressing as it does key issues of self,
mastery, class and gender within its deceptive and transparent framework.
The story centres upon the return from abroad of the young heir to an
English estate, Gerard Roylake, and his encounter with the inhabitants of
a water-mill on his land. On returning from Germany to claim his 'large
landed property',[2] Trimley Deen, Roylake finds the house in the hands of
his socially ambitious step-mother, a woman deeply disappointed to
discover that her stepson's 'principal amusements were derived from
reading books, and collecting insects' (247). Fleeing her society in his quest
for specimens, Roylake comes across the 'venerable timbers of the water-
mill' (249) and the beguiling daughter of the miller, Cristel Toller, with her
'beautiful dusky arms, at once delicate and strong' (251). Roylake is
surprised to see, attached to the 'decrepit building', a new cottage which
stands in 'hideous modern contrast to all that was left of its ancient neighbour' (250). Cristel reveals that the new building houses a lodger whom she
hates. The Lodger then appears, a deaf man with a 'tall and slim' figure and
a 'beautiful face' (255). Alternatively known throughout the text as the
Lodger or the Cur, this individual reveals to Roylake that he is besotted
with Cristel, who has rejected his advances, and expresses jealousy at the
young landowner's arrival on the scene. In the memoirs which he hands to
Roylake, the Lodger recounts the story of his life: he is the son of a freed
female slave from the Southern States and a well-to-do Englishman who
sends his son to Cambridge, after which he becomes a surgeon patronised
by the aristocracy. On his mother's death, the Lodger learns of the

disgraceful conduct of his paternal forebears, and of the 'vile blood' that runs in his veins (264). A severe illness causes his loss of hearing, and he flees society, finally taking up residence at the lonely mill beside 'the ugly river' (271). Roylake is uncertain how to interpret this document, at some points feeling 'sympathy and respect' for the ruined surgeon, at others dismissing him as 'mad' (273). Meanwhile, his step-mother, Mrs Roylake, seeks to introduce him into local society with matrimonial intentions, focusing her efforts on Lord Uppercliff's younger daughter, Lady Lena. The older sister, Lady Rachel, who has married and become an ardent socialist, is to play a decisive part in the plot. Drawn back to the mill, Roylake is implored by the importunate old miller to undertake some repairs to the fabric of the building. Whilst divining 'something devilish' in the Lodger's demeanour, the landowner is persuaded by the beauty of his features to give him the benefit of the doubt, though Cristel urgently warns against trusting him. Later on, returning again to the mill, Roylake comes across the Lodger conducting chemical experiments, his face masked by a white handkerchief. Despite his mounting suspicions, he accepts the Lodger's invitation to tea, but before this event takes place, Roylake is warned off by an ex-pugilist, Mr Gloody, now acting as the Lodger's servant. He ignores the warning and sets off for the mill, discovering that Lady Rachel has been paying a mysterious visit to his host. At tea, the Lodger performs a series of dazzling card-tricks, but on drinking the tea, Roylake falls victim to a poison the effect of which only Cristel's prompt action serves to mitigate. Gloody confirms the existence of a plot to kill the landowner, and Roylake determines now to camp out at the mill in order to keep the Lodger under surveillance. Noting that the mill-boat is missing, Roylake then discovers that Cristel has disappeared, a revelation which drives the Lodger into a fury in which he attempts to shoot the young landowner. The Lodger then suddenly decamps, and Lady Rachel confirms that she had intervened in order to ensure that Roylake should not marry the mill-owner's daughter. Old Toller later dies, and, unable to trace Cristel, Roylake listlessly embarks on a world tour. On his return, he discovers that he has received a death-bed confession from the Lodger, composed in Geneva, and revealing that Cristel had been spirited away on the 'empty' boat by her father's contrivance, and taken off to safety in her wealthy uncle's yacht. 'I say there *was* good in that suffering man', Roylake avers (351), and the tale ends with his marriage to Cristel and peremptory dismissal of Mrs Roylake from Trimley Deen.

This curiously half-hearted text is furrowed with traces of the Gothic: Roylake's relationship with the Lodger, for instance, conforms to Kelly Hurley's definition of the Gothic as 'a genre marked by both attraction towards and aversion from the subject of its obsession', in a strategy of 'occluding that object through mechanisms of textual hysteria'.[3] The tale's structure, a first-person narrative interrupted by the Lodger's memoirs, letters and diaries, bears evidence of the kind of documentary complicatedness redolent of the Gothic, a genre in which both Romantic and late-Victorian manifestations are characterised by the use of embedded narratives, journal extracts and other ostensibly written records, in a drive both to create illusions of verisimilitude and to investigate origins. It is the issue of origins which *The Guilty River* explores with contradictory power and complexity in relation to its delineation of character. Thus Roylake is identified at the outset as looking 'more like a foreigner than an Englishman' (247), having been educated at a German university. Becoming lost and entangled in the forest, the numinous site of German romanticism,[4] he is a 'stranger among [his] own people', lost in Germanic 'solitary meditations' (248). Roylake's sense of humour, according to his step-mother, is 'blunted' by his 'residence in Germany' (285), but he brings with him 'the social habits and the free range of thought of a foreign University' (287) allied with a student predilection for 'tobacco and beer' (287). This Germanic affiliation is reduplicated in the representation of the heroine, since Cristel Toller, as her name indicates, is the daughter of a German mother, and these elective affinities serve to prompt a reading of the story through the lens of European philosophical thought. Paul de Man, whose own investment in this tradition was to prove so problematic, argues that anyone wishing to understand 'modern hopes and anxieties' would 'find Germany to be an inexhaustible mine of information'.[5] If it is true that 'the catastrophes of the twentieth century betray a direct lineage to specifically, German Romantic thought',[6] then one can read *The Guilty River* as inaugurating what de Man nominates as 'a time span of uncertainty and the greatest danger'.[7]

It is the relation between Roylake the great landowner and the deaf Lodger which, it might be argued, conforms to and enacts the parameters of the Hegelian reading of the master–slave dialectic. The Lodger's memoirs reveal that, whilst his father was a well-to-do Englishman, his mother was born 'of slave parents' and 'sold by auction in the Southern States' at the age of eighteen (261), later to be set free and raised socially through her marriage. According to Karl Marx, in the modern world 'each person is *at the same time* a member of slave society and of the public commonweal', because the '*slavery of civil society* is *in appearance* the greatest *freedom*'[8] – a thesis neatly demonstrated here by Mrs Roylake's snobbish enslavement to social climbing. Roylake's baffled love–hate relation with the beautiful Lodger curiously mirrors the Hegelian diagnosis of the confrontation between self and other. As Peter Singer interprets this thinking, the self 'must proceed to supersede the other independent being in order thereby to become certain of itself as the essential being': 'Thus the relation of the two self-conscious individuals is such that they prove themselves and each other through a life-and-death struggle'.[9] In this struggle, which here reaches its climax at the poisonous tea-party, Hegel holds that 'each staked his life and held it of no account',[10] and it is out of this contest that the master–slave relation is born, embodying the dichotomy between independent and dependent consciousness. Wilkie Collins had treated the issue of slavery earlier in his career in the melodrama *Black and White* (1869), which turns on the rivalry between a wealthy West Indian planter, Stephen Westcraft, and a French gentleman for the favours of an heiress, Miss Millburn. In the course of the plot it is revealed that the Frenchman, Maurice de Layrac, is in fact the son of a female slave. At the climax of this farrago, Miss Milburn consents to marry de Layrac despite his compromised origins, though Maurice reflects that '"The slave blood runs in my veins – the slave nature can bear anything"'.[11] It is not, however, clear that in *The Guilty River* it is the son of the slave who retains this slave mentality, the Lodger displaying a power and mastery which daunts and paralyses the actions of the land-owner. As Hegel remarks, 'the object in which the lord has achieved his lordship has in reality turned out to be . . . not an independent consciousness but a dependent one' – the lord is thus possessed of an 'unessential consciousness'.[12] In this instance, Roylake is held in an almost hypnotic trance by the Lodger, despite his sense of danger:

> 'Men of your age', he resumed, 'seldom look below the surface. Learn that valuable habit, sir – and begin by looking below the surface of Me.' He forced the portfolio into my hand. Once more, his beautiful eyes held me with their irresistible influence; they looked at me with an expression of sad and solemn warning. 'Discover for yourself', he said, 'what devils my deafness has set loose in me; and let no eyes but yours see that horrid sight'. (259)

In his study of the Hegelian thesis, Jonathan Taylor notes that 'the dialectical relation of master and slave is eventually overturned, the master being subsumed in the position of slave, the slave working towards mastery and freedom'.[13] The nearly fatal tea-party dramatically embodies Taylor's point that mastery and slavery are posited upon the 'deferment' of 'the life-and-death struggle', and it is clear that the relation between landowner and lodger, for all its apparent equality, 'is always haunted by past mastery and slavery'.[14] Taylor also touches upon this question, observing that 'mutual poisoning stands as a metaphor for laissez-faire class relations as a whole'.[15]

Collins's poisonous tea-party, it might be said, dramatically embodies the way in which, in Kelly Hurley's definition of Gothic, 'a poisonous society (locus of both environmental and moral contaminants) infected the individual, and the individual passed on the infection to its offspring, and the degenerate offspring infected society'.[16] The Lodger, in a curious anticipation of Sherlock Holmes's procedure with the terrier in *A Study in Scarlet* (1887), has first experimented with the miller's dog in a scenario in which, as Diana Basham argues, the canine represents 'a gap in discourse about the male body'.[17] Following Cixous, Jonathan Taylor argues that 'the master term in any hierarchy must always posit itself as masculine, whilst the slave is always constituted as feminine',[18] a gender hierarchy both endorsed and undermined by *The Guilty River*, where the apparently dominant Gerard Roylake is compromised by his lack of interest in field sports or class ambition, and his countervailing devotion to lepidoptery, whilst the vengeful and embittered masculinity of the Lodger is problematised by his beauty and deafness. The opening scene in Fordwitch Wood, in which a bat 'steals' the moths Roylake has studiously ensnared, sets the tone for the story, the 'idle' landowner becoming the 'victim of clever theft' (245) in his pursuit of the beautiful heroine to the extent that he eventually finds that 'My own moths failed to interest me' (310). On the other side of the equation, the Lodger's stunning looks complicate his role as ultra-masculine villain by endowing him with effeminised sensitivity. He is 'without moustache or beard', with a 'tall and slim' figure and 'beautiful' face (254, 255); his eyes, however, are marked by 'a sinister passion' (258) which can instantly change to 'demoniacal rage and hatred' (259). And yet Roylake fails to discover anything 'devilish in the expression of his face' (277) – the Lodger's seductive beauty being read here as a sign of duplicity in marked contrast to the honestly 'ugly face' of his man-servant, Mr Gloody (305). This ex-pugilist, who seeks to warn Roylake of the plot against him, has been selected by the Lodger on account of his appearance: '"He took me into his service, sir, because I was ugly."' (306). Women also, according to the Lodger, prefer an ugly partner: '"A handsome man matches them on their own ground, and they don't like that"', he informs the landowner (319). Collins appears to be mobilising a tale of male rivalry around an undeclared homo-erotic attraction locked into the rivalrous comedy of 'paranoid gothic'. Within this contestatory scenario, or struggle for supremacy, it is the Lodger who gains the upper hand in a stratagem first signalled by his performance of a series of erotically charged card-tricks for his guests:

> He shuffled the pack by pouring it backwards and forwards from one hand
> to the other, in a cascade of cards. The wonderful ease with which he did it

> prepared me for something worth seeing. Cristel's admiration of his
> dexterity expressed itself by a prolonged clapping of hands, and a strange
> uneasy laugh. As his excitement subsided, her agitation broke out. (322)

As Cristel remarks, "'Conjurers are people who ask riddles, and when one
can't guess them, refuse to say what the answer is'" (323). Deafness was often
equated with clairvoyance, or even with madness, and certainly the riddle
embodied in the master–slave relation, as Taylor remarks, is that 'just as
each stakes his own life, so each must seek the other's death'.[19] Taylor's
ensuing observation that slavery 'is based wholly on a denial of origin',
relying upon 'both the affirmation *and* rejection of male, lineal descent',[20]
is borne out in the Oedipal drama of Collins's story, in which both male
protagonists seek to disavow the name-of-the-father. 'Our mothers',
Roylake ruminates, 'have the most sacred of all claims on our gratitude and
our love', since 'they nourished us with their blood'. By contrast, he reflects,
his heart remained unmoved by the death of his father, 'a bad man' who was
his mother's 'worst enemy' (246), and who sent his son into European exile,
leaving the 'elegant' and class-conscious second wife in residence on the
estate. The Lodger's father was equally an unknown quality, 'hardly better
known' than 'strangers passing in the street'; however, on the death of his
beloved mother, his father's family threaten to publicise the 'calamity' of
his 'slave-birth' (263). A letter to his mother exposes the evil legacy of his
paternal forebears, citing his father's desertion of a pregnant girl who then
commits suicide as 'the most infamous in the list of the family crimes' (264).
Both men are thus haunted by familial guilt and a fantasmatic relation to
the mother: as Cristel tells Roylake, "'You have your mother's face, and your
mother's heart'" (335), whilst the Lodger, on his death-bed, reflects upon
'the family taint, developed by a deaf man's isolation', and claims, 'I am
going to my mother now' (351).

The guilty river of the title is thus imagined as the stream of Darwinian
heredity, that 'moral contamination by the vile [paternal] blood' of which
the Lodger speaks (264), imprisoned in both deafness and 'the inherited evil
lying dormant' in his nature (266). But the issue of inheritance is material
as much as psychological, *The Guilty River* being posited upon a fracture in
the class structure which produces a murderous sexual rivalry. This fracture
is physically embodied in the construction of the water-mill with its 'great
turning wheel' and 'venerable timbers'. On first coming upon it Roylake
observes that the 'wooden cottage attached to it had felt the devastating
march of time':

> A portion of the decrepit building still stood revealed in its wretched old
> age; propped, partly by beams which reached from the thatched roof to the

ground, and partly by the wall of a new cottage attached, presenting in
yellow brick-work a hideou modern contrast to all that was left of its ancient
neighbour. (250)

The contrast here between the 'ancient side of the building' (275) and 'the
ugly modern part' (252) offers a neat manifestation of Marx's observation
that the 'hand-mill gives you society with the feudal lord; the steam-mill,
society with the industrial capitalist', and that thus, the 'hand-mill presupposes a different division of labour from the steam-mill'.[21] The contest
between the two men is then, essentially one of class – a contest between a
representative of the old landed gentry and the newly professionalised
surgeon. Roylake, in his self-absorbed sensitivity, both disowns and culti-
vates his role as landowner in ways nicely illuminated by Georg Lukács's
remark that 'for the capitalist . . . there is the same doubling of personality,
the same splitting up of man into an element of the movement of commodities and an (objective and impotent) observer of that movement'.[22]
Consciousness of one's status, Lukács writes, 'is not directed to the real,
living economic unity but to a past state of society as constituted by the
privileges accorded to the estates': 'Status-consciousness – a real historical
factor – marks class consciousness'.[23] Thus Roylake exhibits and continually denies his landowning status in his patriarchal role with the 'Lodger',
with Old Toller, and even with his step-mother, and enters into a funda-
mentally exploitative relation with the miller's daughter. To be a 'lodger' is
to exemplify the condition of modernity, as defined in Kostas Axelos's
examination of Marxist theory:

> Caught in the engagements of property as if in a great machine, man
> loses his own being, finding himself deprived of all enjoyment and
> naked of any shelter. In vain he tries to take refuge in what is a tomb, a hostile
> lodging, and an alien house.[24]

If the Lodger embodies the displacement and anomie of modernity, the
personification of Cristel Toller harks back to the trope of the Gothic
Persecuted Maiden, a figure, as Michelle Massé observes, who is 'recognis-
able as Freud's hysteric', and one who, in the psychoanalytic family romance
performs 'the utilitarian handmaid's role'.[25] In her conflicted but essentially
passive relations with her father, the Lodger and Roylake, Cristel conforms
to Massé's definition of the Gothic utilisation of the woman's body 'as a
pawn':

> She is moved, threatened, discarded, and lost. And, as the whole person, is
> abducted, attacked, and so forth, the subtext metaphorically conveys anxiety
> about her genital risk.[26]

The truth of the 'Beautiful Soul', as Ortwin de Graef explains in his study of de Man, is founded in 'the repetition of an unexplainable void within, which no realisation of the spirit can fill',[27] the myth being embodied, as de Man himself contends, 'in the shape of a person, feminine, masculine or hermaphrodite'.[28]

This issue of the foundations of personality raises the question of the name, which is an insistent note in Collins's text. *The Guilty River* enacts a drama of signification founded in a performance of naming, since, as David Punter observes, Gothic is a term deployed to 'signify a field of hauntings' but also has to deal with 'the issue of namelessness'.[29] The namelessness of the central figure paradoxically generates alternative nominative strategies – 'the Lodger', 'the Cur' – whilst his final expiry enacts de Man's contention that death 'is a displaced name for a linguistic predicament'.[30] On the other side of the equation, the name of Gerard Roylake embodies aristocratic grace and power, with its echoes of 'roi' and of landed property ('lake'), and that of Cristel Toller hints at both clarity and fragmentation. Collins extends this nominative complication and resonance down to the minor characters like Mr Gloody, the bluff goodness and uprightness of the ex-pugilist's character awkwardly modified by the interruptive consonant which appears to endorse Diana Basham's thesis that the letter 'L' emblematises 'a phallic inscription for the reversible laws of sexuality, history and personal identity'.[31]

In the case of the villain of the piece, however, lack of name signifies a deeper absence or loss marked by his profound deafness. The Lodger has been 'too miserable' to learn the 'finger alphabet' (256), and is thus dependent upon written replies for his conversation, 'living the death-in-life of deafness' (267) in conformity to the Gothic prescription of the 'living entombed'. This predicament generates a language of signs, so that Cristel is able to 'make a sign to the deaf man' (317), whilst on his side the Lodger compulsively breaks through 'the incredible monotony of his articulation' to emit 'a screech, prolonged in its own discord until it became perfectly unendurable to hear' (320). Roylake may make 'an affirmative sign' (321), or deploy 'the language of signs' (322), causing the Lodger to 'understand . . . by a sign' (341), yet he constantly misreads the signs himself. What the Lodger designates 'a deaf man's isolation among his fellow-creatures' (351) becomes a mark of the human condition in Collins's proto-modernist text. The Lodger's deafness is thus a dire sign or manifestation of a more general depersonalisation, a modernist situating of the self on a new level of impersonality, but, as de Man notes, 'in the process of depersonalisation, the self could, to some degree, maintain its power', enriched as it is 'by the repeated experience of defeat'[32] – an insistently German experience in the twentieth century. The process of depersonalisation is at an advanced stage in this text, in which all the characters are furrowed with a perfunctoriness of motivation, an opaque transparency of self created out of a depersonalising tendency to produce what de Man designates a 'consciousness without a subject': in de Manian terms, 'the assertion of a self leads by inference to its disappearance'.[33] *The Guilty River* is traced with elements of that increasing sense of fluidity surrounding basic elements of personality and identity within the period; it is a text, that is, whose motivation is a growing crisis in methods of representation. Collins's characterisation here gestures towards an analysis of economics which would delineate the contradictions between the traditional claims of landed property and the new rival claims of the professionalising middle class, a set of conditions which leads inexorably to the evolution of the economic or empty 'personality' of modernism, an emptiness predicated here by the role of the Lodger as conjuror in a scene which brings to centre stage the notion of the counterfeit as the sign of the fading away of an ordered past and a new climate of 'free' circulation and profit.

It is particularly through the trope of an overwhelming deafness that Collins pursues his Gothic thematics most disturbingly in a fictional ploy which may be contextualised by John Picker's study of 'the complicated presence of sound in literature' that stems from technological change.[34] In theoretical writing of the period, hearing was conceived as a 'bodily form of sympathetic vibration' or a 'kind of microscopic Aeolian harp wired to the brain'[35] – a sympathetic aural receptor which the Lodger now lacks. This conception is echoed by Jonathan Rée, who in his study of deafness and the evolution of sign-language, intriguingly suggests that hearing 'has nothing active in it', being 'mere simple susceptibility'.[36] It was argued by nineteenth-century proponents of sign-language that this system constituted 'a real language, separate from English', and that mimic signs embodied 'a universal natural language, based in innate bodily gestures'.[37] The Lodger, to the contrary, rejects the adoption of the sign, relying upon writing in a Derridean ploy which illuminates the way, in Rée's account, 'writing systems debauch the healthy relationship between the audible voice and subjective meaning by making an obscene visible spectacle of it': thus writing takes on the form of 'an insult to the metaphysical purity of language'.[38] Christopher Krantz has argued that 'textuality becomes the best place for deaf and hearing people to interact' as it is 'a place where they can communicate flawlessly as equals'.[39] Writing knowledge down, as de Man remarks *á propos* Hegel's *Phenomenology,* 'in no way loses (nor, of course, recovers) a here and now that, as Hegel puts it, was never accessible to consciousness or to speech'.[40] The Lodger's insistence upon writing bears out the Hegelian thesis that 'writing is what prevents speech from taking place', and enacts de Man's postulate that 'To write down *this* piece of paper (contrary to saying it) [is] the definitive erasure of a forgetting that leaves no trace'.[41] Hegel had argued that the slave could find a type of freedom in adopting a stoicism which 'teaches withdrawal from the external world' through a 'retreat into one's own consciousness',[42] but the deaf Lodger's passionate nature, whilst cultivating such withdrawal, does not enable such a phlegmatic posture.

Although the Lodger rejects sign language on the grounds of its arbitrariness, he seeks consolation in love and nature; indeed, his deafness emulates a Benjaminian 'muteness' of nature – for Benjamin, the 'world of nature' is driven by forces which 'appear concentrated in the silent world'.[43] In Benjamin's postulate nature takes on a name and yet remains mute, whilst the work of art is to be conceived as a form of cultural ruin, like Old Toller's water-mill, signifier of Collins's arbitrary welding together of Gothic and modernist features. The Lodger's apparently allegorical status, as a deaf wanderer, gestures towards that sense adumbrated in Benjamin of allegory as triggered by historical crisis, whilst Collins's text in its blank imperviosity also resounds with pre-echoes of de Man's definition of allegory as telling the story 'of the failure to read'[44] – *The Guilty River*, that is to say, allegorises unreadability by offering a pseudo-knowledge of its own impossibility. Modernism is generated, according to de Man, by 'a genetic movement of gradual allegorisation and depersonalisation'.[45] It is significant that, for de Man, deafness is figured as a type of failed reception or duplicitous communication system that is characteristic of modernism, or even of language itself – as de Man observes,

> To the extent that language is figure (or metaphor or prosopopeia) it is indeed not the thing and, as such, it is silent, mute as pictures are mute. Language, as trope, is always privative.[46]

In *The Guilty River*, the Lodger's chronic deafness may also be construed as an emblem of racial disablement, a sign of that de Manian 'wound of a fracture that lies hidden in all texts'.[47] For Hegel, the enslavement of the African peoples signalled 'a place of advance' from the putative barbarism of an 'isolated sensual existence', enabling 'a mode of being participant in a higher morality and the culture connected with it',[48] but the Lodger, despite his translation into bourgeois society and successful medical career, can never, within this trajectory, slough off the mark of his maternal origins. He carries with him, in the political unconscious of Collins's racially motivated text, the unmistakeable signs of his African descent and is condemned to isolation and rejection by the Victorian cultural hegemony.

Mariaconcetta Costantini interestingly argues that a diachronic analysis of
Wilkie Collins's oeuvre 'will show that his reflection on the limits of colonialism and on the value of difference was part of a revisionary project that
he carried out in the span of over thirty years'.[49] *The Guilty River* thus shares
with other late-Victorian texts what Ronald Thomas has defined as 'the
blindness of the culture' in relation to race, a blindness tied ineluctably to
imperial policy: 'Without the race-theory that regards the physiological
"signs" of African descent as indicators of illness and inhumanness ... imperial ambitions on the "dark continent" could not have been pursued with
the force they were'.[50] As in the detective fiction considered by Thomas, to
which Collins had made so notable a contribution, there is a link between
America, 'the lost colony of an earlier Imperial moment, and Africa, the
dark colony of the New Imperialism'. In such texts, the 'tell-tale marks of
identification are glazed over, perhaps, by a mask of our own skin colour or
a family romance', but 'the subversive criminal kind is hiding there just the
same – lurking in our houses'.[51] In his fertile analysis of 1890s detective
fiction, Thomas demonstrates its implication in the racialised practice of
eugenics and criminology, a practice in which 'what presents itself as objective anatomical analysis is in fact deeply informed by a consistent set of
cultural biases and political interests'. The Lodger's deafness and poisonous
designs register this historical moment, a conjuncture in which, as Thomas
observes, 'the middle class saw itself as "menaced" by subversive elements
from the outside and inside alike', as national identity 'became increasingly
exclusivistic, defensive, and conservative'.[52] The Lodger resembles other
mixed-race characters such as Ezra Jennings in *The Moonstone*, in Costantini's
terms 'a mongrel, who is blamelessly forced to cope with the problems of
cross-cultural identity', or Ozias Midwinter in *Armadale*, who, in parallel
to the Lodger is the son of Creole woman and a dissolute Englishman, and
thus 'relegated to the margins of British society'.[53] *The Guilty River*
embodies these tendencies not only in relation to the socially 'impure'
Lodger but also in Roylake's attitude to the 'thorough radical' Lady Rachel
(298), seen as an internal class enemy and 'mock republican' (310), the 'she-
socialist' (313) who, ironically, intervenes to preserve class-distinctions by
blocking the landowner's romance with the miller's daughter. Where the
Lodger's beauty and slimness marks out his androgyny, Lady Rachel resembles 'a jolly young man' (310) in a pattern of behaviour which both
transgresses and reinforces class boundaries and national hegemony. Apart
from his obsession with Cristel, the Lodger insists upon his aversion to
young women, who are 'repellent' to him (267), in a behavioural structure
which gestures towards a symptomatic Decadence. By contrast Lady
Rachel, in her adoption of radical politics and an activist life-style, evinces

New Womanish tendencies which are contained by the plot. Both Lady Rachel, in her unfeminine assertiveness, and the Lodger, in his withdrawal and guilt-ridden androgyny, register an early tremor of that 'cultural anarchism and decay' which, as Linda Dowling observes, would dominate the 1890s in a 'lurid vision of cultural apocalypse'.[54] Indeed, Dowling's diagnosis of a 'linguistic demoralisation' constituted by a 'silent subversion of a high Victorian ideal of civilisation by the new comparative philology imported from Germany'[55] is especially pertinent to *The Guilty River* with its Germanic background.

Such cultural anxieties, obscurely rooted by Collins in European metaphysics and the West Indian slave-plantations, are focused and objectified in the topography of the action, and notably in the 'ugly river' Loke which threads its way through the action. At the outset, in a resonant set-piece which reverses romantic thematics, 'the ugliest stream in England' is delineated as the site of the criminal plot:

> The moonlight, pouring its unclouded radiance over open space, failed to throw a beauty not their own on those sluggish waters. Broad and muddy, their stealthy current flowed onward to the sea, without a rock to diversify, without a bubble to break, the sullen surface. . . . On the opposite bank, a rank growth of gigantic bulrushes hid the ground beyond, except where it rose in hillocks, and showed its surface of desert sand spotted here and there by mean patches of heath. A repellent river in itself, a repellent river in its surroundings, a repellent river even in its name. (249)

The Lodger is drawn to this scene, turning his back on 'a dirty manufacturing town' but pursuing the course of the river which runs through it (271). This river is peculiarly connected, in the Lodger's dreams, with Cristel Toller: '"Look at the stealthy current"', he adjures Roylake, '"that makes no sound"', and he sees her 'floating away from me on those hideous waters' (294), as she will do later, when the hero thinks he sees the 'mill-boat, beyond all doubt, and nobody in it' (339). At only one point in the narrative is the scene inflected with 'a wild gleam of beauty' in a moment of visionary romanticism:

> Our gloomy trees and our repellent river presented an aspect superbly transfigured, under the shadows of the towering clouds, the fantastic wreaths of the mist, and the lurid reddening of the sun as it stooped to its setting. Lovely interfusions of sobered colour rested, faded, returned again, on the upper leaves of the foliage as they lightly moved. The mist, rolling capriciously over the waters, revealed the grandly deliberate course of the flowing current, while it dimmed the turbid earthy yellow that discoloured and degraded the stream under the full glare of day. (314)

This revelatory moment is, significantly, associated in Roylake's mind with memories of his mother, as he 'learnt from her to be grateful for the beauty of the earth' (314). Here momentarily is made manifest what de Man, in his analysis of Hölderlin, designates 'a perfect equality between the inanimate object that is the river and a human consciousness'.[56] Shortly after the publication of *The Guilty River*, William James would postulate of consciousness that 'It is nothing jointed, it flows', and he went on:

> A river or a stream are the metaphors by which it is most naturally described. *In talking of it hereafter, let us call it the stream of thought, of consciousness, or of subjective life.*[57]

Where Freud would postulate a hierarchical model of the mind, James emphasises a streamlike flow: the landowner is of that class, in the Lodger's definition, who 'seldom look below the surface' (259). Elsewhere, James, in summarising his philosophical pragmatism, curiously echoed the thematics of Collins's novella: 'It is a turbid, muddled, gothic sort of affair without a sweeping outline and with little pictorial nobility'.[58] Yet Collins eschews or neglects this interiority with the result that the registrative function of the Loke lies rather in its symbolisation of history, its insistent ugliness a representation of what Marx designated 'the contradictions between the river of capital which flows on in proportion to the impetus it already possesses and the narrow basis on which the conditions of consumption rest'.[59] In *The Guilty River* there is, on the part of both characters and author, what Lukács defines as a 'failure to perceive the true driving forces that lie beneath the surface': 'behind that flowing river stands revealed an unchanging essence, even though it may express itself in the incessant transformations of the individual objects'.[60] The property-owning class (Roylake), the rentier class (the Lodger), and the proletariat (Old Toller, Gloody) all embody in Marxist terms the same human self-alienation, but it is the landowner who 'feels at home in this self-alienation', whilst others are destroyed by it.[61] History may, in *The Guilty River*, be conceived in Thomas Hardy's terms as 'rather a stream than a tree',[62] but if so Collins's River Loke appears to obliterate a history which then returns to furrow the text with premonitions of disaster. The Loke, as it were, flows backwards towards the prehistory of the characters in German metaphysics and Caribbean slavery: the novella is shadowed or defaced by the parameters of the master/slave dialectic in a trajectory which leads towards a climactic moment of rupture, illumination and ruin. This moment is registered in the text first by the explosive charge of the Lodger's pistol but then more spectacularly when, immediately following this murderous attempt, Roylake sees 'a rocket soar into the sky, from behind the promontory' (341).

The hero becomes preoccupied by the 'extraordinary appearance of the rocket, rising from the neighbourhood of a lonely little village' (342), lighting up the 'dimly-flowing river' (343) momentarily in a decisive inter-ruption of the flow of history. Although later explained as the signal-rocket from the yacht of Cristel's uncle, the episode retains a charge of significance and enigma which, in a sense, relate it to Walter Benjamin's declaration that

> The Romantic appeal to dream life was an emergency signal; it pointed less towards the way home of the soul to its motherland, than to the obstacles that already barred the way.[63]

Michael Löwy explicates Benjamin's theory by postulating that revolu-tionary action is 'not swimming with the stream but is a fierce struggle against the blind forces of history', and he justly identifies the principle of Benjaminian revolution in this writing as 'an explosion of the historical continuum'.[64] Benjamin's version of history as catastrophe is pertinent to a reading of *The Guilty River* in its tracing of race-theory, ownership and capital and its bland deafness to the onset of modernity, the political uncon-scious of the text appearing to endorse Benjamin's remark that 'Before the spark reaches the dynamite, the lighted fuse must be cut'.[65] Lightning, as Wład Godzich remarks, 'cannot be said to be hidden before its manifesta-tion', but rather expresses itself 'fully in the instant of its illumination', 'producing in its instantaneity a moment of perfect presence'.[66] *The Guilty River*, with its soaring rocket, thus curiously accords with the Frankfurt School theory of art: in Adorno's prescription, the 'phenomenon of fireworks is prototypical for artworks'. In this diagnosis, Collins's racial and existen-tial text takes the form of what Adorno terms 'an ominous warning, a script that flashes up, vanishes, and indeed cannot be read for its meaning'.[67] Such unreadability would notoriously mark the reception of Whistler's painting, *Nocturne in Black and Gold*, subtitled *The Falling Rocket*, to which Ruskin took such great exception in 1877. In this iconoclastic picture, according to W. M. Rossetti's account, 'across the trees, not high above the ground, shoots and fizzes the last and fiercest light of the expiring rocket'.[68] The Lodger's affliction signals, as it were, a type of resistance to the coming 'administered world', and it is the text's dissonance and contradictoriness, its ability to destroy its own imagery, which endows it with an accidental power and insight: as Adorno phrases it, in its ability to signal a Benjaminian 'dialectic at a standstill', 'art is profoundly akin to explo-sion'.[69] The subversive literary text interrupts the flow of historicist thought embodied in the river; history is, to the contrary, 'immanently sedi-mented' in the artwork.[70] Collins's marketable writing here strangely serves, as Adorno argues of Kafka, to 'violate the collusion of the novel reader by the explosive empirical impossibility of what is narrated'.[71] *The Guilty River* possesses, in its confused memorability, something of 'the unsurpassable noblesse of fireworks' since it seeks oblivion, aspiring 'not to duration but only to glow for an instant and fade away'.[72] If, as Hölderlin remarks, 'Streams must/ Seek themselves the path', it is clear that in the dynamics and blanknesses of Collins's text the contrastive elements of river and rocket mark a fracture in time between a Whig belief in progress and the onset of an explosive and uncontrollable modernity.

Geoffrey Hartman notes that, in Benjamin, the 'chiasmus of hope and catastrophe is what saves hope from being unmasked as only catastrophe', the flow of 'homogeneous time' being subjected to interruption by images which 'flash up into or reconstitute the present'.[73] As de Graef notes of Hölderlin's poem, whilst 'the line of the Rhine on the map . . . readily supports the developmental unity demanded on the ontological level, the destiny of "man" . . . can be established in such a narrative only through the introduction of historical catastrophe'.[74] It is this sense of the catastrophic and the redemptive that Collins's Lodger, in his hypnotic deafness, so tragically embodies.

CHAPTER 6

Stevenson's *The Ebb-Tide*

Missionary Endeavour in the Islands of Light

Religion is strictly and essentially a civilising process.,
Revd John Angell James (1819)[1]

and the islands float, unmoored and moisture laden
lidded with dream and dew
and find no anchor of love, no hover
of hope in their back-
yard: they can find no safe hollow
the sun rises and sets, rages
bleeding bleeding the pages of history's horror

Edward Kamau Brathwaite, 'Harbour'[2]

In a critical scene towards the beginning of Robert Louis Stevenson's South Sea novella, *The Ebb-Tide* (1894), the trio of stranded beachcombers, Davis, Herrick and Huish, contemplate their future with a sense of finality:

> 'Don't speak to me, don't speak to me. I can't stand it,' broke from
> [Herrick].
> The other two stood over him, perplexed.
> 'Wot can't he stand now?' said the clerk. ''Asn't he 'ad a meal? *I'm*
> lickin' my lips.'
> Herrick reared up his wild eyes and burning face. 'I can't beg!' he
> screamed, and again threw himself prone.
> 'This thing's got to come to an end,' said the captain, with an intake
> of the breath.
> 'Looks like signs of an end, don't it?' sneered the clerk.
> 'He's not so far from it, and don't you deceive yourself,' replied the
> captain.
>
> (ET, 17–18)[3]

The Ebb-Tide may be read as a symptomatic text of the *fin de siècle*, from historical, literary and theological perspectives. Historically it dramatises and examines issues thrown up by the massive process of imperial expansion and exploitation, a historical conjuncture which has generated the 'simple and hard story of exile, suffering and injustice among cruel whites' recounted by Taveeta on board the *Farallone* (ET, 47). In literary terms, the narrative reinflects or misreads a seminal group of pre-texts, notably the rebellious sub-plot of *The Tempest*, the narrative of the mutiny on the *Bounty*, and the boys' adventure tale epitomised by *The Coral Island*. Theologically, Stevenson's story reinscribes a blasphemous or heretical version of the New Testament in which wine is turned to water, there is a parodic last supper, and crucifixion motifs emerge in a transgressive account of missionary zeal. In his authoritative account of the Polynesian mission field, Niel Gunson observes that 'missionary enthusiasm' was regarded as 'something extraordinary', a phenomenon which was taken as a sign 'that the "latter days" referred to in the scriptures were commencing in reality'. He goes on, in words peculiarly applicable to Stevenson's fictional man of God, Attwater, 'It was in this context of millennial dawn that the missionary saw himself as a man of destiny'.[4]

Stevenson's text is certainly shadowed by apocalyptic traces; as Andrew Porter observes of the late-nineteenth century, 'religious revival, national and international upheaval, and missionary enthusiasm were both signs of the millennium's approach and preparations for it'.[5] In *The Ebb-Tide* symptoms of millennial degeneration are everywhere: thus, the three adventurers 'had made a long apprenticeship in going downward; and each, at some stage of the descent, had been shamed into the adoption of an *alias*' (ET, 4). This modernist sense of self-shaping, shifting identity, of the adoption of masks and aliases and the historically constructed instability of selfhood, which even extends to the naming of the abducted schooner *Farallone*, marks out the American sea-captain Davis/Brown, the cultured but weak-willed Englishman Robert Herrick/Hay, and the evil Cockney clerk Huish/Hay/Tomkins as figures in a tropical scenario of decadence, exemplars of those European races who, the narrator tells us, 'carry activity and disseminate disease' through 'the island world of the Pacific' (ET, 3). As Vanessa Smith argues in relation to *The Ebb-Tide*, 'in the era of Pacific colonialism, romance is figured as degenerate'.[6] Thus Herrick accepts failure as 'his portion' (ET, 6), Davis is haunted by the guilt of drunkenly losing an earlier ship, and Huish is at the outset laid low by a disease that 'shook him to the vitals' (ET, 8). Thinking of his courtship, Herrick writes to his sweetheart, 'That was the beginning, and now here is the end' (ET, 20), and his foreboding 'sentiment of coming change' (24), signified by his inscription of the fate motif from Beethoven, is curiously fulfilled in the narration. Indeed, one of the most telling moments on the mysterious island of Zakynthos, as Attwater and Herrick walk towards the beach, points forward to a global loss of humanity in an image which anticipates that more apocalyptic beach-scene in Wells's *Time Machine* published the year after *The Ebb-Tide*:

> All around, with an air of imperfect wooden things inspired with wicked activity, the land-crabs trundled and scuttled into holes. (ET, 84)

In anticipation of Foucault's predication of the moment when 'man would be erased, like a face drawn in sand at the edge of the sea',[7] Stevenson fixes and identifies this degeneracy as a linguistic and philological decline. The ability to maintain and sustain a narrative is problematised several times over: first, by Herrick's Arabian Nights dream, which Huish dismisses as 'bloomin' drivel' (ET, 9); secondly, by the letters home written by the trio as a last resort; and thirdly, by the fraudulent letter dictated by Huish prior to his murderous attack on the master of the island, Attwater. Each of these documents serves to allegorise the work of reading. Stevenson remarks *à propos* Herrick's love of Virgil that 'the demand for literature, which is so marked a feature in some parts of the South Seas, extends not so far as the dead tongues' (ET, 4), and *The Ebb-Tide* is haunted by the anxiety that, as Linda Dowling has expressed it, English is set to become 'simply another dead language in relation to living speech'.[8] Writing came to epitomise, in Dowling's account, the key instance of 'decay in language', the 'monuments of dead language' being precisely those 'works of literature'[9] whose identity Stevenson had debated with Henry James. The privileging of writing over speech which was thought to embody civilisation in the Victorian period collapses in the movement from metropolis or academy to the imperial margins. As Dowling puts it,

> in removing linguistic authority from great authors and investing it in the populace of an expanding British empire, linguistic science plainly appeared to enfranchise the barbarous usages of the underclass and the 'outlandish' voices of the circumference.[10]

Stevenson, noting the prevalence in the islands of 'an efficient pidgin', termed 'Beach-la-Mar', predicted that it would 'almost certainly become the tongue of the Pacific'.[11] This encounter between educated, demotic and 'outlandish' voices is superbly dramatised in the linguistic jousting between the university graduate Attwater, a man of 'stalwart size' significantly 'dissolved' in a Wildean 'listlessness that was more than languor' (71), the Cockney Huish, and the American Davis:

> 'Dr Symmonds is your partner, I guess?' said Davis.
> 'A dear fellow, Symmonds! How he would regret it, if he knew you had been here!' said Attwater.

> "E's on the *Trinity'All,* ain't he?'asked Huish.
> 'And if you could tell me where the *Trinity'All* was, you would confer
>   a favour, Mr Whish!' was the reply.

(ET, 94)

The virtually genocidal missionary zeal which Attwater has brought to his island enacts that larger contradictory project through which, in Dowling's account, 'the efforts of those missionaries whose aim was to carry English and its civilising values to every corner of the Empire' ended 'by betraying the hope that it would fix English forever as the *lingua communis*'.[12]

It seems as if each of the trio embodies what Walter Benjamin, referring to Rimbaud, designated 'the attitude of the footloose vagabond who puts himself at the mercy of chance and thus turns his back on society',[13] but it is Huish, with his roots in Hackney Wick, who embodies most clearly the contemporary debate over urban 'degeneration', 'the dwarfish person, the pale eyes and toothless smile' (ET, 7) all functioning as signifiers within a taxonomy of decay. His array of aliases alerts the reader to the impropriety or incongruity of the proper name which is blocked out, like the name of the *Farallone*, to render his personality blank or hollow in an act of open concealment that problematises the work of naming and signification. Contemporary eugenic theory was particularly exercised over what Karl Pearson designated 'the shallow hysterical cockney of today',[14] and it is significantly the clerk, prey to 'so ugly a sickness' (ET, 8), who manifests that 'weakened capacity for resistance' which, as William Greenslade notes, 'made the individual progressively vulnerable to disease or a degraded environment whose moral effects expressed themselves as a pathology of the will'.[15] The term 'Cockney', Dowling remarks, is not simply a signifier of social class; rather, 'it is an attempt to name something perceived to exist unnervingly outside all known categories of order, rank, or status'.[16] Anna Johnston has pertinently commented on the 'evangelical concentration on two specific constituencies – the British poor and the colonised "heathen"' in a project of categorisation in which the '"dark" faces of the British urban poor resembled those of the "benighted heathen"'.[17] Johnston comments on the fact that 'missionaries were regular witnesses to instances of white degradation in colonial environments' to a degree that prompted 'evangelical and imperial suspicion that colonial climates caused racial degeneracy'.[18] But if Huish is, in Attwater's definition, 'Whitechapel carrion' (ET, 104), each member of the trio participates in what Greenslade refers to as 'the deconstruction of the *hubris* of turn-of-the-century apostles of progress, empire and conquest':[19] ejected from the domestic/feminised space of home, these lawless beachcombers recreate a phantasmatic zone of play and reckless adventure in the South Seas, their residual boyishness offering a bleak parody of Ballantyne's three youthful heroes in *Coral Island*. In the feckless careers of the beachcombers, and in the countervailing moral rigidity and traderly enterprise of Attwater, Stevenson examines, in Homi Bhabha's phrase, 'the fragile margins of the concepts of Western civility and cultural community put under colonial stress'.[20]

In a critique of both missionary and literary exploration of the South Seas, Neil Rennie characterises the beachcomber as 'an absconder from his society', and yet one who is, paradoxically, a 'representative of that society' through his act of having 'discarded social identity with the adoption of the sobriquet', in a strategy which represents a 'desire to escape – both from civilisation and from savagery'.[21] The contrast is starkly underlined when, on board the *Farallone*, Huish and Davis fall into a drunken state whilst the allegedly cannibalistic Kanakas manfully stick to their duty and to their Bible readings: the beachcomber becomes, as Rod Edmond observes, the 'type of the white savage', one who embodied Britain's 'half-hearted colonial presence' in the South Pacific in a diasporic process which rendered the islands 'an imaginary zone or dream territory on to which European concerns could be projected'.[22] Stevenson's trio, which ultimately becomes a 'quartette', functions as a synthetic British imperial subject constantly redefining itself through a studious obliteration of origins: thus, Herrick's letter to his fiancée is premised upon his having first 'scratched out the beginning to [his] father' (ET, 19); and Davis, 'sunk in drunkenness', tires of attempting to paint out the name of the disease-ridden *Farallone* and leaves it 'part obliterated and part looking through' (ET, 45) so that, as Attwater later ominously observes, 'It can still be partly read' (ET, 90), like the characters of his visitors. These acts of partial obliteration may be related to the colonial misrecognition of the native physiognomy, a ploy which Gayatri Spivak designates as 'the placing of the face "under erasure"' in a process which keeps the face 'abundantly visible though crossed out by a draining of affect'.[23] Such native invisibility is eerily embodied in Davis's vision of 'two metallic objects, locomotory like men', whose 'heads were faceless', when Attwater's servants don the diving helmets as a form of 'armour' (ET, 122–3). Thus it is, earlier in the narrative, that the native crew of the *Farallone* are robbed of their identities by Davis in an ascription of colonial renonimation, subordination and effeminisation, becoming 'Sally Day', 'Dungaree', 'Uncle Ned' and so on (ET, 36). Even before arriving in the South Pacific, as Julia Reid demonstrates, Stevenson's anthropological studies were prompting him to elaborate a 'perception of the savagery lurking at the heart of *soi-disant* civilisation', and his subsequent composition of the journals posthumously published as *In the South Seas* is marked by a sense of 'the vulnerability of colonised cultures and the pain involved in relinquishing traditional beliefs and customs'.[24]

'"There ain't no land here"', exclaims the captain when the island is sighted (ET, 63). Zakynthos first appears as 'a greenish, filmy iridescence', a 'reflection from the lagoon', and is categorised in seafaring manuals as an island which 'from private interests would remain unknown' (ET, 64). As 'the undiscovered, the scarce-believed in' (ET, 67), Zakynthos, like the name of the schooner, exists under erasure, to be approached 'underhand like eavesdroppers and thieves' (ET, 68) by the feckless trio. In its symbolic configuration, so 'slender' 'amidst the outrageous breakers, so frail and pretty' (ET, 68), with its translucent lagoon, the island becomes, in Pierre Macherey's terminology, 'a *model* of the fable or reverie', embodying a meditation on 'the theme of origin'[25] in the paradoxical form of a drama of declension. This is because origins, as Macherey observes, also imply 'the special moment of rupture, the moment of *loss* of origins'.[26] Like *Robinson Crusoe*, *The Ebb-Tide* centres upon the figure of 'the ideological father', but in the nineteenth-century island narrative 'the hero is replaced by a group', a transgressive 'family of men'.[27] Macherey is here discussing Jules Verne's *The Mysterious Island*, but whilst Verne's island forms a natural laboratory, Stevenson's may be described as a spiritual testing ground, Verne's conquering bourgeoisie here transformed into a depleted and spiritually bankrupt remnant. The problematic of colonial history reinflects the literary project, undermining the Enlightenment scenario of *Robinson Crusoe* and its imitators through what Diana Loxley, in her trenchant analysis of *Treasure Island*, identifies as 'a journey of acquisition'.[28] Thus the social instability exemplified by 'lawlessness and criminality' is ascribed not to the native other but to the internalised 'system of European cultural identification'.[29] *The Ebb-Tide* rewrites Stevenson's favoured romance form, with its stress on 'adventure and freedom' and 'unconstrained scope for heroic action',[30] as a sombre reflection on the issues of duplicity, mutiny and murder which were reassuringly contained in *Treasure Island*. Whereas Stevenson's romance for boys distinguishes clearly between authorised and unauthorised quests for treasure, in *The Ebb-Tide* these distinctions are collapsed, the traditional encounter with the castaway transformed into a confrontation with a fearsome religious zealotry. Already in *Treasure Island*, as Loxley perceives, Stevenson has inscribed 'a prospective vision of the break-up and disintegration of a colonial system',[31] and *The Ebb-Tide* fulfils the logic of that vision. In this literary tradition, Elizabeth Deloughrey notes, 'the island is simultaneously positioned as isolated yet deeply susceptible to migration and settlement',[32] both settler and migrants bringing depletion and expropriation in their wake.

In the course of an idiosyncratic interpretation of his collection of diving outfits as the armature of divine grace, Attwater demands of the
bemused agnostic Herrick, "'Fond of parables?'" (ET, 82), and earlier
Herrick's magic carpet fantasy is classed as a 'parable' (ET, 9). As a text
saturated in religious terminology and centring upon issues of missionary
and colonial activity, *The Ebb-Tide* takes the form of an ineluctably blasphemous or heretical narrative, a meditation upon Attwater's claim that
'religion is a savage thing like the universe it illuminates' (ET, 83). The
tale bears the imprint of an endlessly ventriloquised religious debate in
which characters discover themselves in hell, adopt cruciform postures and
invoke the efficacy of the communion wine. Scriptural quotation saturates
the text as both verbal echo and dramatic scenario, but the militantly
homiletic rhetoric of Attwater is repeatedly critiqued by a narrative in
which characters are shown to be prone to the workings of supernatural or
magical categories. The missionary is dismissive of native religions as
'some mumbo-jumbo whose very name is forgotten' (ET, 94), yet the
evangelical desire at times to equate Christianity with a civilising modernity is undermined by the dominant trope of atavism which paradoxically
is to be traced in the European adventurers rather than the indigenous
people of the islands. *The Ebb-Tide* marries theological earnestness with
'imperial Gothic' in a bravura display of insoluble contradiction: the
national mission of suppressing idolatrous superstition in the indigenes is
handled dialectically, so that it is the whites who prey upon each other
beneath the totemic sign of the ship's figurehead, the symbol of Anglo-
American reversion. As in *Dracula*, there is a suggestion here that moral
perversion can be transmitted by physical contact – smallpox has killed
both the captain and mate of the *Farallone* (ironically given the
Bunyanesque names Wiseman and Wishart), whilst the bulk of Attwater's
native islanders function as both 'carrier' and destroyer of European civility. Indeed, like the morally insane Renfield in Bram Stoker's novel,
Attwater, a curiously enervated version of the Muscular Christian, is
afflicted with 'homicidal and religious mania' in the very excess of his sac-
rilegiously overweening evangelism,[33] coming upon the islanders as 'a
judge in Israel, the bearer of the sword and scourge' (ET, 84).

The way in which the plot hinges upon the conflict between the trio and
Attwater bears out Neil Rennie's observation that, during the early nineteenth century, 'a proliferation of "sailors' sects" throughout the islands
represented themselves as alternatives to missionary teaching'; indeed, the
resolution of this plot, and Attwater's previous history, endorses Rennie's
contention that force 'must precede discourse in encounters with peripheral
societies'.[34] Attwater's accumulation of pearls and marine junk, as well as

his insistence on creating 'a business, and a colony, and a mission of my own' (ET, 84), embodies that wider Pacific process through which, in Rennie's phrase, 'property becomes parable'.[35] From its opening scene in the 'tiny, pagan city' (ET, 3) to the closing homily of the unlikely convert Davis – '"Why not come to Jesus right away, and let's meet in yon beautiful land?"' (ET, 130) – *The Ebb-Tide* reimagines the gospel story as a narrative of heresy contaminated by echoes of Fletcher Christian's cry during the *Bounty* mutiny, 'I am in Hell'. Huish, marking himself as one of the damned, one ultimately destined to suffer 'hell's agonies, bathed in liquid flames' (ET, 126), rejects Herrick's fairy-tale as 'like the rot there is in tracts' (ET, 9), and later recites a meaningless comic song 'baleful as a blasphemy' (ET, 78) – though the captain later declares he will have 'no blasphemy in [his] boat' (ET, 122). Earlier, Davis, confessing his guilt at the wreck of the *Sea Ranger*, exclaims, '"Guess I sent her to hell"' (ET, 19), whilst after the confrontation with Attwater, Herrick tells the American, '"Go to hell in your own way!"' (ET, 107). Rejecting Herrick's proposal of a joint suicide, Davis remarks, '"Get thee behind me, Satan"' (ET, 29), but it is the captain himself who nominates the sinking of the *Sea Ranger* as 'that day I was damned' (ET, 55). In a resonant echo of the central image of Christianity, *The Ebb-Tide* first presents Attwater, appealing to the unbeliever Herrick to 'come to the mercy seat', spreading 'his arms like a crucifix ' (ET, 86), and then Herrick himself, who had earlier 'drained for months the cup of penitence' (ET, 6), 'stretched upon a cross, and nailed there with the iron bolts of his own cowardice' (ET, 109). Significantly, Stevenson, recounting the 'grind' of completing *The Ebb-Tide*, claimed the right 'to brag a little after such a crucifixion'.[36]

The narrative turns crucially upon a heretical reversal of Christ's miracle at Cana (John 2:1–10), in the revelation that the bulk of the plundered cargo of champagne is plain water. Christ's beneficent act is here countered by a sordidly materialist transaction, the signifying function of both the champagne, and of Attwater's sherry, bearing out Roland Barthes' definition of wine as a 'converting substance' which is 'capable of reversing situations and states, and of extracting from objects their opposites'.[37] The conversion here, so appalling to the beachcombers, precisely denotes the fictive nature of capital and the fluidity and commodified quality of identity in a system founded in exchange. Davis is earlier described as 'paying his shot with usury as he had done many a time before' (ET, 16), and boasts of dealing in '[d]epreciated dollars' (ET, 38). Patrick Brantlinger has noted how Victorian fiction in general registers 'both the substantiality of British power and prosperity and its insubstantiality, its basis only in credit',[38] and this lack of substance and investment in the fictive informs the whole enterprise of the *Farallone*. Indeed, Peru, the putative market for Davis's cargo and source of the influenza outbreak, possesses a double signification: it was a nation singled out by Marx as an economy lacking a developed money system, but, in a significantly Oedipal inversion, was also the country which esteemed the works on marine engineering by Thomas Stevenson whilst professing ignorance of his son's literary endeavours.[39] The range of implication involved in the bogus cargo and commission of the crime of barratry, and in Huish's Benedictine and Davis's Madeira (ET, 12), focuses not only religious but also aesthetic issues with its hint at Stevenson's belated turn from romance to realism in his South Seas writings, a complex suggestively reinscribed in Paul Valéry's poem, 'The Lost Wine':

> Once on a day, in the open Sea
> (Under what skies I cannot recall),
> I threw, as oblation to vacancy,
> More than drop of precious wine . . .
>
> Who decreed your waste, oh potion?
> Did I perhaps obey some divine
> Or else the heart's anxiety,
> Dreaming blood, spilling the wine?
>
> Its habitual clarity
> After a mist of rosiness
> Returned as pure again to the sea . . .
>
> The wine lost, drunken the waves! . . .
> I saw leaping in the salt air
> Shapes of the utmost profundity . . .

Indeed, in the storm scene, in which the captain sits 'in the boat to windward, bellowing orders and insults', with 'a bottle between his knees' (ET, 51), the *Farallone* is transformed into a veritable *bateau ivre*.

   In the massively impervious figure of Attwater, Stevenson reimagines the double personality, what he designated 'that strong sense of man's double being',[40] earlier embodied more sensationally in *Dr Jekyll and Mr Hyde*. As Mariaconcetta Costantini has argued, Attwater's 'perverse incarnation' as a 'godlike figure' is 'confirmed by his exalted and self-centred demeanour, by his ruthless control over the natives, as well as by the many religious metaphors of the text, which make him appear as a strict "paternal" dominator'.[41] And yet, despite the missionary's physical mass, his name suggests a lack of fixity or rootedness, water being, in Gaston Bachelard's terms, a 'transitory element', an emblem of 'the essential ontological metamorphosis between heaven and earth'. 'A being dedicated to water', Bachelard goes on, 'is a being in flux'.[42] In that sense, all Stevenson's characters here are subject to what the narrator designates 'the mobility of fluids' (ET, 119). The first sight of the master of Zakynthos, with his 'gentleman's' voice, 'huge' figure and countervailing 'listlessness', presents him as a nearly indecipherable character marked out by an 'eye of an unusual mingled brilliancy and softness', sign of both his 'unimpaired health and virility' and his 'devastating anger', his dark complexion 'hardly distinguishable from that of a Tahitian' balanced by his 'white drill, exquisitely made' (ET, 71–2). This enigmatic physiognomy bears out Jonathan Crary's account of the way in which the face in western culture appertains 'to a human being both as a physiological organism and as a privatised, socialised individual subject': the face is both a symptom of physiological function and, 'in its relative impenetrability, the mark of the success or failure of a process of self-mastery and control'[43] – a self-mastery to which Herrick, in the weakness of his moral constitution, never attains, discerning 'the roaring of the maelstrom' in his 'bedevilled and dishonoured soul' (ET, 88).

Ann Colley provides a detailed account of Stevenson's reciprocal relations with London Missionary Society missionaries in Samoa and of his ambivalent attitude to the wider South Seas Christian mission, but concludes that 'ultimately he never failed to defend or support it', perhaps in deference to his mother. She also detects an aura of hero-worship in Stevenson's relations with individual missionaries such as Fr Dordillon, Robert Maka, the Revd George Brown and especially the Revd James Chalmers, men who, she observes, 'remained intrepid and always self-reliant'.[44] It is no accident that, in his dual role as pearl fisher and fisher of souls, Attwater enacts what Laura Chrisman has defined as the uncertain relation between a mid-Victorian ideology of missionary endeavour 'and its late nineteenth-century and anti-liberal opposite, an essentialist Social Darwinism'.[45] Niel Gunson demonstrates that the early nineteenth-century missionary was characteristically an artisan or 'mechanic',[46] but Attwater is one of the new influx of gentleman missionaries recruited from Oxbridge in the 1880s, a member of what Brian Stanley nominates a 'new generation of highly educated missionaries . . . heavily influenced by ideas of a broadly imperialist nature'.[47] Stanley's notation of a concurrent rise of the rifle corps in the English public school system contextualises the Winchester rifle that accompanies Attwater on board the *Farallone* and those menacing abilities as a 'fine shot' (ET, 88) demonstrated in his account of the execution of a hapless native, his prompt killing of Huish and his pyrotechnical display in pinning Davis against the figurehead. In the dramatic rendition of Attwater's conflictual and dominating persona *The Ebb-Tide* resonates with echoes of the two key records of South Seas missionary labour, William

Ellis's *Polynesian Researches* (1829) and John Williams's *Missionary Enterprises* (1837) – it is no coincidence in a text dominated by naming that Huish is able to reveal Attwater's Christian names as William John. These missionary texts, as Rod Edmond observes, project the Polynesian as 'a contradictory and unstable figure which produces unease at every level'.[48] It is this unease that motivates both Attwater's chilling account of his treatment of the two natives, 'Sullens' and 'Obsequiousness', which culminates in the suicide of the former and cold-blooded shooting of the latter, and his enforced marriage of the 'too pretty' native girl to his male servant, since, as he tells Herrick, a man 'never knows when he may be inclined to be a fool about women' (ET, 89). Attwater exerts an implacable mastery over islanders and beachcombers alike; however, as Homi Bhabha has written of missionaries in India, 'the word of divine authority is deeply flawed by the assertion of the indigenous sign, and the very practice of domination in the language of the master becomes hybrid – neither one thing nor the other'. The missionary programme constantly runs up against the 'incalculable colonised subject', 'always untrustworthy', who produces 'an insoluble problem of cultural difference for the very address of colonial cultural authority'.[49] Estrangement of the basis of colonial rule generates what Bhabha characterises as 'traditions of colonialist treachery',[50] and it is this hybridisation of effect, power and betrayal which *The Ebb-Tide* traces so potently, imaging it in that performance of doubleness whose traces furrow the colonial text: Zakynthos functions here as what has been aptly nominated 'a metaphysical contact zone'.[51] When Attwater imposes his will upon the island, Davis remarks ominously that 'he looks at us and laughs like God' (ET, 102). As Spivak argues, for imperialism 'as social mission, God's image is that of the governor', the fleeting glimpse of the native girl he has bestowed in marriage confirming both how 'in the context of colonial production, the subaltern has no history and cannot speak', and how 'the subaltern female is even more deeply in shadow'.[52]

Before landing on the uncharted island, the captain speculates, '"A pearling island the government don't know about? That sounds like real estate"' (ET, 65), and after meeting Attwater he affirms that the missionary has been 'doing great business': '"It's pearl and shell, of course"' (ET, 77). As Attwater informs Herrick, he has run the island as 'a business, and a colony, and a mission of my own' (ET, 84). He has enriched himself through the colonising process – he tells Herrick that the contents of his safe will yield 'a moderate fortune' when the time arises 'to place the pearls upon the market' (ET, 89). But Attwater's form of piracy leaves his plunder rotting in the sheds, since he fails to circulate his capital: '"Here are ten years' accumulation from a lagoon where I have had as many as ten divers going all day long"', he boasts to Herrick (ET, 89). The missionary is both capitalist and miser, both types, in Marx's account, driven by a 'passionate chase after value': 'The ceaseless augmentation of value', Marx argues, 'which the miser seeks to attain by saving his money from circulation, is achieved by the more acute capitalist by means of throwing his money again and again into circulation'.[53] The sinews of the spirit thus serve the accumulative power of the western economic system, but undermine the principle of exchange to which the beachcombers themselves adhere; or perhaps, as Christopher Lane suggests, the notion of exchange as the motive for empire is transformed into the exchange of desire amongst men.[54]

Paul Claudel once observed that, as a commodity, pearl 'has no value other than its beauty':

Its appearance on the market devalues all other goods; it changes their price; it brings disquiet to the banks, it threatens the balance of all transactions. For it carries with it an element that is absent from any number: I am speaking of that spiritual covetousness which comes from contemplation.[55]

In the accumulation of his hoard of pearl Attwater exercises a 'spiritual covetousness' which exemplifies the agency 'given over to the coloniser' that Spivak identifies as his 'brutal insertion into the circuit of the same'.[56] Attwater's memorable dinner party, with the 'variety and excellence' of the fare (ET, 92), and the rich comfort of the surroundings, embodies the way in which, in Spivak's words, 'imperialism has always already historically refracted what might have been an incommensurable and discontinuous other into a domesticated other that consolidates the imperial self'.[57] The richness of the food, the sensuous cat, the silently attentive native servants, all combine to produce a domestic scenario whose eeriness is made manifest when Attwater strikes his silver bell:

The note rose clear and strong; it rang out clear and far into the night and over the deserted island; it died into the distance until there only lingered in the porches of the ear a vibration that was sound no longer. 'Empty houses, empty sea, solitary beaches!' said Attwater. 'And yet God hears the bell! And yet we sit in this verandah on a lighted stage with all heaven for spectators! And you call that solitude?' (ET, 94)

The musical 'bar of silence' that ensues, 'during which the captain sat mesmerised' (ET, 94), offers a hint as to the implications of this scene. From the outset, Attwater dominates by the 'brilliancy' of his gaze, and he now exerts over his guests the power of the mesmerist, freeing them from the responsibility of choice as they secretly plot his murder, in a scenario of seduction and coercion. It might be noted that the whole of *The Ebb-Tide* is textually overcoded with occult reference and implication, commencing with Herrick's practice of using the *Aeneid* as a means of divination (ET, 4) and his memory of the ring of skulls in *Der Freischütz* (ET, 9). In prophesying a miserable end for Herrick, even the compromised sea-captain becomes 'like one in whom the spirit of divination worked and might utter oracles' (ET, 30), and his new commission is inhabited by a 'doom that seemed to brood upon the schooner' (ET, 50). As he listens to Herrick's warning, the drunken captain sees him as 'a ghost', whilst Herrick, himself a 'poor ghost' (ET, 20), inspecting Attwater's 'heap of lumber' retrieved from wrecked ships, sees the 'commonplace ghosts of sailormen' (ET, 81). Huish's demurral at the dinner party, '"This ain't a spiritual séance"' (ET, 95), and the 'mesmerised' state into which the captain falls, underscore the quasi-spiritualist implications of a scene in which Herrick sits 'spellbound' (ET, 93).[58] When threatened by Attwater's rifle, Davis is compelled to put his hands up, 'mesmerised with fury' (104), and later, at the crisis of the action beneath the figure-head, the captain stands open-mouthed, 'as the mesmerised may follow the mesmeriser' (ET, 124). As Alison Winter observes in her history of mesmerism, the 'consecrated character' of the missionary 'was not so different from that of the mesmerist', and the dinner party offers, like a late-Victorian séance, 'an intense moment of spiritual or psychological blending'.[59] In the 'lists of love', Stevenson suggested elsewhere, men and women contend 'like rival mesmerists'.[60] But it was clerical mesmerists, as Winter explains, who dreamt of rendering hypnotism 'an "engine in education", a tool for missionaries working abroad' in what she nicely terms 'the open sea of mesmeric experimentation'.[61] Elements of social class were a crucial factor in this connection; thus, as Winter demonstrates, those 'more susceptible to magnetic influence' were 'naturally guided by their moral and social superiors' and became, like Herrick, Davis and Huish, 'more vulnerable to sinful thoughts'.[62] Jenny Bourne Taylor has further shown how mesmerism 'could be pressed into service to support a higher spiritual authority, manifested by the superior power of the mesmeriser over his subjects'.[63] Indeed, Attwater's insistence upon the quality of his sherry, and the portentous shattering of the wine bottle, with its echo of Christ's warning against putting new wine into old bottles 'else the bottles break' (Matthew 9:17), calls up parodic traces of the Last Supper more clearly defined in the manuscript, which speaks of Herrick's alarm lest 'the cloth be sullied with domestic murder' in a 'hateful mockery' of 'breaking bread' (ET, 170). Such resonances are underlined by Herrick's agonised consciousness of himself as 'the third guest' (ET, 92) in a textual knot which synthesises the role of Judas and the episode on the road to Emmaeus. The wine also serves to conjure memories of the catastrophic transmutation of the ship's cargo – as Winter records, 'mesmerised subjects actually perceive water as evil'.[64] Indeed in the 'momentous silence' evoked by Attwater (ET, 95) at dinner, as the bell 'rang out clear and far' (ET, 94), the ghostly name of the ship seems to return in a kind of spectral revenance which marks, in its partially obliterated name, the erasure and return of writing. The missionary's civilised brutality, like that of Conrad's Mr Kurtz, may signify what has been termed 'the least palatable of all spectrality effects, the suspicion that the culmination of the civilising process may in fact be no more than a higher phase of barbarism'.[65]

In her analysis of imperialism, Hannah Arendt offers a perceptive account of the spectrality which arises when 'the gentleman and the criminal' operate outside 'all social restraint and hypocrisy'. So it is that, in *The Ebb-Tide*, the whites share not only a skin colour, but what Arendt designates 'the impact of a world of infinite possibilities for crimes committed in the spirit of play'. According to Arendt, the resultant 'combination of horror and laughter' allows 'for the full realisation of [the white man's] own phantomlike existence' and participation in a repertoire of 'ghostlike events' played out against the backdrop of a 'world of savages'.[66] Witness how, as well as functioning as parodic Last Supper, the dinner-party uncannily replicates key features of the Freudian 'totem feast', involving 'a violent, jealous father' whose death and sacrifice is plotted by his 'expelled' sons. As Freud observes, the 'primal father' is 'the envied and feared model' for the sons who, by killing and eating him, acquire his strength. The conflictual posture of Herrick *vis-à-vis* Attwater reinflects Freud's exposition of the way the rebellious sons conjoin hatred with love and admiration, whilst the fraternal complicity of Davis's party hints at those 'homosexual feelings and activities' which motivate the male primal horde.[67]

In the persona of surrogate father-figure and lawless law-giver, Attwater is, as he concedes, no 'philanthropist': '"I dislike men, and I hate women"', he declares to Herrick (ET, 85). Hence the uncanny relish with which he accounts for the island deaths through smallpox: '"Twenty-nine deaths and thirty-one cases, out of thirty-three souls upon the island. That's a strange way to calculate, Mr Hay, is it not?"' (ET, 73). The absent father is a recurrent theme here – witness Davis's claim to be 'the father of a family' he never sees (19), Herrick's sentimental vision of 'the white head of his father' (ET, 4–5), his magic-carpet ride to visit the 'old folks' (11) and indeed his self-definition, hesitating at the 'open door' of suicide, as 'the prodigal son come home' (ET, 107). It is often argued that the imperial father exerts his power through the efficacy of nomination, and so it is that Attwater bestows names upon his territory and 'subjects' – 'Zakynthos', 'Sullens', 'Obsequiousness', 'Mr Whish' – in an act of colonial categorisation that endorses Homi

Bhabha's critique of the 'cultural mummification' which stems from 'the coloniser's avowed ambition to civilise or modernise the native in a process that leads to a validation of violence in the very definition of the colonial space'.[68] In *The Ebb-Tide* that space is surprisingly dominated by a female figure – namely, the ship's figurehead first glimpsed from the deck of the *Farallone*:

> Only, on the top of the beach and hard by the flagstaff, a woman of exorbitant stature and as white as snow, was to be seen beckoning with uplifted arm. The second glance identified her as a piece of naval sculpture, the figurehead of a ship, that had long hovered and plunged into so many running billows, and was now brought ashore to be the ensign and presiding genius of that empty town. (ET, 70)

'Women were excluded', Stevenson noted laconically of *Treasure Island*,[69] and this gender exclusivity also permeates *The Ebb-Tide*, with its multiple layers of homosocial rivalry, paternity and male bonding. However, if Attwater wields the law of the father, it is this 'defiant deity', 'her helmeted head tossed back, her formidable arm apparently hurling something' (ET, 80), who presides as pre-Oedipal phallic mother over the male adventurers immured in their primary narcissism. Stevenson's editors note the popularity of bare-breasted female figures on the nineteenth-century clipper, observing that 'women were believed to be unlucky on board ship, but a naked woman was believed to have the power to calm a storm' (ET, 144). The bare-breasted female, however, had already figured in the iconography of the French Revolution, signifying what Linda Dowling terms 'an emergent realm of irrational and unknowable forces'.[70] The original of Attwater's figurehead was spotted by Stevenson on Penrhyn Island in 1890 and described by him as 'a very white and haughty lady, Roman nosed' (ET, xxvi), and its resemblance to the mother-queen-empress is hardly fortuitous. But in her threatening whiteness it may be that the statue also hints at a *fin-de-siècle* female vampirism, produced, as Alexandra Warwick notes, by 'the disruption and reversal of gender hierarchies', imagined as 'a horse-woman of the Victorian Apocalypse' portending the 'end of the "race" and the slow death of the British Empire on its throne':[71] in the words of Samoan poet Albert Wendt, 'this tropical paradise is all a vampire's lie'.

The figurehead's 'leprous whiteness' (ET, 70) might also be related to the pervasive thematics of disease in Stevenson's novella, standing as an emblem of the lives destroyed by European imperial conquest. The dying author had, paradoxically, travelled to the South Seas in search of restoration, 'not unwilling to visit like a ghost, and be carried like a bale, among scenes that had attracted [him] in youth and health'.[72] The smallpox which has decimated Attwater's island and killed the European sailors on board the *Farallone* was traced, in nineteenth-century medical discourse, to the African slave trade, the guilt of which, as Debbie Lee notes, 'defined Britain as a sick society'.[73] The guilt is focused, Lee goes on to suggest, in the spectral female in *The Ancient Mariner* – she who is as 'white as leprosy', and whose appearance causes the sailors to drop down 'one by one'; in this scenario it is the white woman 'who becomes the expression of alterity through disease', an alterity virulently embodied in 'morally reprehensible diseases such as syphilis', which were notoriously transmitted to the Pacific by the early European explorers.[74] The South Sea islands had for some time been regarded as special sites of contagion, with leprosy a particular focus for concerns crystallised in Henry Wright's ominously entitled study, *Leprosy: An Imperial Danger*, published in 1889. Leprosy was thought to be contagious, and this led to the establishment of several island leper colonies, including one on Molokai in the Hawaiian group, heroically presided over by a Catholic priest, Father Damien. Shortly after the missionary's death, Stevenson visited Molokai and, when endorsing Damien's work, concluded ruefully, 'there are Molokais everywhere'.[75] As Rod Edmond remarks, the whites of Honolulu regarded leprosy as 'a just punishment for a diseased culture characterised by sexual promiscuity'.[76] Indeed, some contemporary medical opinion insisted that leprosy was nothing other than the fourth stage of syphilis.[77]

In this racial context it is feasible, therefore, to view Attwater, with his graveyard full of natives, as assuming the role of Hyde to Fr. Damien's Jekyll. We may note that the graveyard is filled by 'many mounds', and that the missionary quotes from Gray's 'Elegy' when contemplating this site of death, which he ominously describes as '"the main scene of my activity in the South Pacific"' (ET, 84). Brantlinger notes that the belief that 'savagery was vanishing of its own accord from the world of progress and light mitigated guilt and sometimes excused or even encouraged violence toward those deemed savage'.[78] Attwater likes to contemplate the natives in their graves, '"plucked of their lendings, their dead birds and cocked hats"' (ET, 85), and expresses, in this scene, a sense of that 'proleptic elegy' which, as Brantlinger suggests, takes on the tone of 'self-fulfilling prophecy'. The missionary effort, as he argues, 'lent support to Social Darwinism and its offshoot, the eugenics movement',[79] a postulate illustrated not only by Attwater's killing of the native 'Obsequiousness' but also by his elimination of the Cockney Huish, a specimen, in his eyes, of 'Whitechapel carrion' (ET, 104). In its collocation of femininity and disease, however, the 'exorbitant' female figurehead may also refract a more domestic contemporary controversy, the furore during the 1880s over the Contagious Diseases Acts passed in the 1860s: the melodramatic posture and defiant mien of the figurehead suggests the role played by the 'avenging mother' at the centre of the debate, Josephine Butler. Functioning, in Judith Walkowitz's terms, as 'omniscient narrator, stage manager, and supportive, grieving mother',[80] 'the beautiful and histrionic figure of Butler' helped to secure the repeal of the Acts in 1886 by taking upon herself 'the role of prophet and suffering magdalen'.[81] It is before this potent and over-determined female figure that Herrick wishes 'he might have bowed down . . . in that hour of difficulty' (ET, 80).

Aside from this momentary supplication of the female, *The Ebb-Tide* is exclusively predicated upon a male sexual/textual erotics issuing out of a projected literary collaboration between Stevenson and his stepson, Lloyd Osbourne. In *Double Talk*, Wayne Koestenbaum analyses Stevenson's self-confessed 'infatuation' with Lloyd as a 'craving and a problem', and examines the pervasive 'queerness' of *The Ebb-Tide* and its numerous sexual *double-entendres*.[82] He also pertinently notes the significance of the name of Attwater's absent partner, Dr Symmonds, relating it to Stevenson's friend, John Addington Symonds, who participated in another male collaboration, with Havelock Ellis, to publish *Sexual Inversion* (1897). As Ed Cohen remarks, in his memoirs Symonds was compelled to represent the story of his sexual orientation as one in which he would 'constitute his character as a divided one', a strategy which could be expressed *'only as a double life'*.[83] The genesis of *The Ebb-Tide* lays bare issues of 'homotextuality' and an exclusiveness of gender orientation, both of which are borne out when, in a scene enacting the ferocity of male desire for mastery and disavowal of the feminine, Attwater fires his rifle and creates a 'black hole' that 'marred the whiteness of the figurehead' (ET, 126).[84]

This violent moment of patriarchal assertion is preceded by the most potent challenge to Attwater's regime – namely, Huish's deadly plot to utilise vitriol, a substance which, as he instructs the appalled captain, will 'burn to the bone' (ET, 116). This 'happlication of science' appears 'too damned hateful' (ET, 117) even to the reckless Davis, but in the end the 'stakes were so high' (ET, 118) that he accedes to the plan. The key to this episode lies in Huish's curious definition of vitriol as 'medicine in a bottle' (ET, 116). And indeed the 'horror of the medicine in the bottle' is, at the climax of the tale, powerfully encoded in the landscape:

> The isle shook before them like a place incandescent; on the face of the lagoon, blinding copper suns, no bigger than sixpences, danced and stabbed them in the eyeball; there went up from sand and sea, and even from the boat, a glare of scathing brightness; and as they could only peer

abroad from between closed lashes, the excess of light seemed to be changed into a sinister darkness, comparable to that of a thundercloud before it bursts. (ET, 121)

The concept of a deadly medicinal potion is adumbrated earlier, both in the cough mixture, defined as 'first-rate stuff in a bottle', which Herrick administers in his dream (ET, 9), and in the 'syrup for the kids' (ET, 12) desiderated by Davis in a sentimental moment. In its shocking reversal of healing medicinal properties, the Cockney's vitriol functions as an emblem of Attwater's missionary endeavours in a way which is illuminated by Derrida's essay on 'Plato's Pharmacy'. The *pharmakon*, Derrida argues, operates as 'both remedy and poison',[85] its ambivalence here translated into the contradictory valency of Attwater's evangelising programme carried out under the watchful gaze of the ship's figurehead. Instead of 'quickening life', the *pharmakon* can at best 'only restore its monuments'.[86]

Derrida's observations on the relation between logos and paternity are also pertinent to a reading of *The Ebb-Tide*, since he locates the origins of logos in the father–son relation, arguing that 'the specificity of writing' is 'intricately bound to the absence of the father' – the free-wheeling adventurism of the beachcombers is thus licensed by this absence until they come up against the tainted surrogate father-figure of the missionary. In the Derridean scenario the 'distress of the orphan' is founded in a wish 'to do away with the father', encompassed by the *pharmakon* as a 'poisoned present'.[87] Significantly, the efficacy of the *pharmakon* is associated, Derrida writes, with 'spellbinding powers of enchantment, mesmerising fascination . . . akin to witchcraft and magic'.[88] This is dramatically borne out here, and more generally in Stevenson's South Seas writing, where it has been pertinently observed, 'Magic and money are both currencies inextricably connected to the colonial market'.[89]

Following Attwater's clinical despatch of Huish, bathed in the 'liquid flames' of his own vitriol (ET, 126), and his sharp-shooting display against Davis, *The Ebb-Tide* drifts to an inconclusive ending. As the *Farallone* is consumed by fire, Herrick and Davis are left, as at the opening, on the beach, but whilst Herrick continues to drift irresolutely, Davis remains (like the protagonist of Matthew Arnold's best-known poem) 'suppliant on the beach' (ET, 128), claiming to have 'found peace' as a disciple of the missionary, and calls upon the atheistic Herrick to join him: '"Oh! Why not be one of us? Why not come to Jesus right away, and let's meet in yon beautiful land?"' (ET, 130). A materialist reading of *The Ebb-Tide* as a parable of imperial decline and religious heresy is, as Adorno asserts of cultural texts, only possible 'if it is mediated through the *total social*

process'.[90] Yet there remains in Stevenson's novella a haunting excess of signification that may be located in the figure of light which dominates this
tropical narrative and, as it were, transcends its social determinants.
Herrick's account of himself 'on a bright beach, the sky and sea immoder-
ately blue, and the great breakers roaring outside on a barrier reef' (ET, 20)
echoes Stevenson's prescription of how, 'if the book be eloquent', its words
'should run then resound in our ears like the noise of breakers',[91] and both
descriptions might be framed by Baudrillard's notion that 'ideology appears
as a sort of cultural surf frothing on the beachhead of the economy'.[92]
Stevenson's aesthetic sense of a pattern of 'colours and sounds' creating
'imitative lines'[93] produces a work in which the 'exuberant daylight and the
blinding heaven of the tropics picked out and framed the picture' (ET, 32).
Ann Colley notes how the South Seas missionaries worked to promote 'the
image of the "gleaming light" of Christianity',[94] but here the linguistic
encoding of light is generated out of a sense of estrangement: for Stevenson,
as he himself reflected, 'English was a foreign tongue'.[95] As a Scot, it may
be that his language, in Foucauldian terms, 'always seems to be inhabited
by the other, the elsewhere, the distant', so that it becomes 'hollowed out
by distance'.[96] This process of linguistic difference and the fascination of
distance produces the phantasm of light which reaches its apotheosis in the
approach to the island:

> Here a multitude of sea-birds soared and twinkled and fished in the blue
> waters; and there, and for miles together, the fringe of cocoa-palm and
> pandanus extended desolate, and made desirable green bowers for nobody to
> visit, and the silence of death was only broken by the throbbing of the sea.
>   The airs were very light, their speed was small; the heat intense. The decks
> were scorching underfoot, the sun flamed overhead, brazen, out of a brazen
> sky; the pitch bubbled in the seams, and the brains in the brain-pan.
> (ET, 68)

This intensity of light in the South Pacific gestures towards that 'white
mythology' of which Jacques Derrida has written in his analysis of the
entanglement of European metaphysics and knowledge with metaphor:

> Presence disappearing in its own radiance, the hidden source of light, of
> truth, and of meaning, the erasure of the visage of Being – such must be the
> insistent return of that which subjects metaphysics to metaphor.

Derrida later postulates of this claim to epistemological mastery that the
'sensory sun, which rises in the East, becomes interiorised, in the evening
of its journey, in the eye and heart of the Westerner'.[97] And Paul de Man
has written of the topos of light that it 'implies space which, in turn, implies

the possibility of spatial differentiation', being a 'play of distance and proximity that organises perception'. He adds:

> Whether the light emanates from outside us before it is interiorised by
> the eye . . . or whether the light emanates from inside and projects the
> entity, as in hallucination or in certain dreams, makes little difference.

In addressing the poetry of Shelley, de Man writes in terms applicable to
the problematics of interpreting *The Ebb-Tide*, 'Light covers light, trance
covers slumber and creates conditions of optical confusion that resemble
nothing as much as the experience of trying to read *The Triumph of Life*, as
its meaning glimmers, hovers, and wavers, but refuses to yield the clarity
it keeps announcing'.[98] The performance of doubleness which marks
Stevenson's characters in *The Ebb-Tide* is refracted into a seaborne 'carnal
stereophany' (in Barthes' phrase) to generate that 'excess of light' which
'changed into a sinister darkness' (ET, 121), and triggers this heretical
account of imperial and theological adventure.

CHAPTER 7

Dr Doyle's Uncanny Prognosis

Sherlock Holmes and The Final Solution

Did you see the gas vans?
No ... yes, from the outside. They shuttled back and forth.
I never looked inside; I didn't see Jews in them. I only saw things from outside.
Frau Michelson, wife of a Nazi schoolteacher at Chelmno[1]

I found myself regarding [Holmes] as an isolated phenomenon, a brain without a
heart, as deficient in human sympathy as he was pre-eminent in intelligence.
A. Conan Doyle, 'The Greek Interpreter' (1893)[2]

In so delineating the great detective, Dr Watson unwittingly lays bare a profound ideological contradiction at the heart of Conan Doyle's literary success, a fracture in the Sherlock Holmes saga so deep that it may be read as an ominous step towards Nazi race-law and its ghastly implementation in Eastern Europe. Indeed, Conan Doyle's entire oeuvre is marked by many sub-textual and uncannily prescient anticipations of the terrors of the Third Reich in a writing project which is superbly and disturbingly attuned to the future cataclysm: the Enlightenment project which reaches its fictional apotheosis in the career of the great detective dialectically leads mankind, as the Frankfurt School perceived, to the gates of Auschwitz. Thus, for instance, the notorious killing off of Holmes, recounted by Watson 'with a heavy heart' (CSH, 469), exhibits an apparently conclusive resolution of 'The Final Problem' (1893) which casts its shadow forward to that more overwhelming 'final solution' propounded fifty years later at the 1942 Wannsee Conference.[3] It might be noted that, in 'The Final Problem', Holmes is said to have just helped in resolving 'a serious international complication' and is 'engaged by the French government upon a matter of supreme importance' (CSH, 469). Thus Dr. Watson is surprised, in the spring of 1891, to see the detective 'paler and thinner than usual', and his knuckles 'burst and bleeding'. In response to this surprise, Holmes turns to the subject of his arch-enemy, Professor Moriarty, describing him as one who occupies 'a pinnacle in the records of crime' (CSH, 469, 470) – a brilliant mathematician, Moriarty possesses 'hereditary tendencies of the most diabolical kind'. According to Holmes, ' "A criminal strain ran in his blood, which, instead of being modified, was increased and rendered infinitely more dangerous by his extraordinary mental powers" ' (CSH, 470–1). Moriarty is designated the 'Napoleon of crime', one who 'sits motionless, like a spider in the centre of its web, but that web has a thousand radiations'. If there is 'a man to be removed', the professor is behind it, functioning as the 'central power'. Indeed, the 'horror at his crimes', Holmes remarks, is lost in 'admiration at his skill' (CSH, 471). But now, having his net around the arch-criminal and his accomplices, Holmes gleefully anticipates 'the rope for all of them' (CSH, 471). In return, when confronting Holmes at Baker Street, the professor predicts the detective's 'inevitable destruction' at the hands of 'a mighty organisation' (CSH, 472). With their Baker Street premises burnt down in an arson attack, Holmes and Watson take the train, first to Strasbourg and thence on to Geneva. 'In the homely Alpine villages or in the lonely mountain passes', Holmes can never forget 'the shadow which lay across him', but looks forward to the 'extinction of the most dangerous and capable criminal in Europe' (CSH, 477).

Whilst staying at Meiringen, the pair visit the nearby Reichenbach Falls, of which Watson offers a depiction that calls upon the terminology of the literary sublime:

> It is, indeed, a fearful place. The torrent, swollen by the melting snow, plunges into a tremendous abyss, from which the spray rolls up like *the smoke from a burning house*. The shaft into which the river hurls itself is an immense chasm, lined by glistening coal-black rock, and narrowing into a creaming, boiling pit of incalculable depth, which brims over and shoots the stream onward over its jagged lip. The long sweep of green water roaring forever down, and the thick flickering curtain of spray hissing forever upward, turn a man giddy with their constant whirl and clamour. We stood near the edge peering down at the gleam of the breaking water far below us against the black rocks, and listening to the half-human shout which came booming up with the spray out of the abyss. (CSH, 478; italics added)

The doctor's vision refracts Friedrich von Schiller's thesis, in his 1801 definition of the sublime, when he postulated that nature 'drags down with her in a *single* collapse both the important and the trivial', and adjured his readers to 'stand face to face with the evil fatality [observing] the terrifying and magnificent spectacle of change which destroys everything and creates it anew'.[4] On receipt of what turns out later to be a bogus message, Watson abandons Holmes and returns to the hotel; then, realising his error, the doctor hastens back to the Falls, where he observes 'two lines of footmarks' in the 'blackish soil' which is 'ploughed up into a patch of mud'. Holmes's valedictory letter speaks of his 'final discussion' with Moriarty, and Watson recognises the probability that the detective and his arch-enemy and double[5] are both lost 'deep down in that dreadful cauldron of seething water and swirling foam' (CSH, 479, 480). Yet, as Watson acknowledges, there remain behind a group of 'injudicious champions' who endeavour to clear the name of Moriarty (CSH, 480).

This apocalyptic scene curiously and powerfully foreshadows a very particular philosophical encounter which took place at Davos in Switzerland, the resort favoured during the early 1890s by Conan Doyle and his ailing wife.[6] The philosophical confrontation was between the leading neo-Kantian, Ernst Cassirer,[7] and Martin Heidegger, and in the course of their discussion Heidegger advocated a Kierkegaardian 'leap into exis-tence', an acceptance of 'the hardness of fate', predicated upon that 'fallenness' through which *Dasein*, human being-there, loses itself in its immersion in social existence and the world of things. For Heidegger, philosophy and poetry were, in this moment, two human enterprises located 'proximately on high mountain tops separated by an abyss'.[8] In contradis-tinction to his own position, Heidegger would associate Cassirer's Kantian Marburg school with a system which 'brings about that the dead is made alive, not for the living, but for the dead who have ventured beyond the suicide of existence'.[9] In Adorno's account, by 'situating the sublime in overpowering grandeur' the Kantian sublime affirms its 'complicity with powerlessness'; however, in conceding that 'towering mountains are eloquent not as what crushes overwhelmingly but as images of a space liber-ated from fetters and strictures',[10] Adorno's theorisation might gesture not only towards Heideggerian existentialism but also towards the Führer's cultivation of the Hitlerian will at his alpine retreat, the Berghof. Elsewhere, Adorno satirises the intellectual involved in 'wrestling bouts arranged and contested by inwardness', scenes of contestation which are 'rigged', since 'whether he confront the abyss of Being or the harrowing experience of the Senses', like the great detective, the philosopher always 'falls on his feet'.[11]

Dr Watson's unwonted eloquence in this passage aptly demonstrates or enacts the way in which, according to Paul de Man, rhetoric 'radically suspends logic' – Holmes's key quality – by opening up 'vertiginous possi-bilities of referential aberration'.[12] Walter Benjamin significantly ascribed similar qualities to Hölderlin's Greek translations, in which 'meaning plunges from abyss to abyss until it threatens to become lost in the bottom-less depths of language'.[13] Indeed, both philosophical and fictional scenarios appear to act out what Eve Kosofsky Sedgwick, in her influential definition of 'paranoid Gothic', categorises as 'a residue of two potent male figures locked in an epistemologically indissoluble clench of will and desire'.[14] Ten years before the Davos confrontation, during the 1919 'war emergency semester', Heidegger had declared, 'we stand before an abyss: either an abyss of nothingess, e.g., absolute objectivity, or a successful leap into *another world*'.[15] The onset of this other world was ambivalently dealt with by Gilbert Ryle in his perceptive 1929 review of *Being and Time*, an account which, whilst hailing the book as a phenomenological break-through, characterised it with foreboding as 'an advance towards disaster'.[16] However, a further fall seems as likely as a leap – in his 1935 commentary on Sophocles, Heidegger would propose with Sherlockian aptness that

> The more towering the summit of historical *Dasein*, the deeper will be the abyss for the sudden fall into the unhistorical, which merely thrashes around in issueless and placeless confusion.[17]

To recommence, Doyle's 'The Final Problem' turns upon the predicate of a gifted but hereditarily warped mastermind who, it might be argued, resembles Himmler, sitting at the epicentre of a criminal network. Moreover, the recurrent motif of violence marking 'The Final Problem' in some ways adumbrates the culture of the Nazi SS and SA in 1930s Germany – the firing of Baker Street mirrored in the burning of the Reichstag, whilst the entraining of the protagonists from the metropolis into the dream/nightmare space at the heart of Europe offers the most terrible portent of the future. In his bloodless asceticism and his functioning as 'a brain without a heart', it is clear that Holmes duplicates the role of his antagonist, and stands in a dialectical relation with his author, who once declared, 'If I don't kill him soon he'll kill me'.[18] It is at the aptly named *Reich*enbach Falls that Watson will peer into the depths which would, fifty years later, confront European Jewry with what Walter Benjamin in 1938 would term 'the radiating abyss of the Nazi hell'[19] – an abyss whose exis-tence remains unacknowledged by those 'injudicious champions' and revisionists who persist in denying the facts of the Holocaust.

Sherlock Holmes's rooms in Baker Street see few more dramatic entries than that of the 'pompous' schoolmaster, Thorneycroft Huxtable, in 'The Adventure of the Priory School' (1904). Despite his dignity and 'solidity', Dr Huxtable proceeds to sink to the floor, becoming what Watson terms a 'majestic figure prostrate and insensible upon our bearskin matting' (CSH, 539). The mystery which the teacher unfolds is that of an abduction from the elite Priory School in the Peak District – the boy in question is the son of an eminent former Cabinet Minister, the Duke of Holdernesse, who is, as Holmes affirms, 'one of the greatest subjects of the Crown' (CSH, 540). The school principal tells how the duke's secretary, James Wilder, had announced the boy's arrival at the commencement of the summer term, adding that the duke was separated from his wife who is now resident in the south of France. The boy, Lord Saltire, has disappeared from the school one night without any sign of struggle, his absence rendered more problematic by the simultaneous absence of a second person – namely, 'Heidegger, the German master' – he too is 'missing', having in his case climbed down the ivy-clad walls. Commenting on this disappearance, Dr Huxtable adds, '"His bicycle was kept in a small shed beside this lawn, and it also was gone"' (CSH, 541). No trace is found of the boy or of the 'silent, morose' German teacher, and Holmes and Watson are soon to be found in the 'cold, bracing atmosphere of the Peak country', interviewing the duke, 'a tall and stately person' with 'a drawn, thin face' and nose 'grotesquely curved and long', his pallid complexion in stark contrast to a 'long, dwindling beard of vivid red' (CSH, 543). Holmes promptly draws a sketch-map of the area, which, with its various tracks across the moor, reveals the direction of Heidegger's flight, and the boy's cap is found in a gypsy caravan, as a result of which the travellers are placed 'safe under lock and key' (CSH, 546). With 'high hopes' the pair set off across 'the peaty, russet moor' (CSH, 547) and come upon a set of cycle tracks, but Watson's certitude is quickly dashed by the detective:

> 'A bicycle, certainly, but not *the* bicycle,' said he. 'I am familiar with forty-two different impressions left by tyres. This, as you perceive, is a Dunlop, with a patch upon the outer cover. Heidegger's tyres were Palmer's, leaving longitudinal stripes. Aveling, the mathematical master, was sure upon the point. Therefore, it is not Heidegger's track.' (CSH, 547)

Finding a second set of tracks, 'like a fine bundle of telegraph wires', the two men stumble upon the scene of the crime, the gorse 'dabbled with crimson' and the heather replete with 'dark stains of clotted blood' (CSH, 548). They discover first the bicycle 'horribly smeared and slobbered with blood' and then the 'unfortunate victim', killed by 'a frightful blow upon the head which had crushed in part of his skull' – it is 'undoubtedly the German master' (CSH, 549). After encountering the ill-tempered publican of a nearby inn, the two catch a glimpse of the duke's secretary cycling past with 'a face with horror in every lineament' (CSH, 552). Holmes proceeds to solve the crime with his customary aplomb, identifying the second set of cycle tracks as Wilder's, and deducing that it is the secretary who has abducted the boy in collusion with the landlord, who killed the pursuing Herr Heidegger. Faced with this *dénouement*, the duke confesses that Wilder is his illegitimate son from a previous liaison, and had harboured a 'fanatical' hatred for the legitimate heir. Holmes roundly berates the proud aristocrat, who assures him that Wilder will now 'go to seek his fortune in Australia' (CSH, 558). Holmes announces with some satisfaction that 'the gallows await' the publican, and the tale concludes with the detective's perfunctory advice that the duke should make amends to his estranged wife.

This bafflingly transparent case offers itself as a text with multiple implications, not least those surrounding the resonant coincidence of naming. Three years before the publication of this tale, Sigmund Freud would confess to experiencing 'a slightly disagreeable feeling when one comes across one's own name in a stranger'[20] – a feeling doubly entertained by Conan Doyle's reader. Thus, 'Aveling, the mathematical master' (CSH, 547), takes on the name of the dissolute lover of Eleanor Marx, Edward Aveling, whilst the German teacher shares a surname with one of the greatest philosophers of the modern period.[21] We might note that at Stonyhurst College, the young Conan Doyle had been an adept student of the German language under the tutelage of Fr. Baumgarten, and he went on to spend a further year of study close to the German border at Feldkirch in Austria from 1875 to 1876.[22] This experience may have prompted some remarks in one of the Brigadier Gerard tales, where the hero intuits beneath the 'homely surface' of German life a sense of 'devilry', and concludes that 'there was something terrible in this strong, patient Germany – this mother root of nations'.[23] Diana Basham has postulated that Germany became, for Conan Doyle, 'the murderous other of his writing about British manhood, and also a covert part of its meaning', and furthermore claims that Holmes's 'massive egotism and sense of limitless power' serve to 'conform to the fascist pattern' of masculinity.[24] In 'His Last Bow' (1917), which takes place at the opening of the Great War, 'the most terrible August in the history of the world', Holmes will remark presciently, '"Though unmusical, German is the most expressive of languages"' (CSH, 970, 979). The vexed question of German identity and will, so pressing in the pre-war period, is adumbrated by Herr Heidegger's role as teacher. As Alexander Düttmann puts it, the issue for the German language is, 'can it transform the foreign language into itself, can it thereby immunise itself against the foreign body?'[25] – an issue which would be played out in the coming theatre of war on the Western Front. The linguistic question is crucial since, as Düttmann adds in a phrase nicely applicable to the hapless German teacher, 'the language he feels impelled to speak is the language of his potential murderers'.[26] Elsewhere Düttmann argues, in terms which mirror the fortuitous doubling of the name 'Heidegger', that 'the other is always the one who can come and also comes at any moment, *who is already there*'.[27] That 'something terrible' which Brigadier Gerard sensed in German culture will be inextricably enmeshed in a linguistic possibility: the two Heideggers, like Holmes and Moriarty, share what John Irwin, in his analysis of detective fiction, calls 'the mysterious relationship of sameness and difference that constitutes self-identity'.[28] In his role as expounder of German linguistic rules and his violent death, the schoolmaster's career in early-Edwardian England is a portent of what is to come in 1914 and its aftermath. Basham annotates what she astutely defines as the 'power of the letter "H" to signal a double identity in Doyle's writing',[29] a power she finds peculiarly concentrated in this story, centring as it does upon the Duke of Holdernesse, Dr Huxtable, Herr Heidegger and Reuben Hayes in a case investigated by Sherlock Holmes and John H. Watson – a linguistic patterning, it may be urged here, to be reduplicated by the chief architects of Nazism, Adolf Hitler, Heinrich Himmler, Herman Göring and the master-mind of the Final Solution, Reinhard Heydrich. Discussing Poe's 'William Wilson', in which the narrator is confronted by a stranger bearing his own name, Nicholas Royle notes how the tale 'seems to be implicitly immersed, and explicitly to culminate, in a funny cross-talk involving death, the double and telepathy',[30] and such 'cross-talk' is similarly to be discerned subtextually in Conan Doyle's text. Walter Benjamin, with divinatory clarity, postulated that a 'man's name is his fate',[31] whilst his colleague Adorno argued that 'German words of foreign derivation are the Jews of language'.[32] In his later spiritualist phase, Conan Doyle would observe that 'spirits have the greatest difficulty in getting names through to us'; he also speculated that 'the earth name is a merely ephemeral thing, quite disconnected from the personality'.[33]

It might therefore be suggested that Conan Doyle's school-teacher fortuitously alerts the reader to the central role of language and naming in the thought of Martin Heidegger, epitomised by his reflections on the links between Greek and German cultural identity. Düttmann observes that in Heidegger's thought 'The benaming of name (the name "Germania" as the name of a certain mission and a certain heritage) strives to represent this coming, to enforce the return'.[34] But this act of 'benaming' in the 1930s opens a terrifying vista – as is revealed, for example, in Lyotard's account of 'the mother, language, failed, prostituted, which will have died through the eructation of Hitlerian will'.[35] We note that it is the absence of the mother, in Conan Doyle's tale, which enables the abduction of the heir and the consequent murder of Herr Heidegger; but we may add that it is also the motherland/fatherland which is summoned in Heidegger's university addresses of the early 1930s with their plea to preserve 'at the most profound level the forces that are rooted in the blood and soil of a *Volk*'. Teachers, in this view, are carriers of a mission who 'must really advance to the outermost positions where they will be exposed to the dangers of the world's constant uncertainty'; thus, what Heidegger terms 'the spiritual mission of the German *Volk*' is tied to 'the highest service to the *Volk* in the state'.[36]

In warning of a *'fierce battle'* to be fought by teachers 'in the National Socialist spirit', Heidegger urged that this spirit must not be 'suffocated by humanising, Christian ideas'.[37] Martin Heidegger and Conan Doyle, both trained in Jesuit theology, similarly abandon that discipline in favour of a national imperial mission imbued with a sense of what Heidegger termed a 'hard race with no thought of self', 'a race that lives from constant testing' involved in 'a battle to determine who shall be the *teachers* and *leaders*'.[38] In his 'Hymn to Empire' (1911) Conan Doyle invited the deity to 'Set Thy guard over us', protecting the British imperialists 'From the palm to the pine,/ From the snow to the line/ Brothers together/ And children of Thee', and in a second poem he hailed the white 'Empire Builders' as 'ministers of wrath/ Building better than they know'.[39] Visiting the United States in 1894, he had asserted, 'I believe in the future supremacy of the English speaking races', and he anticipated a time when 'America and England joined in their common Anglo-Saxonhood, with their common blood, will rule the world'.[40] There are echoes of this vision in Heidegger's belief, inspired by the rise of National Socialism, that it was essential that each subject's life 'will be rooted in the *Volk* as a whole, and in its destiny' in a project involving 'the will to build *a living bridge* between the worker of the "hand" and the worker of the "head"'.[41] This strain of thinking emerges out of nineteenth-century philology, a line of thinking, as Martin Kayman remarks, which 'could do little more than spiritualise the race-oriented biology it sought to replace, underpinning its infinite regression with a mythical, primal "Ur-text", expressive of a collective *Völksgeist*'.[42] The complex lines of affiliation between Conan Doyle's popular fiction and the abstruse realms of Heideggerian thought may be equivocally traced, for instance, with reference to Benjamin's exploration of language in his early essay, 'On Language as Such' (1916), which posits a post-lapsarian Babel of arbitrary signs and argues that translation or language-teaching accentuate an alienation endemic in all languages. Language is, in this reading, a 'foreign friend' which renders men and women alien within their own homeland; for both Heideggers, it may be that, in the philosopher's phrase, 'Coming to be at home is thus a passage through the foreign': 'the law of the encounter between the foreign and one's own is the fundamental truth of history'.[43] This is a process of alienation which would come to pass with a deadly signification in the 'Germanisation' of certain Polish place-names, Oświęcim–Auschwitz, Brzezinka-Treblinka.

Düttmann's suggestion that the 'speculative moment of the German language' will reveal 'the possibility of "absolute horror" along with that of genuine knowledge'[44] might serve as a frame for the central moment of detection in Conan Doyle's story – Holmes's reading of the tyre tracks in a bravura interpretation of the doctor's sketch-map. The scenario is a 'great rolling moor', 'a peculiarly desolate plain' which is 'intersected with a thousand sheep paths' and at one point 'widens into a morass' (CSH, 546, 547). Holmes strides across the moor 'eagerly observant of every muddy stain upon the mossy surface', and proceeds with his exposition of the 'forty-two different impressions left by tyres' (CSH, 547).[45] It might be noted that the technology of the bicycle, its replaceability and repetitive motion, is suggestive of a radically distinct temporality of biological repetition that is marked and registered in the story's reduplicated coincidence of naming.

We might also observe that the Peak District topography of 'The Priory School' resembles the Dartmoor of *The Hound of the Baskervilles* (1902),[46] and that Catherine Wynne has aptly related 'viscous landscapes' such as 'bogs, or moors or swamps' to the complexities of colonialism in the work of a writer of Scottish birth, Catholic Irish descent and adopted English gentry identity; thus, according to Wynne, 'moor and bog release regressive traits'.[47] Herr Heidegger is lost and then murdered on such a track, whilst his philosophical namesake saw as part of his project the need 'to build a narrow and not far-reaching footpath as a passageway'.[48] Watson's map depicts, indeed, the situation envisaged in a poem by Martin Heidegger entitled 'Wege', which speaks of 'paths of thought, going by themselves, vanishing'; as Düttmann glosses this, 'It is only a path if it strays from itself: it is its own straying'.[49] But this 'straying' is surveyed and demarcated in the detective's sketch-map, thus bringing the desolate moorland under surveillance. These kinds of map, it has been suggested, 'entered the law, were attached to ordinances' and thus 'acquired an aureole of science', so that 'the silent lines of the paper landscape foster the notion of socially empty space'.[50] Indeed, Düttmann, in the course of his meditative commentary on the motif of the 'path' in Heidegger and Rosenzweig, suggests that at 'the edge of the path, of the way, of language' we experience 'the name as other' which 'watches us in silence': thus, he suggests, 'we are watched from the end of the path, that is to say, from the limits of language'. For Heidegger, the 'question of the path' invokes the concept of 'the German people, this people which engenders its own spiritual world': they are, he declares, 'on the march', advancing 'along the path of spirit'.[51] Here it may be that our paths divide, for, in Sherlock Holmes's world-view, the cycle tracks offer the opportunity for a positivist display of forensic method, whilst Heidegger argues that the 'essence of Experience of the path is lost when it is identified with method' – what the philosopher designates that 'path upon which we pursue a matter'.[52]

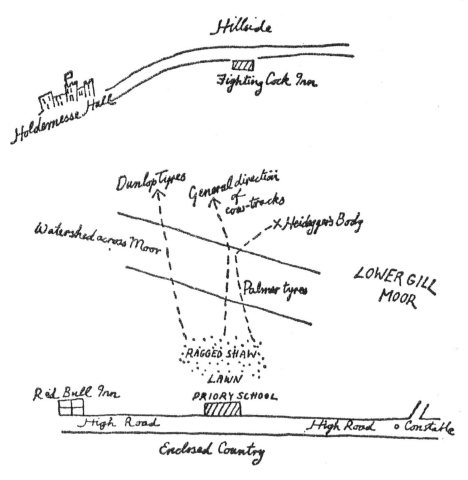

Watson's map of the neighbourhood of the school

It is in the same work that Heidegger suggests that roots are 'alien to the Jewish people which, for this reason, is always found everywhere', and this is why the Jewish people 'is found anywhere, on all paths or ways, but without being found there'.[53] In contrast, for the Jewish Walter Benjamin, 'Method is a digression'.[54] If the name of Herr Heidegger's murderer, Reuben Hayes, serves to hint at Jewish origins in Conan Doyle's story, the sketch-map of tracks ending abruptly suggests a reading of materiality which adumbrates the most cataclysmic event of modern history, an event that Martin Heidegger cunningly sidestepped in his Black Forest hut.[55] In Holmes's work of detection, to adopt a phrase of Leo Bersani, 'the finality of the signifier is both posited and ignored'.[56] This 'finality' is registered in a network of tracks which peter out in empty space, the space of death for both the German master and the putatively Jewish miscreant. The outlines of the sketch-map might also lead to a pondering of its similarities with the railway branch-lines and sidings that served Auschwitz-Birkenau, Treblinka and other death-camps, and to the baffling truth that, as George Steiner has remarked of Heidegger, 'One of the principal works that we have in the philosophy of language . . . was composed almost within earshot of a death camp'.[57] The tracks which Holmes and Watson pursue indefatigably over the moor emblematise that 'trace' which Jacques Derrida perceives as 'the essence of selfhood', an essence constituted 'by the threat or anguish of its irremediable disappearance'.[58] For the German teacher cycling in pursuit of the abducted boy, the path was (in the words of his philosophical namesake) 'interrupted at a decisive place': 'the attempt made on that path', Heidegger says of his early work, 'was running the risk' of reinforcing 'further subjectivity'.[59]

This issue of the overcoming of subjectivity is pressingly inflected in both Heidegger's and Doyle's discourse here – note how, for instance, Heidegger speaks, in 1929, of the way in which

> Profound boredom, drifting here and there in the abysses of our existence like a muffling fog, removes all things and oneself along with them into a remarkable indifference. This boredom manifests beings as a whole.[60]

Sherlock Holmes also knew much about existential boredom, deploying cocaine, tobacco, violin-playing or chemical experiments to allay the tedium of existence between cases. This Heideggerian condition is nicely epitomised in 'The Adventure of the Bruce-Partington Plans' (1908). At the outset of the case Watson depicts London enveloped in 'a dense yellow fog', whilst Holmes, irritated by 'this drab existence', is 'biting his nails, tapping the furniture, and chafing against inaction' (CSH, 913). The great detective, however, is marked out by his ability to watch and wait, a quality classically exemplified by his silent vigil on the moor in *The Hound of the Baskervilles*. Heidegger argues that watching and waiting 'is not an actionless or thoughtless letting things come and go, it is not a closing of one's eyes in the face of some dark foreboding'.[61] Yet it is precisely such a closing of the eyes or averting of the gaze which has marked and compromised the reception of Heidegger's thought consequent upon his vision, however transitory, of National Socialism as 'the possibility of an inner gathering and renewal on the part of the people', and his discernment of 'a path towards the discovery of its historical . . . vocation'.[62] As James Phillips puts it, 'Heidegger defers the emergence of the *völk* precisely in order to think its historicality and thus the poetical'.[63] The interwoven tracks of Holmes's map in 'The Priory School' reflect what Adorno, pondering his own flight from Nazi Germany and Benjamin's more tragic destiny, designated the way the 'lines of our destiny cross each other and form an inextricable interlacing' of 'criss-crossing lines'.[64] In a phrase which ominously calls up the terminating railway-lines at the entrance-arch to Auschwitz, Adorno argues that 'Nothing can be rescued unchanged, nothing that has not passed through the portal or the gateway of its death'.[65]

In 'The Adventure of the Priory School' it is the 'gypsies camped on the moor' who are immediately suspected of the crime, placed 'all safe under lock and key' and promptly forgotten by the narrative (CSH, 546). Conan Doyle was an admirer of George Borrow and an ardent campaigner against legal injustices, and yet this stereotypical ascription of guilt marks several of the Sherlock Holmes tales such as 'Silver Blaze' (1892) and 'The Adventure of the Speckled Band' (1892) in a way which uncannily anticipates Kafka's notion of 'a gypsy literature that had stolen the German child from the cradle'.[66] In an early essay for a Catholic journal, Heidegger referred scathingly to what he termed the 'interesting people' of the avantgarde, and anticipated the 'hour of grace' when the artist 'becomes conscious of the great lie of his gypsy-life'.[67] This type of racially-motivated ascription of guilt would be pursued to its deadly conclusion in Nazi Germany: gypsies were defined as 'social deviants' in the 1933 race laws, some were involuntarily sterilised, and many by 1936 incarcerated in the first concentration camp at Dachau. They were deported to the east in the early days of the war, those at Auschwitz being largely left to their own devices in a separate encampment until July 1944, when 3000 were gassed in a single night. The gypsies were to become a largely forgotten component of the Nazi terror, yet as Inga Clendinnen observes, 'an absence is also an erasure'.[68] The lack of witnesses, so necessary to Sherlock Holmes's bravura displays of theory, foreshadows that catastrophic *'not seeing'* which Shoshana Felman identifies as the crucial feature of the unfolding of the Holocaust: 'the unprecedented, inconceivable advent of *an event without a witness*, an event which consists in planning the literal erasure of its witnesses'.[69] But the detective needs no witness: on the moor, he assures Watson, '"with stains as well as the track to guide us [Herr Heidegger] cannot escape us now"' (CSH, 548) – and yet Herr Martin Heidegger, as is well known, also sought to escape the odium of his Nazi flirtation. This attempt took the form of silence, a refusal to speak about the Holocaust.

Lacoue-Labarthe, in his investigation of Heidegger's silence, remarks upon the absence of any ritual element in the Holocaust:

> Nowhere else, in no other age, has such a will to clean and totally eradicate
> a 'stain' been seen so compulsively, without the least ritual. . . . There was
> not the least 'sacrificial' aspect in this *operation*, in which what was calcu-
> lated coldly and with the maximum efficiency and economy . . . was a pure
> and simple *elimination*.[70]

As Deleuze and Guattari argue, National Socialism 'did not spring from the
sleep of reason but rather from the rationalism that would allow nothing to
remain outside its light'.[71] This is precisely where Conan Doyle's work so
penetratingly discerns and stages the portents of an overweening rationality.
The emphasis upon the 'coldness' and 'efficiency' of the Nazi operation curiously echoes the characterisation of Sherlock Holmes: as Watson observes
of his colleague, 'All emotions . . . were abhorrent to his cold, precise but
admirably balanced mind' ('A Scandal in Bohemia' (1891) CSH, 161).
Indeed, in some respects the great detective, 'a machine rather than a man'
('The Crooked Man' (1893), CSH, 412), offers points of resemblance with
Adolf Hitler, 'a solitary with a charlatan's flair for multiple self-presenta-
tions'.[72] So too does Heidegger, for, as James Phillips points out, in the early
1930s the philosopher 'even alters his moustache in his aggressive design
to become Hitler's *doppelgänger*'.[73]

The opening story of *The Return of Sherlock Holmes*, 'The Adventure of the
Empty House' (1903), gives an account of the detective's escape from the
Reichenbach Falls. Here, Watson expresses the incredulity of the readership
when he asks, '"Is it possible that you succeeded in climbing out of that
awful abyss?"' Holmes tells how he evaded that 'dreadful chasm', his
expertise in Japanese wrestling causing Professor Moriarty to fall over the
brink with 'a horrible scream' (CSH, 486). This, though, was not the end
of Holmes's ordeal, as the professor's accomplice began to shower rocks
down from above, and the detective imagined hearing the arch-criminal's
voice 'screaming at me out of the abyss'. With characteristic understate-
ment he adds, '"It was not a pleasant business, Watson"' (CSH, 487). Conan
Doyle was himself, at this critical juncture of his career, poised on the edge
of disaster both personal and political. His conflicted personal life had
involved him in a chivalric determination to remain technically faithful to
his invalid wife Louise whilst nurturing a passionate but 'Platonic' relationship with Jean Leckie. Moreover, as a liberal and humane supporter of
women's rights, and an ardent interventionist in cases of social and legal
injustice, Conan Doyle was politically embarrassed by his advocacy of the
Boer War, from which he had recently returned. Having gained entry to the
war as a surgeon at the Langman Hospital, Bloemfontein, Conan Doyle
became embroiled in the controversies surrounding the conflict, and

published two widely-read books on the subject, *The Great Boer War* (1901) and *The War in South Africa* (1902), which took the form of an analysis of the 'cause and conduct' of hostilities. This propagandistic effort brought him a knighthood; indeed, as Diana Basham argues, for Conan Doyle the Boer War writing represents 'the focal point of his career',[74] but it was public recognition bought at a psychic cost that was reflected in the subsequent Sherlock Holmes series, most notably in *The Hound of the Baskervilles*.

It might be noted that the thrust of Conan Doyle's second war study, a lengthy pamphlet, was aimed at a defence of the concentration camps designed by Kitchener to 'clear' Boer women and children and African males from outlying areas where the British were confiscating or burning homesteads. The establishment of the camps led to virulent controversy at home, opposition being orchestrated both by feminists such as Emily Hobhouse and Millicent Fawcett, by Liberal MPs such as C. P. Scott and John Ellis, and by the crusading journalist W. T. Stead. Death-rates at the camps rose inexorably towards 12 per cent, due to disease brought in by the large numbers of women and children being deported: in the white camps the death-rate peaked at a rate of 350 per 1000 in 1901, whilst the rate in the black camps was as high as 370 per 1000 in the same year. It was in response to Stead's anti-war propaganda in his newspaper series, *War against War* (1899–1900) and then in his book, *Methods of Barbarism* (1901), that Conan Doyle composed *The War in South Africa*. As Paula Krebs has effectively demonstrated, this response is framed through the medievalising concept of chivalry, a concept which led Conan Doyle indignantly to rebut allegations of British sexual assault on Boer females. But his argument, as Krebs observes, only serves to reveal Conan Doyle's 'lack of language with which to rebut an assertion that masculinity includes the potential to rape'.[75] It was, Conan Doyle stressed, 'the duty of the British, as a civilised people, to form camps of refuge for the women and children'. In attacking Stead and other liberal critics of the camps, Conan Doyle argued that 'the British nation would have indeed remained under an ineffaceable stain had they left women and children without shelter upon the veldt in the presence of a large Kaffir population'[76] – imagery matched and duplicated in Watson's notation of the 'muddy stain upon the mossy surface' of the moor (CSH, 547). The 'stain' which the otherwise liberal Conan Doyle cannot bring himself to acknowledge, the guilt of the imperial concentration camp, is encapsulated in Sherlock Holmes's own admission, in 'The Adventure of Charles Augustus Milverton' (1904), that '"I have always had an idea that I would have made a highly efficient criminal"' (CSH, 577) – a concept further elaborated in 'The Second Stain' (1904). Conan Doyle speaks of Stead's 'harrowing pictures of the moral and physical degradation of the

Boer women' in the camps,[77] a type of degeneracy dialectically posited upon the 'purity' of British military personnel. As Krebs remarks, 'To justify the formation of the concentration camps, Doyle chose to focus on the sexual vulnerability of white women and the necessity for the British government to protect those women'.[78] It is this trope of an uncontainable 'degeneracy' which, it might be said, saturates the text of *The Hound*, whose Dartmoor topography curiously reduplicates that of the South African veldt. In his propaganda war, Conan Doyle is, as Krebs notes, 'at a distinct disadvantage in trying to defend British honour' in a war 'fought for control of land and goldfields';[79] significantly, in *The Hound*, Sir Charles Baskerville's aristocratic wealth is derived from 'South African speculation'.[80] Conan Doyle's insistence that the 'case for the formation of the camps must be admitted to be complete and overwhelming'[81] masks a deep ideological fracture; as Krebs remarks, it was difficult to argue the case that 'the camps were a purely chivalrous gesture'.[82] Conan Doyle's polemical prose here simply reinflects, we might argue, the thematics of romances such as *The White Company* (1891) or the Brigadier Gerard stories whose heroes, as Kenneth Wilson observes, 'behave according to the imagined code of medieval chivalry'.[83] Conan Doyle did not, however, feel able to extend this chivalry to his opponents, claiming that Emily Hobhouse's 'political prejudices were known to be against the Government', and that 'the defects in sanitation' at the camps were 'due to the habits of the inmates': 'To overcrowd a tent' he avers, 'is hygienically almost impossible'.[84] This medically sanctioned opinion contrasts starkly with Hobhouse's observation that when the twelve people 'who occupied a bell-tent were all packed into it', 'there was no room to move, and the atmosphere was indescribable'.[85] Hobhouse was in fact debarred from visiting some of the worst camps, such as the one at Standerton where the latrine consisted of 'one long narrow trench with a pole across it lengthwise on which people were expected to perch'.[86] To counter such accounts, *The War in South Africa* ponderously assembles positive countervailing testimony from other participants in the conflict as to the nature of the camps, including an officer from the Kroonstad camp who enthuses, in terms which anticipate the playing of the band at Auschwitz, 'We have cricket, tennis, and croquet for them, and they are all jolly well treated'.[87] Whilst Conan Doyle acknowledges a problem with the death-rate, his medical opinion is that this is mitigated by the fact that 'the death-rate among children is normally quite remarkably high in South Africa'. Doyle concludes with the claim that 'we have looked after our enemies far better than our friends'.[88] Krebs's critique of this position is judicious:

> To justify the formation of the concentration camps, Doyle chose to focus on
> the sexual vulnerability of white women and the necessity for the British
> government to protect those women. He could then ignore the economic
> vulnerability of the same women – a vulnerability created by the British
> when they burned farms and crops.[89]

If we loop back to the plot of 'The Priory School', we might note that it
involves the abduction of the legitimate heir by his illegitimate half-brother
in an act which exemplifies Leo Bersani's contention that the 'illegitimate,
the unauthorised, do not merely disrupt the straight line' but also 'establish another line, a possible (unfaithful) double'.[90] However, it is the
doubling of thought implicated in the nomination of Herr Heidegger
which opens up the more troubling aspects of 'The Priory School'. Indeed,
Conan Doyle's robust defence of the South African concentration camps is
strangely reinflected in the perceptive and sensitive anticipations of Nazi
terror that feature elsewhere in his *oeuvre*. As Paul de Man remarks, 'The
future is present in history only as the remembering of a failed project that
has become a menace'.[91] In an early pre-Sherlock Holmes story, 'That Little
Square Box' (1881), for instance, the hero uncovers what he suspects to be
an anarchist plot to blow up a transatlantic liner and ascribes it to 'desperate
emissaries' who seek 'to sacrifice themselves, their fellow-passengers, and
the ship, in one great holocaust'. In a subsequent discussion of the justification for the 'indiscriminate murder' involved in the bombardment of
Paris, a second character remarks, '"It seemed right enough to German
eyes"'.[92] Whilst in this farcical case the suspect container houses only a flock
of homing-pigeons, Major-General Heatherstone's Afghan diaries, in *The
Mystery of Cloomber* (1888), more overtly countenance the extermination of
subject-peoples and, indeed, a Professor Challenger story published in the
period immediately prior to the Great War, *The Poison Belt* (1913), would
afford a still deeper resonance in the context of the century of 'total war'. In
this fantasy, the group of men which had first accompanied Professor
Challenger in *The Lost World* (1912) is summoned to his Surrey home to
observe the passage of the earth through a deadly cloud of poison gas which,
Challenger announces on their arrival, has already killed off 'the less developed races': '"There are deplorable accounts from Africa"', he tells his
auditors, '"and the Australian aborigines appear to have been already exter-
minated"'. He adds, with a strangely Hitlerian inflection, '"The Slavonic
population of Austria is down, while the Teutonic has hardly been
affected"'. When Lord John Roxton exclaims, '"universal death – it's
awful!"' the professor suggests that it is '"not, in my judgement, a matter
for apprehension"'.[93] The group proceed to enjoy 'a merry meal', admiring

the 'elemental greatness' of their leader and 'the sweep and power of his understanding', even as 'the invisible tide of Death was slowly and gently rising around' them (PB, 241). To delay the effects of the gas, the professor has made his wife's boudoir 'as airtight as is practicable' (PB, 243), whilst the progress of the poison cloud across the earth is marked by 'terrible racial rioting': 'It was death – painless but inevitable – death for young and old, for weak and strong, for rich and poor, without hope or possibility of escape' (PB, 247). In urging his wife to accept death without a struggle, Professor Challenger's 'tender' voice reveals to the narrator a different character trait, 'very far from the bullying, ranting, arrogant man who had alternately amazed and offended his generation' (PB, 249). Viewing the conflagrations which begin to dot the countryside, the narrator reflects that 'Cremation is surely the best burial' (PB, 259), and observes the idyllic landscape of the Weald now transformed into a type of 'terrible Golgotha strewn with the bodies of the human race' (PB, 267). He imagines a journalistic account of scenes in St Paul's depicting a 'packed mass of despairing humanity, grovelling at this last instant before a Power' (PB, 268). The poison cloud passes over, leaving in its wake a 'deadly silence' and a 'pall' 'round the ruins of humanity' (PB, 279). Venturing into London, the group discover a city of the apparently dead, 'the fate of the children' filling the narrator 'with the strongest sense of intolerable injustice' (PB, 281). With the evaporation of the cloud comes a 'great awakening', but the *Times* is left to speculate upon the nature of human existence and the 'abysses' that 'may lay upon either side of it' (PB, 301).

This is a text of the Great War period in which Conan Doyle eerily assembles some key elements of the Nazi Holocaust – the sealed chamber, the lethal gas, the demonic leader, the categorisation and decimation of 'lower' races, the final days in Hitler's bunker – these combining to form a set of tropisms marking a ruinous cultural context, an Edwardian England which Doyle, with telepathic insight, represents as hovering on the verge of catastrophe.[94] The characters surrounding Professor Challenger act out the pathology of a historical conjuncture in a fantasmatic reduplication anticipatory of the real; as George Steiner has argued of the twentieth century, 'it is difficult to conjecture a bestiality, a lunacy of oppression or sudden devastation, which would not be credible'.[95] The political unconscious of Conan Doyle's poetics and structure prompts and enables a consideration of both the 'devastation' of the Great War with its poison gas and of the 'bestiality' of the Holocaust. These events horrendously mirror Heidegger's contention that it is Western philosophy which is responsible for the 'homelessness' of mankind, and the deep cause of the current 'forgetting of Being'; indeed, they also figure as what Anson Rabinbach designates 'the insurmountable horizon of philosophical reflection against which any account of Western thought would have to be measured'.[96] Conan Doyle's melodramatic fantasy sheds a riddling light upon the Heideggerian hypothesis of a 'fall' in thought from Plato onwards, but it may be, as Rabinbach posits, that Heidegger's concern for the revealing/concealing of Being marks 'an attempt to remove himself from all ethical considerations or demands of responsibility'.[97] It was National Socialism, as Heidegger phrased it in 1935, which would enable Germany to fulfil its historic mission because it was 'the most metaphysical of nations': the role of Germany, that is to say, was to 'move itself, and thereby the history of the West, beyond the centre of their future "happening" and into the primordial realm of the Greeks'.[98] As Rabinbach notes, Heidegger was, with Albert Speer and others, a member of the 'Hellenist' wing of the National Socialist party, one who looked for a lighting-concealing advent of Being posited upon the necessity for man to stand in that 'openness' or 'clearing' which becomes crucial in his later thinking. Such a 'clearing' is gestured towards in *The Poison Belt* in 'the whole widespread landscape' of the Weald; as the narrator remarks, 'Nowhere in the blue heaven or on the sunlit earth was there any foreshadowing of a catastrophe' (PB, 245). For Heidegger, Rabinbach concludes, 'National Socialism and the war was not a catastrophe for its victims, only a catastrophe for the advent of Being'.[99]

In Conan Doyle's *oeuvre*, the manifestation of 'catastrophe' would assume its most potent fictional embodiment in his wartime pot-boiler, *The Valley of Fear* (1915), a work whose broken-backed structure may be read as a rhetorical strategy for coping with the complex distortions of the Great War. Whilst the first part of *The Valley* is a conventional Sherlock Holmes mystery, the second part abandons the detective and centres upon the criminal activities of a brotherhood known as the 'Scowrers' in an industrial valley in the USA. In delineating the clandestine violence of this brotherhood, Conan Doyle's text compulsively foreshadows the rise of the SA and the SS some fifteen years later, and the subsequent apocalyptic scenario of the industrialised death-camps. The Scowrers are led and dominated by Boss McGinty, 'a high public official, a municipal councillor, and a commissioner of roads' who exercises his 'secret powers' in a 'pitiless' fashion. The Boss combines 'fine features' and a 'frank bearing' with 'dead, dark eyes, deep and remorseless', so that his enemies find themselves 'face to face with an infinite possibility of latent evil' (CSH, 826). The Scowrers, despite a campaign of criminality and violence through which the county becomes 'a place of terror' (CSH, 819), are never brought to justice because, as Ettie Shaffer, a 'blond and fair-haired' German 'type', explains to the hero, '"no witness dares to appear against them"' (CSH, 820, 824). Another character,

Brother Morris, tells the hero how, having joined the lodge, he found himself impelled to participate in mass-killings at a lonely farmhouse which leave the men's hands 'crimson to the wrist'. Morris goes on, in terms resonant with implication for the Nazi death-camps, '"Look down the valley! See the cloud of a hundred chimneys that overshadows it! I tell you that the cloud of murder hangs thicker and lower than that over the heads of the people. It is the Valley of Fear, the Valley of Death. The terror is in the hearts of the people from the dusk to the dawn"' (CSH, 842). As an observer in the train remarks, '"I guess hell must look something like that"' (CSH, 818). It is at this seat of industry, where in the 'growing gloom there pulsed the red glow of the furnaces' that the 'murder society' of the Scowrers holds sway (CSH, 816, 822), imposing its rule of terror as 'the flames of the frequent furnaces' are to be seen 'roaring and leaping in the darkness' (CSH, 818). The Scowrers operate as a secret society, their initiation ceremonies directed by Boss McGinty, 'a priest presiding over some diabolical ritual', and each official displays a 'medallion as emblem of his office' (CSH, 832). At the close of the proceedings, 'these men, to whom murder was familiar' pause for 'refreshment and for harmony'. As the narrator remarks, with chilling anticipation of the culture of the death-camps, 'the tender or pathetic in music could move them to tears' (CSH, 837). This aesthetic cultivation runs in tandem with a reign of terror – one 'terrible winter' witnesses a series of mutilations and killings which leaves a 'shadow' on the valley:

> Darkly the shadow lay upon the Valley of Fear. The spring had come with running brooks and blossoming trees. There was hope for all Nature bound so long in an iron grip; but nowhere was there any hope for the men and women who lived under the yoke of the terror. Never had the cloud above them been so dark and hopeless. (CSH, 853)

Like the National Socialists, the Scowrers, men 'whose hands had . . . been reddened a dozen times', mask their actions in the language of working-class rights; yet they were, the narrator comments, 'as hardened to human murder as a butcher to sheep' (CSH, 861).

The Valley of Fear may thus be read as a melodramatic critique of industrial production, predicating the ills of modernity upon the manufacturing process and consequent depredation of nature. In that sense Conan Doyle's tale is cognate with Heidegger's rejection of a nihilistic modern culture arising out of what Michael Zimmerman terms 'the same one-dimensional disclosure of entities that simultaneously gave rise to the industrial forms of working and producing'.[100] Heidegger had absorbed the influence of the *Völkisch* movement which, in cultivating the folk-roots of the 'old'

Germany, rejected commercial, industrial and utilitarian values – what the poet Stefan George in 1911 characterised as 'the urban-progressive contamination' which had established 'the satanically inverted, the America-world, the ant-world' of modern life.[101] Rationality had, in this view, sapped the potency of Germanic blood in an emasculation jointly ascribed to Marxist and Liberal thought. And yet *Völkisch* writers concurred in locating the spirit of the folk within the state, hence the paradoxical enthusiasm they displayed at the onset of the Great War, with its colossal investment in mechanised armaments. *The Valley of Fear*, written in 1914–15, may be construed as a confusedly allegorical response to that war. It is a curious thought that Conan Doyle, in his espousal of empire and antipathy to industry, shared with Heidegger a contradictory and complex set of ideas which issued in proclamations such as the Rector's somewhat chilling announcement, in July 1933, that 'Whoever does not advance the struggle, remains left behind', and his call for a 'hard stock' of Germans who would live by 'constant testing'.[102] We might note that Heidegger associated empire with the emergence of technology, arguing in his 1942 lecture on Parmenides that the imperial 'arises from the essence of truth as correctness in the sense of direction-giving, arranging security of the security of domination'[103] – an ensemble of ideas which similarly underpins Conan Doyle's concentration camp literature. Two years earlier, as the war was getting underway, Heidegger had explicitly referred to 'the connection of English imperialism with the Calvinist ethic'.[104] Whilst the philosopher did not subscribe to the biological race-theory underpinning National Socialist ideology, as Zimmerman notes, 'he was certainly aware of the concentration camps for political prisoners . . . set up near Freiburg' in 1933.[105] Zimmerman's study goes on to outline Heidegger's gradual swerve away from a National Socialism increasingly devoted to a strengthening of the technological era, and his own wish, expounded in his mystical readings of Hölderlin, for a mood of receptiveness and 'releasement' which should free mankind from its enslavement to the machine.

There remain, however, the troubling issues raised by Heidegger's 'silence', that catastrophic failure to address the issue of the Holocaust which stands in dramatic contrast to Conan Doyle's wholehearted espousal of the concentration camp as a place of refuge. As Lyotard has argued, we may take 'Auschwitz' as a referent which demonstrates the impossibility of any single authoritative discourse about history – striving for totality, in his view, being compatible with Nazism itself. There is, that is to say, a continuum of explanation or 'fact' surrounding the Final Solution. Naïve historical realism is always inflected by the aesthetics of emplotment and point of view. Consideration of the Shoah may, therefore, entail a refusal of narrative closure in a process of continuous investigation of the depths of the Western Imaginary, such a trajectory producing a multifaceted reading which would inevitably create its own aporia or hermeneutic challenge. Thus, the Holocaust bears a freight of excessive implication which can never be defined. This can never justify the fact that Heidegger's only specific reference to the death-camps, as is well known, was to include them in a roll-call of the evils of modern technology:

> Agriculture is now a motorised food industry, the same thing in its essence as the production of corpses in the gas chambers and the extermination camps, the same thing as blockades and the reduction of countries to famine, the same thing as the manufacture of hydrogen bombs.[106]

In his promulgation of a poetic setting for the emergence of the truth of Being and the clearing of the self-concealing which becomes a 'pathway' to the numinous, and in his urgent stress upon the impressment of 'that which is', Heidegger after the 'turn' in his thinking would speak no intelligible word about the Shoah. But then, as Habermas would ask, 'can the planned murder of millions of human beings . . . be made understandable in terms of the history of Being as a fateful going astray?'[107] Heidegger's profound meditations on the work of art and the poetics of being, dialectically related as they were to the events of the war, might be said to have been parodically anticipated by Conan Doyle's passionate espousal of the claims of spiritualism. Indeed, the philosopher specifically juxtaposed spiritualist and materialist claims in the aftermath of the war, proposing that 'In whatever manner beings are interpreted',

> whether as spirit, after the fashion of spiritualism; or as matter and force, after the fashion of materialism; or as becoming and life; or as representation, will, substance, subject, or energeia; or as the eternal recurrence of the same – every time, beings as beings appear in the light of Being.[108]

To move towards a conclusion, this chapter's bizarre and scandalous juxtaposition of Arthur Conan Doyle and Martin Heidegger seems to illuminate the imperial context of the Final Solution as an event which owes its origins to the West's long history of domination of its others: the Judeocide may be interpreted, from this perspective, as a limit case of the 'enlightened' West defending itself against alien cultures and identities, a defence already dramatised parodically in the treatment of the racial other in many Sherlock Holmes stories. For the Nazis, the Jews functioned as the enemy within to be balanced against the Bolshevist enemy without. Indeed, the terrible singularity of the Final Solution, its sheer enormity, is both revealed and refracted by the institutionalisation of the concentration camp

to which Conan Doyle lent his name, in a series of propagandistic 'docu-
mentations' which confirm the West's sense of privilege and superiority. In
these stories, Sherlock Holmes seems to embody, in his fictional mastery, a
fantasmatic version of that racial supremacy which would fuel Nazi
thinking. Moreover, in the denigration and disavowal of his popular
creation Conan Doyle unwittingly participates in his own problematic
insertion within the antinomies of circulation and production. In the
Sherlock Homes stories the Jew carried the burden of an ascribed parasitism
as middleman or intellectual in ways often identified with criminality.
Again, the male self-cultivation and misogyny of the *Freikorps* is uncannily
anticipated in both the homosocial Baker Street brotherhood of Holmes and
Watson and in their rivalrous contest with Professor Moriarty. Joseph
Kestner has appositely noted the way in which Holmes and Watson become
'two fellows sharing rooms, a male fantasy of domesticity without the intru-
sion of female presence'; it is, Kestner adds, 'a reconsolidation of masculine
space echoing the corresponding arenas of the regiment, the troop-ship, or
the university medical environment'. Kestner interestingly underlines the
complexities of this bonding in relation to Dr Watson's imperial injury,
arguing that the 'wounded male body, and the fact that the wounding
occurred in a defeat, acknowledge Doyle's focus on the masculine script'.[109]

There is, though, yet another way of reading the uncanny or unimagin-
able conjunction of Conan Doyle and Martin Heidegger, and that is to trace
it to a concern with 'spirit'. We may note that Conan Doyle had diagnosed
Germany's problem in the aftermath of the Great War as an absence of spirituality, writing that 'All other life was at its highest, but spiritual life was
dead'.[110] In his later years the novelist devoted much time and energy to
the study and practice of spiritualism, an avocation which culminated in
the two-volume history of spiritualism, published in 1926, in which he
identified the only school of thought antithetical to the spiritualist movement: 'That is the school of materialism, which holds the world in its grip
at present'.[111] Conan Doyle defines 'the typical materialist state' as pre-war
Germany, and argues that all religions have 'been tried and all have failed',
having 'lost all contact with the living facts of spirit'. A person who has
tried all religions 'finds himself in a valley of gloom', but, on discovering
'proof of independent existence', 'is no longer in a valley but upon the ridge
beyond'. For Conan Doyle, 'revealed religion and metaphysical philosophy
are equally helpless before the advancing tide'.[112] As Diana Basham argues,
spiritualism offers itself, in such writings, 'as a new revelation of Higher
Law, a new religious dispensation or sacred code able to provide material
evidence for a beleagured human spirituality, and thus hold its own against
the encroachments of a materialistic and empirical science'.[113]

It is true that Heidegger's early thought, summed up in *Being and Time* (1927), eschews consideration of the spirit, but in the unprecedented events which ensued, the question became pressing. His lectures and essays begin to take on an urgent sense of the impress of modernity as it is revealed in technology, and his response insists upon a 'clearing' for the self-concealing of being which will mark a pathway to the numinous. Like Conan Doyle, Heidegger would, in the Hölderlin lectures, critique a thinking which 'remains everywhere metaphysical' because 'remnants of the Christian world view' which both writers reject, 'remain operative everywhere'. But, in a unique inflection, Heidegger argues that 'metaphysics first begins to achieve its supreme and utter triumph in our century as modern machine technology' – that is to say, paradoxically, 'Modern machine technology is "spirit"'.[114] In his readings of poetic texts in the 1930s and 40s, Heidegger stresses the poetical setting into work of the truth of being in ways which suggest parallels with the politically opposed Frankfurt School. For both Heidegger and the Frankfurt School, humanity has learnt to dominate nature through an 'enlightened' repression of the self, in an act of self-concealment. As Habermas says of this conjuncture and the concept of 'instrumental reason', 'In the moment of its most extreme acceleration, history congealed into nature and faded into the Golgotha of a hope become unrecognisable'.[115] In terms which recall the characterisation of Sherlock Holmes, Habermas notes Horkheimer and Adorno's project of assessing 'the cost incurred in the usurpation of reason's place by a calculating intellect'. The altered trajectory of Heidegger's thinking, Habermas suggests, takes him from the consideration of *Dasein* as representing 'the existentially isolated individual in his move toward death' to 'the collective *Dasein* of a fatefully existing and "in-each-case-our" people [*Volk*]'.[116] In the Rectoral Address of 1933, Heidegger would speak of 'the *Dasein* of our people': the Führer, he argues, 'asks nothing of the people', rather, 'Our will to the self-responsibility of the people wills that each people find the greatness and truth of its determination'.[117] It is through this altered emphasis, as David Farrell Krell annotates it, that 'Heidegger's discourse of spirit would legitimise National Socialism', whilst he simultaneously 'takes his distance' from the movement in considering 'what will prove to be anything but a *spiritualised* politics of "earth and blood"'.[118] Heideggerian thought here circles round what Krell terms, in an argument also applicable to Conan Doyle's fictional school-master, the concept of the German nation 'as guardian of the sacred fire of philosophy, of the ancestral hearth of thought, of the domesticity of spirit, of *Geist*, in one sole language'.[119]

Heidegger, like Conan Doyle in his history of spiritualism, searches for an originary event of being in a thought-movement which marks an evasion

or circumventing of unbearable social realities: the metaphysical 'spiritualism' which is critiqued in *Being and Time* is liberated with a vengeance in
the more avowedly Hegelian Rectoral Address or the *Introduction to
Metaphysics* (1935). Within this complex web of discourse, David Wood
suggests, 'What spirit and the spiritual achieves for Heidegger is a way of
thinking concrete institutions (university, state, leader) while maintaining
Dasein's openness to Being'. Spirit, in Heidegger's new definition, is
'primordially attuned, knowing resoluteness towards the essence of Being'
– as Wood observes, this represents an ominous 'regimentation of the
Spirit'.[120] Certainly Heidegger will postulate during the period of wartime
crisis that 'Spirit as spirit is communal spirit', and 'it is "spirit" in historical human beings that determines historicality'.[121] The question of the
spiritual for Heidegger at this conjuncture is thus, as Jacques Derrida
argues, ineluctably 'inscribed in contexts with a high political content', in
a way which reverses or undermines the role of the 'metaphysical ghost' or
'spectral silhouette' of spirit in *Being and Time*.[122] The wartime lectures on
Hölderlin urgently situate spirit within the boundaries of a homeland.
Culture, Heidegger insists, 'is always already only the consequence of a
"dwelling", of a being "at home" of spirit', and this 'dwelling' is significantly transformed only when, 'for the sake of what is its own', spirit 'wills
the unhomely, the foreign'.[123] The Rectoral Address of 1933 had assured
its audience that the '*uncertainty of entities in their totality*' bestowed upon 'our
people' the 'most intimate and extreme world of danger': 'in other words
its true *spiritual* world'.[124] Derrida succinctly remarks of the Rector's
address, 'One could say that he spiritualises National Socialism',[125] and this
process is carried further in the *Introduction to Metaphysics*, where Europe is
depicted as 'caught in a vice between Russia and America'. This situation
is all the more 'fatal', Heidegger argues, 'in that the destitution of spirit
derives from Europe itself', and has been 'definitively determined, on the
basis of Europe's own spiritual situation'. It is 'the questioning of the question of Being' which is the fundamental issue 'for a reawakening of spirit'
in a strategy which will 'master the danger of a darkening of the world' and
enable 'a taking up of the historial mission of our people'.[126] As Derrida
glosses this, spirit is to be 'awakened' by 'the taking charge of the sending,
of a *mission*, the historial mission of *our people*, as the middle of the West'.[127]
It came as no surprise that Adorno, in a trenchant critique, categorised
occultism as 'connected by thought-patterns' to anti-semitism: 'The
hypnotic power exerted by things occult resembles totalitarian terror: in
present-day processes the two are merged'. Advocates of the spiritual,
Adorno remarks, 'inveigh against materialism' and yet 'they want to weigh
the astral body'.[128]

Arthur Conan Doyle was to die in 1930, prior to the unfolding of those events in Nazi Germany which his work had telepathically staged and dramatised with stunning diagnostic potency and insight. In 'The Adventure of the Priory School', the German teacher Herr Heidegger is murdered whilst 'On the path': '"He fell wounded"', Holmes postulates, '"he stood up – he remounted – he proceeded. But there is no other track"' (CSH, 548). In Derrida's complex reading of Heidegger, spirit is affined to 'the blow, the strike, the imprint' or 'the bad blow',[129] whilst in Conan Doyle's portentous short story, Herr Heidegger has suffered 'a frightful blow upon the head' (CSH, 549). Gilbert Ryle's 1929 review of *Being and Time*, ruminating upon the philosophical 'bankruptcy and disaster' he discerned in the book, observed that 'one of the characteristics of my whole being is that *qua* Life it terminates in Death – *terminates* in Death without finding its *completion* in it'.[130] This termination without completion, here visited upon the fictional German master, would find its unthinkable apotheosis in the death-camps.

In the poem 'Todtnauberg', written after a post-war visit to Heidegger's ski-hut, the Jewish poet and Holocaust survivor Paul Celan recalls how he signed the philosopher's log-book with 'hope of a thinking man's coming word in the heart' – that confession of remorse which never came. Whilst Sherlock Holmes struggles to establish a connection between 'the missing boy and this German master' (CSH, 541), in his most famous poem, 'Todesfuge', Celan would incorporate the insistent refrain, 'Death is a Master from Germany'. When Derrida considers Martin Heidegger, he discerns, in the philosopher's ruminations on spirit, 'two paths of thought here crossing under Heidegger's step' which he relates to 'a certain crossing of *our* paths': the trail, suggested by Heidegger's reading of Trakl, leads back to 'the spirituality of a promise' which is 'foreign' to both Christianity and Platonism. Yet this trail ultimately 'appears to be scarcely passable, even as the impassable itself'.[131] Reflecting upon the period of composition of *Being and Time*, Heidegger ruminated, 'I always followed only an unclear trace of the right path'.[132] We may note with John Bayley how Celan, 'deeply interested in the language of the philosopher', invented compounds such as *heideggangerisch*, 'moorwandering'. Bayley, indeed, argues that, in 'Todtnauberg', 'the feel of the moor, the *Hochmoor*, haunts his poem, which is also haunted by a kind of silence, perhaps that of the philosopher himself': 'The dumb sense of the wet moor, without human response in it, is silent and expressionless'.[133]

Adorno once remarked that 'Heidegger was *in favour* of false trails',[134] to the extent that, in Deleuzian terminology, the philosopher 'lost his way along the paths of the reterritorialisation'.[135] On the high moorland of the

Peak District, Holmes and Watson 'frequently lost sight of the track', yet 'always succeeded in picking it up once more'. Eventually, however, 'No further help from the tracks could be hoped for' and, in a type of existential limit-situation, Holmes can barely 'save himself from falling' (CSH, 548, 550). These strangely intertwining paths that trace a bizarre link between Sherlock Holmes and Martin Heidegger would ultimately lead, in the apotheosis of Enlightenment metaphysics, to the portals of mass extermination.

Notes

Introduction

1   T. W. Adorno, *Aesthetic Theory*, tr. Robert Hüllot-Kentor (London: Continuum, 1997), 286.

2   Steven Galt Crowell, 'Heidegger and Husserl', in *A Companion to Heidegger*, ed. Hubert L. Dreyfus and Mark A. Wrathall (Oxford: Blackwell, 2005), 56.

3   Adorno, *Aesthetic Theory*, 228–9.

4   T. W. Adorno, *Minima Moralia*, tr. E. F. N. Jephcott (London: NLB, 1974), 226.

5   Walter Benjamin, 'The Task of the Translator', tr. Harry Zohn, in *Walter Benjamin: Selected Writings*, vol. 1, ed. Marcus Bullock and Michael Jennings (Cambridge, Mass.: Harvard University Press, 1996), 258–9.

6   Walter Benjamin, *The Origin of German Tragic Drama*, tr. John Osborne (London: Verso, 1977), 201.

7   Walter Benjamin, cited in Irving Wohlfarth, 'The Measure of the Possible', in *The Actuality of Walter Benjamin*, ed. Laura Marcus and Lynda Nead (London: Lawrence & Wishart, 1998), 15.

8   Cited in Wohlfarth, 'The Measure', 18.

9   Wohlfarth, 'The Measure', 19.

10 Benjamin, *The Origin*, 44, 29.

11 Benjamin, *The Origin*, 32.

12 Friedrich Nietzsche, cited in Paul de Man, *Blindness and Insight* (London: Methuen, 1983), 102.

13 Adorno, *Aesthetic Theory*, 211.

14 Adorno, *Aesthetic Theory*, 178.

15 Richard J. Bernstein, *The New Constellation* (Cambridge: Polity Press, 1991), 146.

16 De Man, *Blindness and Insight*, 107.

17 Søren Kierkegaard, *Either/Or*, tr. Alastair Hannay (Harmondsworth: Penguin, 1992), 394, 395.

18 Kierkegaard, *Either/Or*, 482, 483.

19 Kierkegaard, *Either/Or*, 486, 489.

20 Timothy J. Reiss, *The Uncertainty of Analysis* (Ithaca, N.Y.: Cornell University Press, 1988), 98–9.

21 Fredric Jameson, *Marxism and Form* (Princeton: Princeton University Press, 1974), xii.

22 Jameson, *Marxism and Form*, xii, xiii.

23 Jameson, *Marxism and Form*, xix.

24 See for instance Roger Ebbatson, *Lawrence and the Nature Tradition* (Hassocks:

Harvester Press, 1980), and *An Imaginary England* (Aldershot: Ashgate, 2005).

25 Timothy Clark, *The Poetics of Singularity* (Edinburgh: Edinburgh University Press, 2005), 156.

26 Richard Jefferies, *Field and Hedgerow* (London: Longmans, Green & Co., 1910), 98. This essay, 'Swallow Time', was first published in the *Standard* in 1886 and reprinted by Jefferies' widow in this posthumous collection.

I   Tennysonian Shadows: 'In the Garden at Swainston'

1   Ann Thwaite, *Emily Tennyson* (London: Faber, 1996), 279. For a detailed account of the Simeons and their estate see L. G. Whitbread, 'Tennyson's "In the Garden at Swainston"', *Victorian Poetry* 13 (1975), 61–9.

2   Robert Bernard Martin, *Tennyson: The Unquiet Heart* (Oxford: Clarendon Press, 1980), 487.

3   Thwaite, *Emily Tennyson*, 471.

4   Martin, *Tennyson*, 487.

5   Martin, *Tennyson*, 488.

6   *Tennyson: A Selected Edition*, ed. Christopher Ricks (Harlow: Longman, 1989), 620.

7   *Tennyson: A Selected Edition*, 620. The Cabinet Edition of 1874 prints line 10 as 'Still in the house of his coffin the Prince of courtesy lay'.

8   Marylu Hill, 'Julia Margaret Cameron's Photographic Illustrations of Tennyson's *Idylls of the King*', *Victorian Poetry* 40 (2002), 448.

9   Letter of 7 December 1843, cited in Helen Groth, *Victorian Photography and Literary Nostalgia* (Oxford: Oxford University Press, 2003), 1.

10 William Henry Fox Talbot, *Athenaeum*, 9 February 1839, cited in Groth, *Victorian Photography*, 136.

11 Alison Chapman, *The Afterlife of Christina Rossetti* (Basingstoke: Macmillan, 2000), 105.

12 Roland Barthes, *Camera Lucida*, tr. Richard Howard (New York: Noonday, 1981), 82.

13 John D. Rosenberg, *Elegy for an Age* (London: Anthem Press, 2005), 68.

14 It may be significant for the poem that in nature it is only the male nightingale which sings.

15 Darrel Mansell, 'Displacing Hallam's Tomb in Tennyson's *In Memoriam*', *Victorian Poetry* 36 (1998), 98–9.

16 Mansell, 'Displacing Hallam's Tomb', 100.

17 George Steiner, *In Bluebeard's Castle* (London: Faber & Faber, 1971), 81.

18 Mansell, 'Displacing Hallam's Tomb', 103, 106.

19 Mansell, 'Displacing Hallam's Tomb', 108.

20 Angela Leighton, 'Touching Forms: Tennyson and Aestheticism', *Tennyson Research Bulletin* 7 (2001), 225.

21 Søren Kierkegaard, *Either/Or*, tr. Alastair Hannay (Harmondsworth: Penguin, 1992), 151.

22 Peter M. Sacks, *The English Elegy* (Baltimore: Johns Hopkins University Press, 1987), 23, 37.

23 Gerhard Joseph, 'Tennyson, Freud and the Work of Mourning', *Victorian Poetry* 36 (1998), 129.

24 W. David Shaw, *The Origins of the Monologue: The Hidden God* (Toronto: Toronto University Press, 1999), 131.

25 Peter Allen, *The Cambridge Apostles* (Cambridge: Cambridge University Press, 1978), 133.

26 Hallam Tennyson, *Alfred Lord Tennyson: A Memoir*, vol. 1 (London: Macmillan, 1897), 72–3.

27 Paul de Man, *The Rhetoric of Romanticism* (New York: Columbia University Press, 1984), 78, 120.

28 Sigmund Freud, 'Mourning and Melancholia', *The Standard Edition of Sigmund Freud*, vol. 14 (London: Hogarth Press, 1975), 249.

29 Sacks, *The English Elegy*, 7, 8.

30 Sigmund Freud, *The Interpretation of Dreams*, tr. James Strachey (Harmondsworth: Penguin, 1976), 157, 473, 476.

31 C. J. Jung, *Selected Writings*, ed. Anthony Storr (London: Fontana, 1983), 91.

32 Jung, *Selected Writings*, 93.

33 T. S. Eliot, *Collected Poems* (London: Faber & Faber, 1974), 60.

34 Hélène Cixous and Catherine Clément, *The Newly-Born Woman*, tr. Betty Wing (Minneapolis: University of Minnesota Press, 1986), 79.

35 John Schad, *Victorians in Theory* (Manchester: Manchester University Press, 1999), 37.

36 Marion Shaw, *Alfred Lord Tennyson* (Hemel Hempstead: Harvester Wheatsheaf, 1988), 143, 151, 160.

37 Kelly Hurley, *The Gothic Body* (Cambridge: Cambridge University Press, 1996), 4.

38 Walter Benjamin, *The Origin of Tragic German Drama*, tr. John Osborne (London: NLB, 1977), 135.

39 *The Letters of Alfred Lord Tennyson*, ed. Cecil Y. Lang and Edgar F. Shannon, vol. 1 (Cambridge, Mass.: Harvard University Press, 1981), 213.

40 Karl Marx and Friedrich Engels, *The Communist Manifesto*, in *The Essential Left* (London: Unwin, 1960), 33.

41 Isobel Armstrong, *Victorian Poetry* (London: Routledge, 1993), 31, 35.

42 Jacques Derrida, *Specters of Marx*, tr. Peggy Kamuf (London: Routledge, 1994), 41.

43 Marx and Engels, *Communist Manifesto*, 14.

44 Derrida, *Specters of Marx*, 40.

45 Jack Kolb, 'An Unrecorded Sonnet by Hallam', *Victorian Poetry* 15 (1977), 374.

46 T. Vail Motter (ed.), *The Writings of Arthur Hallam* (London: Oxford University Press, 1943), 233.

47 Derrida, *Specters of Marx*, 40.

48 Karl Marx, *A Contribution to the Critique of Political Economy*, tr. S. W. Rayazanskaya (New York: International Publishers, 1970), 109.

49 Marx and Engels, *Communist Manifesto*, 29.

50 Derrida, *Specters of Marx*, 154, 156.

51 Karl Marx, *Eighteenth Brumaire of Napoleon Bonaparte*, in *Collected Works*, vol. 11 (New York: International Publishers, 1979), 125.

52 Derrida, *Specters of Marx*, 45.

53 Martin, *Tennyson*, 95.

54 It was this book which helped to prompt Thomas de Quincey's writings on Afghanistan. See John Barrell, *The Infection of Thomas de Quincey* (New Haven: Yale University Press), 13–14.

55 John O. Waller, *A Circle of Friends: The Tennysons and the Lushingtons of Park House* (Columbus: Ohio State University Press, 1986), 151.

56 Waller, *A Circle of Friends*, 158.

57 Cited in Waller, *A Circle of Friends*, 183.

58 Waller, *A Circle of Friends*, 138, 188.

59 Cited in Waller, *A Circle of Friends*, 191.

60 Waller, *A Circle of Friends*, 197.

61 On his deathbed Lushingon appears to have urged the reluctant Venables to marry his sister Emily, a consummation never to be achieved.

62 Edward Said, *Orientalism* (London: Routledge & Kegan Paul, 1978), 94, 45.

63 Earl Grey, *The Colonial Policy of Lord John Russell's Administration*, vol. 1 (London: Bentley, 1853), 14.

64 Thomas Richards, *The Imperial Archive* (London: Verso, 1993), 3.

65 Catherine Hall (ed.), *Cultures of Empire* (London: Routledge, 2000), 14.

66 Christopher Lane, *The Ruling Passion* (London: Duke University Press, 1995), 16, 17.

67 Lane, *The Ruling Passion*, 4.

68 Lane, *The Ruling Passion*, 2.

69 Armstrong, *Victorian Poetry*, 15, 12.

70 Cited in Christopher Ricks, *Tennyson* (London: Macmillan, 1972), 28n.

71 Rosenberg, *Elegy for an Age*, 33.

2 Fair Ships: A Victorian Poetic Chronotope

1 Matthew Arnold, *Selected Prose*, ed. P. J. Keating (Harmondsworth: Penguin, 1970), 209.

2 Arnold, *Selected Prose*, 209.

3 Arnold, *Selected Prose*, 222.

4 Arnold, *Selected Prose*, 225.

5 *Tennyson: A Selected Edition*, ed. Christopher Ricks (Harlow: Longman, 1989), 665. Subsequently cited as Ricks.

6 Charles Tennyson Turner, 'On Board a Jersey Steamer' (1868), *Collected Sonnets* (London: Kegan Paul, 1880), 265. See Roger Evans, 'Tennyson's "Crossing the Bar": A Family Connection', *Notes & Queries* 46 (1999), 478–9.

7   A. C. Swinburne, 'Prelude' (1871), *Songs Before Sunrise* (London: Heinemann, 1918), 8. Swinburne's poem goes on conventionally to connote death with sunset, with the dying soul left 'Helmless in middle turn of tide'.

8   Linda M. Shires, 'Tennyson's Gender Politics', in *Victorian Sages and Cultural Discourse*, ed. Thaïs Morgan (New Brunswick: Rutgers University Press, 1990), 52.

9   T. W. Adorno and Max Horkheimer, *The Dialectic of Enlightenment*, tr. John Cumming (London: Allen Lane,1973), 83.

10   Ricks, 666.

11   Paul de Man, *The Resistance to Theory* (Minneapolis: University of Minnesota Press, 1986), 84, 85.

12   Ricks, 357.

13   Sigmund Freud, *The Interpretation of Dreams*, tr. James Strachey (Harmondsworth: Penguin, 1976), 471.

14   Freud, *Interpretation of Dreams*, 528.

15   Ricks, 331.

16   Sigmund Freud, 'The Uncanny', *Art and Literature*, tr. James Strachey (Harmondsworth: Penguin, 1985), 347.

17   Freud, 'The Uncanny', 364, 365.

18   Freud, 'The Uncanny', 365.

19   George P. Landow, *Images of Crisis* (London: Routledge & Kegan Paul), 1982, 17.

20   Landow, *Images of Crisis*, 200.

21   J. A. Froude, *Thomas Carlyle* (1884), cited in Aidan Day, *Tennyson's Scepticism* (Basingstoke: Palgrave, 2005), 38.

22   Cited in Jürgen Habermas, *The Philosophical Discourse of Modernity*, tr. Frederick G. Lawrence (Cambridge: Polity Press, 1987), 54.

23   Alison Winter, '"Compasses All Awry": The Iron Ship and the Ambiguities of Cultural Authority in Victorian Britain', *Victorian Studies* 38 (1994), 69.

24   *The Sermons and Devotions of Gerard Manley Hopkins*, ed. Christopher Devlin (Oxford: Oxford University Press, 1959), 157.

25   John T. Irwin, *The Mystery to a Solution* (Baltimore: Johns Hopkins University Press, 1994), 50.

26   *Sermons and Devotions*, 23, 137.

27   Christina Rossetti, *Letter and Spirit* (London: SPCK, 1883), 11.

28   Daniel Brown, *Hopkins' Idealism* (Oxford: Clarendon Press, 1997), 258.

29   Brown, *Hopkins' Idealism*, 278.

30   *The Journals and Papers of Gerard Manley Hopkins*, ed. Humphry House and Graham Storey (Oxford: Oxford University Press, 1959), 225.

31   Brown, *Hopkins' Idealism*, 203.

32   'Barnfloor and Winepress', *Gerard Manley Hopkins: Selected Poetry*, ed. Catherine Phillips (Oxford: Oxford University Press, 1996), 24.

33   See especially Sean Street, *The Wreck of the Deutschland* (London: Souvenir, 1992), and Jude V. Nixon, '"Read the Unshakeable Shock Night":

Information Theory, Chaos Systems, and the Welsh Landscape of Hopkins's *The Wreck of the Deutschland*, *Merope* (35–6) (2002), 111–49.

34 W. David Shaw, *Origins of the Monologue: The Hidden God* (Toronto: Toronto University Press, 1999), 162.

35 Cesare Casarino, *Modernity at Sea* (Minneapolis: University of Minnesota Press, 2002), 11.

36 Casarino, *Modernity at Sea,* 14.

37 Casarino, *Modernity at Sea*, 67.

38 Casarino, *Modernity at Sea*, 59.

39 *Selected Poems of Herman Melville*, ed. Hennig Cohen (New York: Fordham University Press, 1991), 118.

40 Herman Melville, *Moby-Dick,* ed. Harold Beaver (Harmondsworth: Penguin, 1972), 296.

41 *Journals and Papers*, 118.

42 In his personal copy of the poem, Melville crossed out 'dead indifference' and substituted 'dense stolidity' (*Selected Poems*, 220).

43 See Brown, *Hopkins' Idealism*, 21–2. It was common practice for men participating in Arctic expeditions to express their responses poetically: see Erika Behrisch, 'Scientific Exploration and Explorers' Poetry in the Arctic, 1832–52', *Victorian Poetry* 41 (2003), 73–89.

44 Christina Rossetti, 'Sleep at Sea', *The Complete Poems*, ed. R.W. Crump (Harmondsworth: Penguin, 2001), 73–6.

45 T. W. Adorno, *Aesthetic Theory,* tr. Robert Hüllot-Kentor (London: Continuum, 1997), 86.

46 Jerome J. McGann, 'Christina Rossetti's Poems', in *Victorian Women Poets*, ed. Angela Leighton (Oxford: Blackwell, 1966), 103.

47 Adorno, *Aesthetic Theory*, 86.

48 Kathryn Burlinson, *Christina Rossetti* (Plymouth: Northcote House, 1998), 71.

49 Dolores Rosenblum, 'Christina Rossetti's Religious Poetry', in *Victorian Women Poets*, 116. This was a poem whose original title, 'Something Like Truth', was changed at the behest of D. G. Rossetti.

50 Adorno, *Aesthetic Theory*, 87.

51 Arthur Conan Doyle, 'The Homecoming of the "Eurydice"', *The Poems of Arthur Conan Doyle* (London: John Murray, 1922), 67. Conan Doyle was a pupil at the Jesuit college of Stonyhurst and its associated preparatory school from 1868 to 1875, and Hopkins studied philosophy at the affiliated college of St Mary's from 1870 to 1873; there is, however, no evidence of contact between the two.

52 Julia F. Saville, *A Queer Chivalry* (Charlottesville: University Press of Virginia), 2000, 134.

53 Paul Gilroy, *Black Atlantic* (London: Verso, 1993), 16.

54 Karl Marx, *Grundrisse*, tr. Martin Nicolaus (Harmondsworth: Penguin, 1974), 411.

55   Eric Williams, *Capitalism and Slavery* (London: Deutsch, 1964), 166.
56   Casarino, *Modernity at Sea*, 37.
57   Casarino, *Modernity at Sea*, 186.
58   Casarino, *Modernity at Sea*, 141.
59   John Schad, *Victorians in Theory* (Manchester: Manchester University Press, 1999), 123.
60   Maureen F. Moran, ' "Lovely Manly Mould": Hopkins and the Christian Body', *Journal of Victorian Culture* 6 (2001), 69.
61   *The Letters of Gerard Manley Hopkins to Robert Bridges*, ed. Claude C. Abbott (London: Oxford University Press), 1955, 27.
62   Casarino, *Modernity at Sea*, 181.
63   Casarino, *Modernity at Sea*, 165.
64   Hans-Georg Gadamer, *Gadamer on Celan*, tr. Richard Heinemann and Bruce Krajewski (Albany: State University of New York Press, 1997), 156.
65   Letter of 8 May, 1885; cited in Norman White, *Hopkins: A Literary Biography* (Oxford: Clarendon Press, 1992), 394.
66   Henry David Thoreau, *Walden*, ed. Michael Meyer (Harmondsworth: Penguin, 1983), 370.
67   Gillian Beer, *Darwin's Plots* (London: Routledge & Kegan Paul, 1983), 232.
68   Richard Jefferies, *The Story of My Heart*, ed. Samuel J. Looker (London: Constable, 1947), 127.
69   *A Nietzsche Reader*, ed. R.J. Hollingdale (Harmondsworth: Penguin, 1977), 207, 208.
70   F. O. Matthiessen, *American Renaissance* (Oxford: Oxford University Press, 1941), 565, 566.
71   Matthiessen, *American Renaissance*, 574.
72   Walt Whitman, *The Complete Poems*, ed. Francis Murphy (Harmondsworth: Penguin, 1975), 437.
73   Gadamer, *Gadamer on Celan*, 67.
74   Thomas Hardy, 'The Convergence of the Twain', sts. VI–XI, *The Complete Poems of Thomas Hardy*, ed. James Gibson (London: Macmillan, 1976), 307.

3   *A Laodicean*: Hardy and the Philosophy of Money

1   Thomas Hardy, *The Complete Poems*, ed. James Gibson (London: Macmillan, 1976), 102.
2   Cited in Anthony Giddens, *Capitalism and Modern Social Theory* (Cambridge: Cambridge University Press, 1971),10.
3   *Simmel on Culture: Selected Writings*, ed. Mike Featherstone and David Frisby (London: Sage, 1997), 245.
4   *Simmel on Culture*, 245.
5   *Simmel on Culture*, 246.
6   *Simmel on Culture*, 247.
7   *Simmel on Culture*, 248.
8   *Simmel on Culture*, 250.

9   Georg Simmel, *The Philosophy of Money*, tr. Tom Bottomore and David Frisby (London: Routledge, 1990), 198.

10   Thomas Hardy, *A Laodicean*, ed. John Schad (Harmondsworth: Penguin, 1997), 8. Subsequently cited in the text as AL.

11   Simmel, *Philosophy of Money*, 198.

12   *Simmel on Culture*, 250.

13   *Simmel on Culture*, 253.

14   Georg Lukács, *History and Class Consciousness*, tr. Rodney Livingstone (London: Merlin Press, 1971), 335.

15   Patrick Brantlinger, *Fictions of State* (Ithaca: Cornell University Press, 1996), 7.

16   Brantlinger, *Fictions of State*, 28–9.

17   Arthur MacEwan, *Debt and Disorder* (New York: Monthly Review Press, 1990), 31.

18   Brantlinger, *Fictions of State*, 45.

19   Brantlinger, *Fictions of State*, 146.

20   John Vernon, *Money and Fiction* (Ithaca: Cornell University Press, 1984), 19, 49.

21   Cited in Giddens, *Capitalism and Modern Social Theory*, 40.

22   Kevin McLoughlin, *Paperwork* (Philadelphia: University of Pennsylvania Press, 2005), 4.

23   Catherine Gallagher, *Nobody's Story* (Oxford: Clarendon Press, 1994), xxiii.

24   *Simmel on Culture*, 178.

25   Mark Seltzer, *Bodies and Machines* (New York: Routledge, 1992), 18.

26   See Nicholas Daly, *Literature, Technology, and Modernity* (Cambridge: Cambridge University Press, 2004), chs.1 and 2.

27   Walter Benjamin, *The Arcades Project*, tr. Howard Eiland and Kevin McLaughlin (Cambridge, Mass.: Belknap Press, 1999), 901.

28   Cited in *A Laodicean*, ed. Jane Gatewood (Oxford: Oxford University Press, 1991), 472. The serial version appeared in the European edition of *Harper's New Monthly Magazine* between December 1880 and December 1881.

29   Peter Widdowson, *Hardy in History* (London: Routledge, 1989), 109–11.

30   Ken Morrison, *Marx, Durkheim, Weber* (London: Sage, 1995), 74.

31   Benjamin, *Arcades Project*, 904, 906.

32   Vernon, *Money and Fiction*, 66, 91.

33   Deborah Parsons, *Streetwalking the Metropolis* (Oxford: Oxford University Press, 2000), 26.

34   Jean Baudrillard, *For a Critique of the Political Economy of the Sign* (St Louis: Telos Press, 1981), 94.

35   Baudrillard, *For a Critique*, 95.

36   Baudrillard, *For a Critique*, 96, 97.

37   Vernon, *Money and Fiction*, 8.

38   Iwan Rhys Morus, 'The Electric Ariel', *Victorian Studies* 39 (1996), 372, 373.

39   Nicholas Royle, *Telepathy and Literature* (Oxford: Blackwell, 1991), 5.

40   George Miller Beard, *American Nervousness* (New York: G.P. Putnam's, 1881), vi–vii. Beard was the first to coin the term 'neurasthenia', which after the publication of his earlier *Treatise on Nervous Exhaustion* (1869) became known as 'Beard's malady'.

41   Emma's role foreshadows Henry James's more extensive employment of a secretary/typist with spiritualist leanings. See Pamela Thurschwell, *Literature, Technology, and Magical Thinking* (Cambridge: Cambridge University Press, 2001).

42   Joe Fisher, *The Hidden Hardy* (London: Macmillan, 1992), 101.

43   E. P. Thompson, 'Time, Work-discipline and Industrial Capitalism', *Past and Present* 38 (1967), 57, 90–1.

44   Peter Galison, 'Einstein's Clocks', *Critical Inquiry* 26 (2000), 385.

45   Simmel, *Philosophy of Money*, 129, 130.

46   Jane Thomas, *Thomas Hardy, Femininity and Dissent* (Basingstoke: Macmillan, 1999), 99.

47   *A Laodicean*, ed. Gatewood, 463.

48   Alison Chapman, 'Mary Elizabeth Coleridge, Literary Influences and the Technologies of the Uncanny', in *Victorian Gothic*, ed. Julian Wolfreys and Ruth Robbins (Basingstoke: Palgrave, 2000),110, 123.

49   David Frisby, 'The *Flâneur* in Social Theory', in *The Flâneur*, ed. Keith Tester (London: Routledge, 1994), 86.

50   Rob Shields, 'Fancy Footwork', in *The Flâneur*, 68.

51   Gaming houses had been abolished in England in 1845. Hardy's scene may be indebted to the opening chapter of *Daniel Deronda*, published five years before *A Laodicean*.

52   *A Laodicean*, ed. Gatewood, 465.

53   Gillian Beer, 'The Reader's Wager', *Essays in Criticism* 40 (1983), 104.

54   Beer, 'The Reader's Wager', 104, 105, 110.

55   Beer, 'The Reader's Wager', 114.

56   Vernon, *Money and Fiction*, 116, 122.

57   *Simmel on Culture*, 178.

58   *Simmel on Culture*, 224.

59   *Simmel on Culture*, 240.

60   Benjamin, *Arcades Project*, 513, 515, 511.

61   Benjamin, *Arcades Project*, 497.

62   Bruce Mazlich, 'The *Flâneur*: From Spectator to Representation', in *The Flâneur*, 47.

63   Mark Durden, 'Ritual and Deception: Photography and Thomas Hardy', *Journal of European Studies*, 30 (2000), 63.

64   Benjamin, *Arcades Project*, 673.

65   Nancy Armstrong, *Fiction in the Age of Photography* (Cambridge, Mass.: Harvard University Press, 1999), 28.

66   Benjamin, *Arcades Project*, 915.

67   Armstrong, *Fiction in the Age of Photography*, 118.

68 Norman H. Holland and Leona Sherman, 'Gothic Possibilities', *New Literary History* 8 (1976–7), 282.

69 Armstrong, *Fiction in the Age of Photography*, 45.

70 Benjamin, *Arcades Project*, 678.

71 John Tagg, *The Burden of Representation* (Minneapolis: University of Minnesota Press, 1993), 37.

72 Durden, 'Ritual and Deception', 65.

73 *The Complete Poems*, 469.

74 Tim Armstrong, *Haunted Hardy* (Basingstoke: Palgrave, 2000), 58, 59.

75 Vernon, *Money and Fiction*, 70.

76 Geoffrey Batchen, *Burning with Desire* (Cambridge, Mass.: MIT Press, 1997),177, 216.

77 On the historical and literary context of anarchism see Barbara Melchiori, *Terrorism in the Late-Victorian Novel* (London: Croom Helm, 1985).

78 Vernon, *Money and Fiction*, 67, 78.

79 Maurice Blanchot, *The Infinite Conversation*, tr. Susan Hanson (Minneapolis: Minnesota University Press, 1993), 394.

80 En route to the USA in 1937 in his flight from Nazi Germany, Adorno would compare himself to Kafka's land-surveyor, whilst expressing relief that Horkheimer's Institute for Social Research 'is not the Castle' (Stefan Müller-Doohm, *Adorno: A Biography*, tr. Rodney Livingstone (Cambridge: Polity, 2005), 231.)

81 Martin Heidegger, *Being and Time*, tr. John Macquarrie and Edward Robinson (Oxford: Blackwell, 1967), 295, 298, 299.

82 *Simmel on Culture*, 174.

83 Zygmunt Bauman, *Modernity and Ambivalence* (Oxford: Polity, 1991), 185, 186, 187.

84 George Steiner, *Heidegger* (London: Fontana, 1992), 129.

85 Heidegger, *Being and Time*, 360, 361, 363.

4 Sensations of Earth: Thomas Hardy and Richard Jefferies

1 Martin Heidegger, *Hölderlin's Hymn 'The Ister'*, tr. William McNeill and Julia Davis (Bloomington: Indiana University Press, 1996), 120.

2 Gilles Deleuze and Felix Guattari, *What is Philosophy?*, tr. Hugh Tomlinson and Graham Burchell (New York: Columbia University Press, 1994), 60.

3 Friedrich Nietzsche, *Ecce Homo*, tr. R.J.Hollingdale (Harmondsworth: Penguin, 1979), 105.

4 Nietzsche, *Ecce Homo*, 66.

5 *A Nietzsche Reader*, ed. R.J.Hollingdale (Harmondsworth: Penguin, 1977), 66, 67.

6 Lennart Björk (ed.), *The Literary Notebooks of Thomas Hardy* (London: Macmillan, 1985), I, 132.

7 Thomas Hardy, *The Return of the Native* , ed. Simon Gatrell (Oxford: Oxford University Press, 1990). Subsequently cited in the text as RN.

8   T. W. Adorno and Max Horkheimer, *Dialectic of Enlightenment*, tr. John Cumming (London: Routledge & Kegan Paul, 1962), 189.

9   Adorno and Horkheimer, *Dialectic of Enlightenment*, 32.

10 Maurice Merleau-Ponty, *The Phenomenology of Perception*, tr. Colin Smith (London: Routledge & Kegan Paul,1962), 81.

11 Walter Benjamin, *Reflections*, tr. Edmund Jephcott (New York: Brace Jovanovich, 1978), 328.

12 Alexander Garcia Düttmann, *The Gift of Language*, tr. Arline Lyons (London: Athlone, 2000), 53.

13 Regenia Gagnier, *Subjectivities* (Oxford: Oxford University Press, 1991), 24.

14 Jean Baudrillard, *Selected Essays*, ed. Mark Poster (Cambridge: Polity, 2001), 115, 158.

15 A moment which recalls the erotic charge felt by the boyish Hardy as the dress of his early patroness, Julia Augusta Martin, brushed against the Stinsford church font (see Michael Millgate, *Thomas Hardy* (Oxford: Oxford University Press, 1985), 47–8.)

16 Björk, *Literary Notebooks*, II, 16.

17 Karl Marx, *Economic and Philosophic Manuscripts of 1844*, in Marx and Engels, *Collected Works*, vol. 13 (London: Lawrence & Wishart, 1975), 272. Subsequently cited in the notes as EPM.

18 EPM, 273.

19 EPM, 273.

20 EPM, 275.

21 EPM, 275.

22 EPM, 276.

23 EPM, 276.

24 Karl Marx, *Capital*, vol. 1, tr. Ben Fowkes (Harmondsworth: Penguin, 1976), 284.

25 Alfred Schmidt, *The Concept of Nature in Marx* (London: NLB, 1971), 130.

26 EPM, 277.

27 Schmidt, *Concept of Nature*, 15, 30.

28 Anson Rabinbach, *The Human Motor* (Berkeley: University of California Press, 1992), 77.

29 Marx, *Capital,* 283.

30 Marx, *Capital*, 283.

31 Marx, *Capital*, 285.

32 T. W. Adorno, *Aesthetic Theory*, tr. Robert Hüllot-Kentor (London: Continuum, 1997), 71.

33 Schmidt, *Concept of Nature*, 45.

34 Schmidt, *Concept of Nature*, 72. On the linguistic communality and carnivalesque properties of the rustics on the heath see Roger Ebbatson, *Hardy: Margin of the Unexpressed* (Sheffield: Sheffield Academic Press, 1993), ch. 6.

35 Karl Marx, *Grundrisse*, tr. Martin Nicolaus (Harmondsworth: Penguin, 1974), 211.

36   Martin Heidegger, *The End of Philosophy*, tr. Joan Stambaugh (New York: Harper & Row, 1973), 86.
37   Gagnier, *Subjectivities*, 168.
38   Richard Jefferies, *The Story of My Heart* (Dartington: Green Books, 2002). Subsequently cited in the text as SH.
39   Hannah Arendt, *The Life of the Mind: Thinking* (London: Secker & Warburg, 1978), 156.
40   On the complex relation between history and ontology in *The Dewy Morn* see Roger Ebbatson, *An Imaginary England: Nation, Landscape and Literature 1840–1920* (Aldershot: Ashgate, 2005), ch. 4.
41   James Phillips, *Heidegger's Volk* (Stanford: Stanford University Press, 2005), 204.
42   Ralph Waldo Emerson, 'History', in *The Portable Emerson*, ed. Mark van Doren (Harmondsworth: Penguin, 1977), 144.
43   Ralph Waldo Emerson, *Nature, Addresses and Lectures* (London: Routledge, n.d.), 15–16.
44   Saree Makdisi, *Romantic Imperialism* (Cambridge: Cambridge University Press, 1998), 12.
45   Cited in Rüdiger Safranski, *Martin Heidegger: Between Good and Evil*, tr. Ewald Osers (Cambridge, Mass.: Harvard University Press, 1998), 3.
46   *Martin Heidegger: Basic Writings*, ed. David Farrell Krell (London: Routledge, 1993), 196. Subsequently cited in the notes as BW.
47   BW, 162, 172.
48   BW, 170.
49   BW, 178.
50   BW, 178, 179, 180.
51   BW, 168, 197.
52   BW, 168, 162.
53   Cited by Albert Borgmann, 'Technology', in *A Companion to Heidegger*, ed. Hubert L. Dreyfus and Mark A. Wrathall (Oxford: Blackwell, 2005), 425.
54   BW, 198.
55   BW, 420.
56   BW, 442.
57   BW, 442.
58   BW, 442, 444, 445.
59   BW, 445.
60   BW, 174.
61   BW, 172,
62   Otto Pöggeler, *Martin Heidegger's Path of Thinking* (Atlantic Highlands, N. J.: Humanities Press, 1989), 172.
63   Paul de Man, *The Rhetoric of Romanticism* (New York: Columbia University Press, 1984), 40.
64   Jacques Derrida, *The Margins of Philosophy*, tr. Alan Bass (Brighton: Harvester, 1982), 39, 40.
65   W. J. Keith, *Richard Jefferies* (London: Oxford University Press, 1965), 132.

66   Richard Jefferies, 'On the Downs', in *Jefferies' England*, ed. Samuel J. Looker (London: Constable, 1945), 93.

67   *Jefferies' England*, 94, 96.

68   *The Notebooks of Richard Jefferies*, ed. Samuel J. Looker (London: Grey Walls Press, 1948), 230.

69   *Notebooks*, 233, 264, 280.

70   *Notebooks*, 283.

71   *Notebooks*, 290.

72   BW, 246.

73   BW, 246.

74   BW, 252.

75   Martin Heidegger, 'On the Essence of Ground' (1929), tr. William McNeill, in *Pathmarks*, ed. William McNeill (Cambridge: Cambridge University Press, 1998), 128.

76   BW, 254.

77   Heidegger, *Hölderlin's Hymn 'The Ister'*, 49.

78   Simon Grimble, *Landscape, Writing and the Condition of England* (Lampeter: Edwin Mellen Press, 2004), 97, 99.

79   Leo Löwenthal, 'Knut Hamsun', in *The Essential Frankfurt School Reader*, ed. Andrew Arato and Eike Gebhardt (Oxford: Blackwell, 1978), 320.

80   Löwenthal, 'Knut Hamsun', 321, 322.

81   Löwenthal, 'Knut Hamsun', 326.

82   Löwenthal, 'Knut Hamsun', 328.

83   Löwenthal, 'Knut Hamsun', 344.

84   Edward Thomas, *Richard Jefferies* (London: Dent, 1938), 162.

85   Thomas, *Richard Jefferies*, 173.

86   Thomas, *Richard Jefferies*,186.

87   Keith, *Richard Jefferies*, 93.

88   Keith, *Richard Jefferies*, 98.

89   Martin Heidegger, *Being and Time*, tr. John Macquarrie and Edward Robinson (New York: Harper & Row, 1962), 440.

90   Maurice Merleau-Ponty, *Themes from the Lectures, 1952–60*, tr. J. O'Neill (Evanston, Ill.: Northwestern University Press, 1970), 83.

91   John Lucas, 'Places and Dwelling', in *The Iconography of Landscape*, ed. Denis Cosgrove and Stephen Daniels (Cambridge: Cambridge University Press, 1988), 87.

92   Safranski, *Martin Heidegger*, 432.

93   Fredric Jameson, *Marxism and Form* (Princeton, N.J.: Princeton University Press, 1974), 119.

94   Raymond Williams, *The Country and the City* (London: Chatto & Windus, 1973), 196.

95   Karl Marx, *Early Writings*, tr. Rodney Livingstone and Gregor Benton (Harmondsworth: Penguin, 1975), 328.

96 Kostas Axelos, *Alienation, Praxis, and Techne in the Thought of Karl Marx*, tr. Ronald Bruzina (Austin: University of Texas Press, 1976), 198.

97 Michel Foucault, *Language, Counter-Memory, Practice*, tr. Donald F. Bouchard and S. Simon (Ithaca: Cornell University Press, 1977), 85. Italics added.

98 Walter Benjamin, *Illuminations*, tr. Harry Zohn (London: Fontana, 1973), 281, 262–3.

99 Eleanor Farjeon, *Edward Thomas: The Last Four Years* (Stroud: Sutton, 1997), 155.

100 *BW*,145, 146,147.

101 *BW*, 152, 157.

102 *BW*, 194, 199.

103 Martin Bidney, 'Rage and Reparation in the Epiphanies of Edward Thomas', *English Literature in Transition* 47 (2004), 292, 294.

104 *The Collected Poems of Edward Thomas*, ed. R. George Thomas (Oxford: Oxford University Press, 1981), 103.

105 Diary entry 21 March 1917; *Collected Poems*, 190.

5 *The Guilty River:* Wilkie Collins's Gothic Deafness

1 Walter Benjamin, *The Origin of German Tragic Drama*, tr. John Osborne (London: Verso, 1985), 45.

2 Wilkie Collins, *Miss or Mrs? The Haunted Hotel. The Guilty River*, ed. Norman Page and Toru Sasaki (Oxford: Oxford University Press, 1999), 246. Subsequent page references are to this edition.

3 Kelly Hurley, *The Gothic Body* (Cambridge: Cambridge University Press, 1996), 155.

4 *The Guilty River*, in telling of the protagonist's infatuation with the miller's daughter, reinflects elements of Schubert's song-cycle, *Die Schöne Müllerin* (1824), settings of poems by Wilhelm Müller.

5 Paul de Man, cited in Ortwin de Graef, *Titanic Light* (Lincoln, Neb.: University of Nebraska Press, 1995), 170.

6 De Man, cited in *Titanic Light*, 124.

7 Paul de Man, *The Rhetoric of Romanticism* (New York: Columbia University Press, 1984), 60–1.

8 Marl Marx, cited in Nancy S. Love, *Marx, Nietzsche, and Modernity* (New York: Columbia University Press, 1986), 149.

9 Peter Singer, *Hegel* (Oxford: Oxford University Press, 1983), 57.

10 G. W. F. Hegel, *The Phenomenology of Spirit*, tr. A. V. Miller (Oxford: Oxford University Press, 1977), 114.

11 Wilkie Collins and Charles Fechter, *Black and White* (London: C. Whiting, 1869), 29. *The Guilty River* may also reimagine some elements of Dinah Craik's *Olive* (1850), which features a young woman named Christal, who is the daughter of a Scottish gentleman and 'a Quadroon lady – one of that miserable race, the children of planters and slaves' (Dinah Craik, *Olive*, ed. Cora Kaplan (Oxford: Oxford University Press, 2000), 272.)

12 Hegel, *Phenomenology*, 117.

13 Jonathan Taylor, *Mastery and Slavery in Victorian Writing* (Basingstoke: Palgrave, 2003), 4.

14 Taylor, *Mastery and Slavery*, 11, 159.

15 Taylor, *Mastery and Slavery*, 57.

16 Hurley, *The Gothic Body*, 69.

17 Diana Basham, *Conan Doyle and the Meaning of Masculinity* (Aldershot: Ashgate, 2000), 138.

18 Taylor, *Mastery and Slavery*, 29.

19 Taylor, *Mastery and Slavery*, 114.

20 Taylor, *Mastery and Slavery*, 78.

21 Karl Marx, *The Poverty of Philosophy* (New York: International Publishers, 1963), 109, 133.

22 Georg Lukács, *History and Class Consciousness*, tr. Rodney Livingstone (London: Merlin Press, 1971), 166.

23 Lukács, *History and Class Consciousness*, 58.

24 Kostas Axelos, *Alienation, Praxis, and Techne in the Thought of Karl Marx*, tr. Ronald Bruzina (Austin: University of Texas Press, 1976), 142.

25 Michelle Massé, 'Psychoanalysis and the Gothic', in *A Companion to the Gothic*, ed. David Punter (Oxford: Blackwell, 2000), 234.

26 Michelle Massé, *In the Name of Love* (Ithaca: Cornell University Press, 1992), 108.

27 De Graef, *Titanic Light*, 165.

28 De Man, cited in *Titanic Light*, 133.

29 David Punter, 'Shape and Shadow: On Poetry and the Uncanny', in *Companion to the Gothic*, 197.

30 Paul de Man, *The Rhetoric of Romanticism* (New York: Columbia University Press, 1984), 81.

31 Basham, *Conan Doyle and the Meaning of Masculinity*, 104.

32 Paul de Man, *Blindness and Insight* (London: Methuen, 1983), 72.

33 De Man, *Blindness and Insight*, 78, 105.

34 John M. Picker, *Victorian Soundscapes* (Oxford: Oxford University Press, 2003), 12. It was Edison's deafness, as Picker demonstrates, which led indirectly to the invention of the phonograph.

35 Picker, *Victorian Soundscapes*, 87.

36 Jonathan Rée, *I See a Voice* (New York: Henry Holt, 1999), 53.

37 Rée, *I See a Voice*, 303.

38 Rée, *I See a Voice*, 322.

39 Christopher Krantz, 'Duncan Campbell and the Discourses of Deafness', *Prose Studies* 27 (2005), 45.

40 Paul de Man, *The Resistance to Theory* (Manchester: Manchester University Press, 1986), 42.

41 De Man, *Resistance to Theory*, 42, 43.

42 Singer, *Hegel*, 62.

43 Letter of 9 December, 1923; *The Correspondence of Walter Benjamin*, ed. Gershom Scholem and T.W.Adorno (Chicago: Chicago University Press, 1994), 224.

44 Paul de Man, *Allegories of Reading*, 206.

45 De Man, *Blindness and Insight*, 176.

46 De Man, *Rhetoric of Romanticism*, 80.

47 De Man, *Rhetoric of Romanticism*, 120.

48 G. W. F. Hegel, *The Philosophy of History*, tr. J. Sibree (New York, Dover, 2005), 99.

49 Mariaconcetta Costantini, 'Weird, Wild, Wise – the Other as a Source of Knowledge in Wilkie Collins's Fiction', *Englishes* 22 (2004), 26.

50 Ronald R. Thomas, 'Revaluating Identity in the 1890s', in *Transforming Genres*, ed. Nikki Lee Manos and Meri-Jane Rochelson (New York: St Martin's Press, 1994), 211.

51 Thomas, 'Revaluating Identity', 211.

52 Thomas, 'Revaluating Identity', 212.

53 Costantini, 'Weird, Wild, Wise', 37, 38.

54 Linda Dowling, 'The Decadent and the New Woman', *Nineteenth-Century Fiction* 33 (1979), 437.

55 Linda Dowling, *Language and Decadence in the Victorian Fin de Siècle* (Princeton: Princeton University Press, 1986), 104.

56 De Man, *Rhetoric of Romanticism*, 295.

57 William James, *Principles of Psychology* (1890), vol. 1 (New York: Dover Publications, 1950), 239.

58 William James, *A Pluralistic Universe* (Cambridge, Mass.: Harvard University Press, 1977), 26.

59 Karl Marx, cited in Lukács, *History and Class Consciousness*, 244.

60 Lukács, *History and Class Consciousness*, 65, 180.

61 Karl Marx, cited in Lukács, *History and Class Consciousness*, 149.

62 *The Life and Work of Thomas Hardy*, ed. Michael Millgate (London: Macmillan, 1984), 179.

63 Walter Benjamin, review of 1939, cited in Michael Löwy, *On Changing the World* (New Jersey: Humanities Press, 1993), 146.

64 Löwy, *On Changing the World*, 139.

65 Walter Benjamin, *One-Way Street*, tr. Edmund Jephcott and Kingsley Shorter (London: Verso, 1985), 80.

66 Wład Godzich, Introduction to de Man, *Resistance to Theory*, xx.

67 T. W. Adorno, *Aesthetic Theory*, tr. Robert Hüllot-Kentor (London: Continuum, 1997), 81.

68 Cited in Robin Spencer, *Whistler: A Retrospective* (New York: Wings Books, 1991), 19.

69 Adorno, *Aesthetic Theory*, 84. In this section, Adorno even speaks, à propos Wedekind, of 'the unspeakable melancholy of the river landscape'.

70 Adorno, *Aesthetic Theory*, 85.

71   Adorno, *AestheticTheory*, 195.
72   Adorno, *Aesthetic Theory*, 28.
73   Geoffrey H. Hartman, *Criticism in the Wilderness* (New York: Yale University Press, 1980), 78.
74   De Graef, *Titanic Light*, 16.

6   Stevenson's *The Ebb-Tide*: Missionary Endeavour in the Islands of Light

1   John Angell James, *The Attraction of the Cross* (1819), cited in Niel Gunson, *Messengers of Grace* (Oxford: Oxford University Press, 1978), 269.
2   *The Penguin Book of Caribbean Verse*, ed. Paula Burnett (Harmondsworth: Penguin, 1986), 262.
3   Robert Louis Stevenson and Lloyd Osbourne, *The Ebb-Tide*, ed. Peter Hinchcliffe and Catherine Kerrigan (Edinburgh: Edinburgh University Press, 1995). All subsequent page references are to this edition.
4   Gunson, *Messengers of Grace,* 332.
5   Andrew Porter, 'Religion and Empire', *Journal of Imperial and Commonwealth History* 20 (1992), 379.
6   Vanessa Smith, *Literary Culture and the Pacific* (Cambridge: Cambridge University Press, 1998), 158.
7   Michel Foucault, *The Order of Things* (London: Routledge, 1974), 387.
8   Linda Dowling. *Language and Decadence* (Princeton: Princeton University Press, 1986), xv.
9   Dowling, *Language and Decadence*, 84.
10   Dowling, *Language and Decadence*, 93.
11   Robert Louis Stevenson, *In the South Seas*, ed. Neil Rennie (Harmondsworth: Penguin, 1998), 10.
12   Dowling, *Language and Decadence*, 100–1.
13   Walter Benjamin, in *Aesthetic Politics*, ed. R. Taylor (London: Verso, 1977), 87.
14   Karl Pearson, *National Life and Character* (London: Dent, 1894), 257.
15   William Greenslade, *Degeneration, Culture and the Novel* (Cambridge: Cambridge University Press, 1994), 20.
16   Linda Dowling, *Hellenism and Homosexuality in Victorian Oxford* (Ithaca: Cornell University Press, 1994), 20.
17   Anna Johnston, *Missionary Writing and Empire, 1800–1860* (Cambridge: Cambridge University Press, 2003), 205.
18   Johnston, *Missionary Writing*, 206.
19   Greenslade, *Degeneration, Culture and the Novel*, 94.
20   Homi Bhabha, *The Location of Culture* (London: Routledge, 1994), 174.
21   Neil Rennie, *Far-Fetched Facts* (Oxford: Clarendon, 1995), 19, 25, 196.
22   Rod Edmond, *Representations of the South Pacific* (Cambridge: Cambridge University Press, 1997), 63, 131.
23   Gayatri Spivak, *A Critique of Postcolonial Reason* (Cambridge, Mass.: Harvard University Press, 1999), 346.

24   Julia Reid, 'Robert Louis Stevenson and the "Romance of Anthropology"', *Journal of Victorian Culture* 10 (2005), 55, 58.

25   Pierre Macherey, *A Theory of Literary Production*, tr. Geoffrey Wall (London: Routledge & Kegan Paul, 1978), 199, 202.

26   Macherey, *Literary Production*, 203.

27   Macherey, *Literary Production*, 209, 211.

28   Diana Loxley, *Problematic Shores: The Literature of Islands* (Basingstoke: Macmillan, 1990), 132.

29   Loxley, *Problematic Shores*, 132.

30   Loxley, *Problematic Shores*, 149.

31   Loxley, *Problematic Shores*, 168.

32   Elizabeth Deloughrey, 'A Litany of Islands: Caribbean and Pacific Archipelagraphy', *Ariel* 32 (2001), 25.

33   On the religious discourse in *Dracula* see Christopher Herbert, 'Vampire Religion', *Representations* 79 (2002), 21–51.

34   Rennie, *Far-Fetched Facts*, 97, 40.

35   Rennie, *Far-Fetched Facts*, 62.

36   Letter of 16 May 1893, cited in R. I. Hillier, *The South Seas Fiction of R. L. Stevenson* (New York: Peter Lang, 1989), 125.

37   Roland Barthes, *Mythologies*, tr. Annette Lavers (London: Vintage, 1993), 58.

38   Patrick Brantlinger, *Fictions of State* (Ithaca: Cornell University Press, 1996), 7.

39   'Thomas Stevenson, Civil Engineer' (1887), R. L. Stevenson, *Essays and Poems*, ed. Claire Harman (London: Dent, 1992), 173.

40   'A Chapter on Dreams' (1888), *R. L. Stevenson on Fiction*, ed. Glenda Norquay (Edinburgh: Edinburgh University Press, 1999), 136.

41   Mariaconcetta Costantini, 'Stevenson's South Seas', *Merope* 35–6 (2002), 222.

42   Gaston Bachelard, *Water and Dreams*, tr. Eileen R. Farrell (Dallas: Pegasus Foundation, 1983), 6.

43   Jonathan Crary, *Suspensions of Perception* (Cambridge, Mass.: MIT, 1999), 99.

44   Ann C. Colley, *Robert Louis Stevenson and the Colonial Imagination* (Aldershot: Ashgate, 2004), 25, 31. Chalmers, a man of imposing build deeply admired by RLS, may have sat as a model for Attwater: Colley notes that, though he was a 'good raconteur', his character betrayed 'a harsh streak' illustrated when, in order to bring a local chieftain to heel, the missionary poured two bottles of acid onto the ground so that 'the fumes went into his face' (34) – an episode which may have been refracted into the vitriol plot in *The Ebb-Tide*.

45   Laura Chrisman, *Re-Reading the Imperial Romance* (Oxford: Oxford University Press, 2000), 4.

46   Gunson, *Messengers of Grace*, ch. 1.

47   Brian Stanley, *The Bible and the Flag* (Leicester: Apollos, 1990), 82.

48   Edmond, *Representations of the South Pacific*, 111.

49   Bhabha, *Location of Culture*, 33.

50   Bhabha, *Location of Culture*, 114.

51   J. M. Harris, 'Robert Louis Stevenson: Folklore and Imperialism', *English Literature in Transition* 46 (2003), 397.

52   Spivak, *Critique of Post-Colonial Reason*, 36, 274.

53   Karl Marx, *Capital*, vol. 1, tr. Ben Fowkes (Harmondsworth: Penguin), 254–5.

54   Christopher Lane, *The Ruling Passion* (Durham, N.C.: Duke University Press, 1995), passim.

55   Cited in Esther Leslie, *Walter Benjamin* (London: Pluto, 2000), 192.

56   Spivak, *Post-Colonial Reason*, 108.

57   Spivak, *Post-Colonial Reason*, 130.

58   In 'The Beach of Falesá' Wiltshire alludes to 'that Blavatsky business in the papers'. (R. L. Stevenson, *South Sea Tales*, ed. Roslyn Jolly (Oxford: Oxford University Press, 1996), 36).

59   Alison Winter, *Mesmerised* (Chicago: University of Chicago Press, 1998), 247, 248. In 1888 Fanny Stevenson had experienced a 'phantasm' of Stevenson's friend Charles Baxter in a telepathic projection which crossed the Atlantic. (See Roger Luckhurst, *The Invention of Telepathy* (Oxford: Oxford University Press, 2002), 195.)

60   'Talk and Talkers' (I) (1882), *Stevenson on Fiction*, 154.

61   Winter, *Mesmerised*, 248, 250.

62   Winter, *Mesmerised*, 257.

63   Jenny Bourne Taylor, 'Fallacies of Memory in Nineteenth-Century Psychology', *Victorian Review* 26 (2000), 102.

64   Winter, *Mesmerised*, 269.

65   David Glover, 'The Spectrality Effect in English Modernism', in *Gothic Modernism*, ed. Andrew Smith and Jeff Wallace (Basingstoke: Palgrave 2001), 41.

66   Hannah Arendt, *Imperialism* (New York: Harcourt Brace, 1968), 70.

67   Sigmund Freud, *Totem and Taboo*, tr. A. A. Brill (Harmondsworth: Penguin, 1938), 189, 192.

68   Bhabha, *Location of Culture*, 43.

69   'My First Book: *Treasure Island*' (1894), *Essays and Poems*, 211.

70   Dowling, *Hellenism and Homosexuality*, 21.

71   Alexandra Warwick, 'Vampires and Empire', in *Cultural Politics at the Fin de Siècle*, ed. Sally Ledger and Scott McCracken (Cambridge: Cambridge University Press, 1995), 219.

72   *In the South Seas*, 5.

73   Debbie Lee, *Slavery and the Romantic Imagination* (Philadelphia: University of Pennsylvania Press, 2002), 55.

74   Lee, 58. See also J. R. Ebbatson, 'Coleridge's Mariner and the Rights of Man', *Studies in Romanticism* 11 (1972). Interestingly, Coleridge, in his 1795 Bristol lecture on the slave trade, had projected a vision of 'the inspired philanthropist of Galilee' returning to Cana, where he would not 'change Water into Wine' but instead exhibit some of the results of the trade, 'Tears and Blood, and

Anguish', and 'the loud Peals of the Lash'. (S.T.Coleridge, *Lectures 1795: On Politics and Religion*, ed. Lewis Patton and Peter Mann (London: Routledge & Kegan Paul, 1971), 248.)

75 Robert Louis Stevenson, *Travels in Hawaii*, ed. A. Grove Day (Honolulu: University of Hawaii Press, 1973), 143.

76 Rod Edmond, 'Abject Bodies/Abject Sites', in *Islands in History and Representation*, ed. Rod Edmond and Vanessa Smith (London: Routledge, 2003), 143.

77 On the career of 'the martyr of Molokai' and Stevenson's involvement in his posthumous reputation see Tony Gould, *Don't Fence Me In* (Bloomsbury, 2005), chs. 3 and 4.

78 Patrick Brantlinger, *Dark Vanishings* (Ithaca: Cornell University Press, 2003), 3.

79 Brantlinger, *Dark Vanishings*, 5.

80 Judith R. Walkowitz, *City of Dreadful Delight* (London: Virago, 1994), 89.

81 Walkowitz, *City of Dreadful Delight*, 90.

82 Wayne Koestenbaum, *Double Talk* (London: Routledge, 1989), 146 ff.

83 Ed Cohen, 'The Double Lives of Man', in *Cultural Politics at the Fin de Siècle*, 93, 94.

84 On these issues see Guy Davidson, 'Homosocial Relations, Masculine Embodiment, and Imperialism in Stevenson's *The Ebb-Tide*', *English Literature in Transition* 47 (2004), 123–41.

85 Jacques Derrida, *Dissemination*, tr. Barbara Johnson (London: Athlone Press, 1993), 70.

86 Derrida, *Dissemination*, 99, 110.

87 Derrida, *Dissemination*, 77.

88 Derrida, *Dissemination*, 115, 105.

89 Harris, 'Stevenson: Folklore and Imperialism', 389.

90 T.W.Adorno, in *Aesthetics and Politics*, 129.

91 'A Gossip on Romance' (1882), *Stevenson on Fiction*, 52.

92 Jean Baudrillard, 'The Political Economy of the Sign', *Selected Writings*, ed. Mark Poster (Cambridge: Polity, 2001), 79.

93 'On Some Technical Elements of Style' (1885), *Stevenson on Fiction*, 95.

94 Colley, *Stevenson and the Colonial Imagination*, 98.

95 'Talk and Talkers' (II) (1882), *Essays and Poems*, 167.

96 Michel Foucault, *The Archaeology of Knowledge*, tr. Alan Sheridan (London: Tavistock, 1972), 111.

97 Jacques Derrida, *Margins of Philosophy*, tr. Alan Bass (Brighton: Harvester, 1982), 268.

98 Paul de Man, *The Rhetoric of Romanticism* (New York: Columbia University Press, 1984), 258, 106.

7 Dr Doyle's Uncanny Prognosis: Sherlock Holmes and the Final Solution

1 Cited in Claude Lanzmann, *Shoah: The Film Text* (New York, Pantheon Books, 1985), 82.

2 *The Penguin Complete Sherlock Holmes* (Harmondsworth: Penguin, 1981), 435. Subsequently cited in the text as CSH.

3 The 'Jewish Problem' was a subject of debate in Germany from Karl Marx (1844) and Richard Wagner (1850), through Wilhelm Marr (1879), Eugen Dühring (1881) and Theodor Herzl (1896), to Louis Brandeis (1915). Sherlock Holmes is a keen Wagnerite and, in 'The Adventure of the Red Circle' (1911), urges Dr Watson to 'hurry' so as not miss the second act of 'a Wagner night at Covent Garden' (CSH, 913).

4 Friedrich von Schiller, *Naïve and Sentimental Poetry and On the Sublime*, tr. Julius A. Elias (New York: Frederick Ungar, 1966), 207, 210.

5 It is notable that Sidney Paget, who illustrated the stories for *The Strand*, portrayed Holmes and Moriarty with similar features.

6 It was during his 1893 stay at Davos that Conan Doyle visited the Reichenbach Falls.

7 It is not the least remarkable conjunction of naming in this entanglement of texts that one of Cassirer's most eminent pupils should be the philosopher of science, Hans Reichenbach (1891–1953), who would flee Nazi Germany for the USA in the 1930s.

8 Cited in Fred Dallmayr, *Life-World, Modernity and Critique* (Cambridge: Polity Press, 1991), 54.

9 Cited in Stephan Kaufer, 'Logic', in *A Companion to Heidegger*, ed. Hubert L. Dreyfus and Mark A. Wrathall (Oxford: Blackwell, 2005), 146.

10 T. W. Adorno, *AestheticTheory*, tr. Robert Hüllot-Kentor (London: Continuum, 1997), 199.

11 T. W. Adorno, *Minima Moralia*, tr. E.F.N. Jephcott (London: NLB, 1974), 134.

12 Paul de Man, *Allegories of Reading* (New Haven: Yale University Press, 1979), 10. It is worth noting, in relation to the plot of 'The Priory School', that de Man's brother Hendrik died in a cycling accident.

13 Walter Benjamin, *Illuminations*, tr. Harry Zohn (London: Fontana, 1973), 82.

14 Eve Kosofsky Sedgwick, *Between Men* (New York: Columbia University Press, 1985), 246.

15 Cited in Richard Wolin, *Heidegger's Children* (Princeton: Princeton University Press, 2001), 218.

16 *Mind*, 38 (1929), 355.

17 Cited in Michael E. Zimmerman, *Heidegger's Confrontation with Modernity* (Bloomington: Indiana University Press, 1990), 105.

18 Cited in Richard Lancelyn Green, ed., *The Uncollected Sherlock Holmes Stories* (Harmondsworth: Penguin, 1983), 65.

19 Walter Benjamin, cited in Michael Löwy, *On Changing the World* (New Jersey: Humanities Publishers, 1993), 171.

20 Sigmund Freud, *The Psychopathology of Everyday Life* (Harmondsworth: Penguin, 1975), 64.

21 Aveling, a disciple of Marx and Darwin, is alleged to have persuaded his

common-law wife, Eleanor Marx, to join him in a suicide pact; whilst his partner died from drinking prussic acid, Aveling, in some accounts, failed to keep his part of the bargain. The mysterious South American tenants in 'The Adventure of Wisteria Lodge' (1908) acquire their clothing from 'Marx and Co., High Holborn' (CSH, 828), and in 'The Adventure of the Veiled Lodger' (1927) the scarred Eugenia Ronder renounces the use of prussic acid as an end to her torment. The maths teacher's name may have been prompted by Frederick Aveling, author of *Britons and Boers* (1899), whilst the name of the German master probably derived from one Heinrich Heidegger, who had published a Swiss travel book in 1792. (See Donald A. Redmond, *Sherlock Holmes: A Study in Sources* (Montreal: McGill-Queen's University Press, 1982), 134.) Intriguingly, Arthur Morrison published a slender short story about the elixir of life entitled 'Dr Heidegger's Experiment' in *The Palace Journal*, 7 August 1889, 148–50. (I am indebted to Anthony Cummins for alerting me to this text.)

22   The complexity of naming in these texts is deepened by recalling Heidegger's action, as Rector of Freiburg University, in attempting to block the academic appointment of Weber's nephew, Eduard Baumgarten, a man the Rector denigrated as having become 'Americanised' and being associated with 'the Jew [Eduard] Frankel'. (See Victor Farias, *Heidegger and Nazism* (Philadelphia: Temple University Press, 1989), 209–11.)

23   Arthur Conan Doyle, 'How the Brigadier Played for a Kingdom' (1896), *The Complete Brigadier Gerard*, ed. Owen Dudley Edwards (Edinburgh: Canongate, 1995), 186, 202.

24   Diana Basham, *Conan Doyle and the Meaning of Masculinity* (Aldershot: Palgrave, 2000), 3, 4.

25   Alexander Garcia Düttmann, *The Memory of Thought*, tr. Nicholas Walker (London: Continuum, 2002), 299.

26   Düttmann, *Memory of Thought*, 302.

27   Alexander Garcia Düttmann, *The Gift of Language*, tr. Arline Lyons (London: Athlone, 2000), 126.

28   John T. Irwin, *The Mystery to a Solution* (Baltimore: Johns Hopkins University Press, 1994), 410.

29   Basham, *Conan Doyle and the Meaning of Masculinity*, 132.

30   Nicholas Royle, *The Uncanny* (Manchester: Manchester University Press, 2003), 190.

31   Walter Benjamin, *One-Way Street and Other Writings*, tr. Edmund Jephcott and Kingsley Shorter (London: NLB, 1979), 116.

32   T. W. Adorno, *Minima Moralia*, 110.

33   Arthur Conan Doyle, *The New Revelation and the Vital Message* (London: Psychic Press, 1981), 53.

34   Düttmann, *Memory of Thought*, 221–2.

35   Jean-Francois Lyotard, *Heidegger and the Jews*, tr. Andreas Michel and Mark S. Roberts (Minneapolis: University of Minnesota Press, 1990), 93.

36 Martin Heidegger, 'The Self-Assertion of the German University' (1933), tr. William S. Lewis, in *The Heidegger Controversy*, ed. Richard Wolin (New York: Columbia University Press, 1991), 33–4, 34, 35, 38.

37 'The University in the New Reich' (1933), tr. William S. Lewis, *Heidegger Controversy*, 44.

38 Wolin, *Heidegger Controversy*, 45.

39 *The Poems of Arthur Conan Doyle* (London: John Murray, 1922), 93, 105.

40 Harold Orel, ed., *Sir Arthur Conan Doyle: Interviews and Recollections* (New York: St Martin's Press, 1991), 132, 60.

41 'National Socialist Education' (1934), *Heidegger Controversy*, 57.

42 Martin A. Kayman, *From Bow Street to Baker Street* (London: Macmillan, 1982), 237.

43 Martin Heidegger, *Hölderlin's Hymn 'The Ister'*, tr. William McNeill and Julia Davis (Evanston: Indiana University Press, 1996), 49.

44 Düttmann, *Memory of Thought*, 303.

45 The pneumatic bicycle tyre was relatively new, having been introduced some fifteen years before the date of this story. The mid-nineties was a period characterised by frenzied speculation in bicycle company stock in a process which created one multi-millionaire, Ernest Hooley, whose fraudulent transactions led him to the bankruptcy court in 1898.

46 In an eerie reduplication or doubling of Conan Doyle's hound, in the early 1930s Adorno was to adopt the pseudonym Hektor Rottweiler, naming himself after 'a fearsome beast', in order that 'no Nazi will ever suspect that it might hide the identity of a non-Aryan writer'. (Stefan Müller-Doohm, *Adorno: A Biography*, tr. Rodney Livingstone (Cambridge: Polity, 2005), 180.

47 Catherine Wynne, *The Colonial Conan Doyle* (Westport: Greenwood Press, 1992), 68, 83.

48 Wolin, *Heidegger Controversy*, 116.

49 Düttmann, *Gift of Language*, 31.

50 J. B. Harley, 'Maps, Knowledge, Power', in *The Iconography of Landscape*, ed. Denis Cosgrove and Stephen Daniels (Cambridge: Cambridge University Press, 1988), 285, 284.

51 Düttmann, *Gift of Language*, 26, 27, 29.

52 Martin Heidegger, *The Principle of Reason*, tr. Reginald Lilly (Bloomington: Indiana University Press, 1991), 8, 12.

53 Heidegger, *Principle of Reason*, 10.

54 Walter Benjamin, *The Origin of German Tragic Drama*, tr. John Osborne (London: NLB,1985), 28.

55 In 'The Adventure of Black Peter' (1904) the villainous sailor of the title is reported as having 'built himself a wooden outhouse – he always called it his "cabin"' (CSH, 561).

56 Leo Bersani, *The Culture of Redemption* (Cambridge, Mass.: Harvard University Press, 1990), 171.

57   George Steiner, *In Bluebeard's Castle* (London: Faber & Faber, 1971), 63.

58   Jacques Derrida, *Writing and Difference*, tr. Alan Bass (Chicago: Chicago University Press, 1978), 230.

59   Lecture on Nietzsche (1940), cited in Jacques Taminiaux, 'Philosophy of Existence', in *Twentieth-Century Continental Philosophy*, ed. Richard Kearney (London: Routledge, 1994), 66.

60   Martin Heidegger, 'What is Metaphysics?', tr. David Farrell Krell, in *Pathmarks*, ed. William McNeill (Cambridge: Cambridge University Press, 1998), 87.

61   Heidegger, *Hölderlin's Hymn 'The Ister'*, 55.

62   Heidegger's later reflections on his 1933 Rectoral Address, cited in Düttmann, *Memory of Thought*, 187.

63   James Phillips, *Heidegger's Volk* (Stanford: Stanford University Press, 2005), 23.

64   Cited in Düttmann, *Gift of Language*, 100–1.

65   T. W. Adorno, *Negative Dialectics*, tr. E.B.Ashton (London: Routledge & Kegan Paul, 1990), 392.

66   Cited in Irving Wohlfarth, 'Walter Benjamin and the German-Jewish Parnassus', *New German Critique* 70 (1997), 30.

67   Cited in Wolin, *Heidegger's Children*, 208.

68   Inga Clendinnen, *Reading the Holocaust* (Cambridge: Cambridge University Press, 1999), 7.

69   Shoshana Felman, 'Film as Witness: Claude Lanzmann's "Shoah"', in *Holocaust Remembrance*, ed. Geoffrey H. Hartman (Oxford: Blackwell, 1994), 96.

70   Philipe Lacoue-Labarthe, *Heidegger, Art and Politics*, tr. Chris Turner (Oxford: Blackwell, 1990), 37.

71   Gilles Deleuze and Felix Guattari, *What is Philosophy?* tr. Hugh Tomlinson and Graham Burchill (London: Verso, 1994), 109.

72   Clendinnen, *Reading the Holocaust*, 100. In 'The Adventure of the Speckled Band' (1891), a story dealing with the persecution of twin girls, Holmes warns his medical colleague, '"When a doctor goes wrong he is the first of criminals"' (CSH, 170) – a deeply ominous remark in the light of Dr Mengele's Auschwitz experiments on pairs of twins.

73   Phillips, *Heidegger's Volk*, 107.

74   Basham, *Conan Doyle and the Meaning of Masculinity*, 207.

75   Paula M. Krebs, *Gender, Race and the Writing of Empire* (Cambridge: Cambridge University Press, 1999), 101.

76   Arthur Conan Doyle, *The War in South Africa* (London: Smith, Elder, 1902), 94.

77   Doyle, *The War*, 94.

78   Krebs, *Gender, Race*, 106.

79   Krebs, *Gender, Race*, 107.

80   Arthur Conan Doyle, *The Hound of the Baskervilles*, ed. Christopher Frayling (Harmondsworth: Penguin, 2001), 16.

81 Doyle, *The War*, 95.

82 Krebs, *Gender, Race*, 104.

83 Kenneth Wilson, 'Fiction and Empire: The Case of Sir Arthur Conan Doyle', *Victorian Review* 19 (1993), 26.

84 Doyle, *The War*, 97.

85 Emily Hobhouse, *The Brunt of the War* (London: Methuen, 1902), 116.

86 Hope Hay Hewison, *South Africa, the Pro-Boers and the Quaker Conscience* (London: Currey, 1989), 189.

87 The perceived decline in soldierly physique during the period of the war provided a fillip to the ongoing eugenics debate, as witness D. H. Lawrence's plan, propounded in 1908, to 'build a lethal chamber as big as Crystal Palace, with a military band playing softly' into which would be led 'all the sick, the halt, and the maimed'. (*The Letters of D. H. Lawrence*, vol. 1, ed. James T. Boulton (Cambridge: Cambridge University Press, 1979), 81.)

88 Doyle, *The War*, 103, 97, 99.

89 Krebs, *Gender, Race*, 106.

90 Bersani, *The Culture of Redemption*, 207.

91 Paul de Man, *The Rhetoric of Romanticism* (New York: Columbia University Press, 1984), 58–9.

92 Arthur Conan Doyle, 'That Little Square Box', *London Society: An Illustrated Magazine* (Christmas, 1881), 55, 61.

93 Arthur Conan Doyle, *The Poison Belt*, in *The Lost World and Other Thrilling Tales*, ed. Philip Gooden (Harmondsworth: Penguin, 2001), 238, 239. Subsequently cited in the text as PB.

94 Conan Doyle introduced a variant on this scenario in one of the last Sherlock Holmes stories, 'The Adventure of the Retired Colourman' (1926), in which the miserly old villain gasses his wife and her lover in a 'hermetically sealed room'. The nozzle of the gas-pipe is concealed by ornamentation, but as Holmes explains, '"At any moment by turning the outside tap the room could be flooded with gas"'. One victim attempts a scribbled message on the wall, and the bodies are dumped in 'a disused well' (CSH, 1120, 1121,1122). In an earlier story set in Cornwall, 'The Adventure of the Devil's Foot' (1910), two characters are driven insane and two killed by the poisonous odour of a tropical plant.

95 Steiner, *In Bluebeard's Castle*, 57.

96 Anson Rabinbach, 'Heidegger's "Letter on Humanism" as Text and Event', *New German Critique* 62 (1994), 3.

97 Rabinbach, 'Heidegger's "Letter"', 11.

98 Martin Heidegger, *Introduction to Metaphysics*, tr. Ralph Mannheim (New York: Anchor Books, 1961), 31, 32.

99 Rabinbach, 'Heidegger's "Letter"', 22.

100 Zimmerman, *Heidegger's Confrontation*, xix.

101 Cited in Robert E. Norton, *Secret Germany: Stefan George and His Circle* (Ithaca: Cornell University Press, 2002), 483.

102 Cited in Zimmerman, *Heidegger's Confrontation*, 75.

103 Cited in Zimmerman, *Heidegger's Confrontation*, 175.

104 Cited in Zimmerman, *Heidegger's Confrontation*, 179.

105 Zimmerman, *Heidegger's Confrontation*, 75–6.

106 Lecture of 1949, cited in Lacoue-Labarthe, *Heidegger, Art and Politics*, 34.

107 Jürgen Habermas, 'On the Publication of the Lectures of 1935', in *Heidegger Controversy*, 197.

108 Martin Heidegger, 'Introduction to "What is Metaphysics"' (1949), tr. Walter Kaufmann, *Pathmarks*, 278.

109 Joseph A. Kestner, *Sherlock's Men: Masculinity, Conan Doyle, and Cultural History* (Aldershot: Ashgate, 1997), 49, 48.

110 Arthur Conan Doyle, *The Wanderings of a Spiritualist* (Berkeley: Ronin Publishing, 1988), 32.

111 Arthur Conan Doyle, *The History of Spiritualism,* vol. 2 (New York: George H. Doran, 1926), 247.

112 Doyle, *History of Spiritualism*, 247, 249, 261–2.

113 Diana Basham, *The Trial of Woman* (Basingstoke: Macmillan, 1992), 108.

114 Heidegger, *Hölderlin's Hymn 'The Ister',* 53.

115 Jürgen Habermas, *The Philosophical Discourse of Modernity*, tr. Frederick Lawrence (Cambridge: Polity Press, 1987), 117.

116 Habermas, *Discourse of Modernity*, 119,157.

117 Cited in Habermas, *Discourse of Modernity*, 157.

118 David Farrell Krell, 'Spiriting Heidegger', in *Of Derrida, Heidegger, and Spirit*, ed. David Wood (Evanston: Northwestern University Press, 1993), 20.

119 Krell, 'Spiriting Heidegger', 34.

120 David Wood, 'The Actualisation of Philosophy', in *Of Derrida*, 81.

121 Heidegger, *Hölderlin's Hymn 'The Ister'*, 127, 128.

122 Jacques Derrida, *Of Spirit: Heidegger and the Question*, tr. Geoffrey Bennington and Rachel Bowlby (Chicago: Chicago University Press, 1987), 6, 24.

123 Heidegger, *Hölderlin's Hymn 'The Ister'*, 137, 131.

124 Cited in Derrida, *Of Spirit*, 36.

125 Derrida, *Of Spirit*, 39.

126 Cited in Derrida, *Of Spirit*, 59, 67.

127 Derrida, *Of Spirit*, 67.

128 Adorno, *Minima Moralia*, 240, 243.

129 Derrida, *Of Spirit*, 106.

130 Ryle, *Mind*, 370, 367.

131 Derrida, *Of Spirit*, 107, 108.

132 Martin Heidegger, *On the Way to Language*, tr. P. D. Hertz (New York: Harper & Row, 1971), 121.

133 John Bayley, *Housman's Poems* (Oxford: Clarendon Press, 1992), 71, 72.

134 Cited in Samir Gandesha, 'Leaving Home', in *The Cambridge Companion to Adorno*, ed. Tom Huhn (Cambridge: Cambridge University Press, 2004), 108.

135 Deleuze and Guattari, *What is Philosophy?*, 109.

Index